For my dearest

I'm so glad that I found
a book that I knew you
would really appreciate
for your 80th birthday

from your
loving husband

Pete

EDWARD DURELL STONE

MODERNISM'S POPULIST ARCHITECT

Dmitri Kessel

EDWARD DURELL STONE

MODERNISM'S POPULIST ARCHITECT

MARY ANNE HUNTING

W. W. NORTON & COMPANY

NEW YORK • LONDON

For information about permission to reproduce selections from this book,
write to Permissions, W. W. Norton & Company, Inc., 500 Fifth Avenue,
New York, NY 10110

For information about special discounts for bulk purchases,
please contact W. W. Norton
Special Sales at specialsales@wwnorton.com or 800-233-4830

Manufacturing by Edwards Brothers Malloy
Book design by Abigail Sturges
Digital production by Joe Lops
Production manager: Leeann Graham

Library of Congress Cataloging-in-Publication Data

Hunting, Mary Anne.
 Edward Durell Stone : modernism's populist architect / Mary Anne Hunting,
PhD. — First Edition.
    p. cm.
 Includes bibliographical references and index.
 ISBN 978-0-393-73301-3 (hardcover)
 1. Stone, Edward Durell—Criticism and interpretation. I. Title.
 NA737.S66H86 2012
 720.92—dc23
                        2012011405

ISBN: 978-0-393-73301-3

W. W. Norton & Company, Inc., 500 Fifth Avenue, New York, N.Y. 10110
www.wwnorton.com
W. W. Norton & Company Ltd., Castle House,
75/76 Wells Street, London W1T 3QT

0 9 8 7 6 5 4 3 2 1

To Tom, with infinite gratitude

To Mary Ives and Henry, with hope that you too will find passion in your work

And in memory of my father, still my pillar of strength

Workers constructing the United States Pavilion theater (1956–58) at the Exposition Universelle et International Bruxelles 1958.

CONTENTS

LIST OF DRAWINGS

PREFACE AND ACKNOWLEDGMENTS

Some ten years ago, Allison Ledes, the late editor, and my former employer, of *The Magazine Antiques*, asked me to write an article about Edward Durell Stone's International Style Richard H. Mandel house in what is now Bedford Hills, New York. I rapidly came to realize that there were only a few scattered articles about Stone, mostly focusing on such early contributions, and little else. I was intrigued. Not because of the man himself (although he is indeed a colorful figure) but because of the deficient commentary about his architecture, and more, the absence of any scholarly examination of it. Curious, I asked, "How could an architect whose name was once a household word fail to sustain lasting appeal?" My presupposition—that there is a deep-seated disconnect between the popular approval and critical dismissal of his work—was central to the rationale of my Ph.D. dissertation, "Edward Durell Stone: Perception and Criticism" (2007).

Fortuitously, at least for me, at about the same time the controversy was peaking over the proposed redesign of Stone's Gallery of Modern Art Building at 2 Columbus Circle in New York City—with educators, journalists, curators, and historians at last beginning to weigh in. The polemic fueled my mission, both then and now, to embrace and understand the criticism of Stone's work without prejudice, rather than to simply, and prosaically, defend his architecture, as has been done. The resulting reassessment of Stone's contributions relative to the transformation and acceptance of Modernism in the United States offers fresh insight into the moment when Stone's "new romanticism" won the approbation of the American people, and it establishes him, fair and square, within the realm of the modern masters.

In all my writing projects I most enjoy the research and the people with whom I encounter along the way. This book is no exception; the names of those who endorsed my effort—building owners or managers, archivists, librarians, press people, editors, curators, architects, designers, preservationists, historians, and photographers as well as my family (especially my mother and husband), friends (the moms in particular), and colleagues—could fill these pages. Although too numerous to list, I am deeply appreciative to each of them.

I am grateful to my devoted mentor, Kevin Murphy of the CUNY Graduate Center and to my very talented friend, Eleanor Gustafson of *The Magazine Antiques* for providing exceptional support on a seemingly daily basis. Cynthia Carris Alonso of Photo Solutions, Alison Poole, architect, and Mary Gladue have similarly been invaluable.

I also would like to acknowledge Richard Guy Wilson of the University of Virginia, Geoffery Stark and Andrea Cantrell (now retired) of the University of Arkansas, architects Harold Spitzer, Christian Bjone, and Ernest E. Jacks, a true southern gentlemen. Descendants of Stone's patrons—among them the Thurnaeur, Galbraith, Morosani, and Graf families—have been equally attentive. My appreciation is also extended to my colleague and dear friend, architectural historian Jill Lord, Rosemarie Haag Bletter of the CUNY Graduate Center, Kate Wood of Landmark West!, Nancy Green and Benjamin Yarling at W. W. Norton, and Abigail Sturges.

Mary Anne Hunting

INTRODUCTION

The animated, nine-year public debate that culminated in 2005 over the proposed redesign of the Gallery of Modern Art at 2 Columbus Circle in New York City by Edward Durell Stone (1902–78) revealed that mid-twentieth-century architecture still incites passionate responses—not only from historians and critics but, just as Stone had hoped, from "everyone, the man in the street, the uneducated man, the uninformed man."[1] The circumstance of his courageously provocative building, lost to a near total makeover (see page 148), demonstrates that even after a quarter century of modernist revisionism and postmodernist criticism, the numerous reevaluations, many of them undiscerning, fell short of capturing the meaningful role played by such paragons of modern architecture during the cold war era. Understandably, then, a more comprehensive historical awareness is called for if sound decisions are to be made about the fate of other momentous modernist buildings by Stone and his contemporaries too.

On the completion of the John F. Kennedy Center for the Performing Arts (1958–71) in Washington, D.C., J. William Fulbright, the Democratic senator from Stone's hometown in Fayetteville, Arkansas, enthusiastically hailed Stone as a "populist architect."[2] Stone was enormously successful, widely recognized, and hugely influential during his more than forty-year career—framed by the Great Depression of 1929 and the Oil Embargo of 1973. Importantly, his architecture served as a vital link between the avant-garde and its elite clientele (who traditionally considered the art world their domain) and the middle class that emerged after World War II.[3] Stone's revisionist attitude toward Modernism certainly anticipated 1970s Postmodernism, which similarly embodied a critique of the aesthetic and ideological assumptions of Modernism. Though Postmodernism had no specific style because it was fundamentally pluralistic, Stone shared many of the same visual themes as means of cultural expression, including historical reference, contextualization, regionalism, truth to structure, and simple (though often superficial) detail.

But because Stone grasped, and represented in built form, the ethos of the moment by incorporating popular tastes maligned by formalistic modernists, he is still not comfortably situated in mainstream histories of Modernism. While the most current appraisals of his architecture go beyond formalist criteria and utilize diverse methodologies and insights from other disciplines, the complex yet fundamental interrelationship between Stone, popular consumption, and the mass media has not been thoughtfully considered. Thus, this more inclusive examination of Stone's production and its critical fortunes provides the opportunity to identify his legacy of effectively reconciling Modernism with popular culture. By exposing dramatically shifting viewpoints, the media's increasing command over public opinion, and new types of patronage, it expands the dialogue about the second generation of modern architects, and more specifically the members

Gallery of Modern Art
(1958–64; redeveloped),
2 Columbus Circle,
New York City. *Arnold Eagle*

of what has sometimes been called the "Ballet School." First used in the early 1960s by the architectural historian Reyner Banham to describe the ornamented, classically oriented buildings of Eero Saarinen (the architect Stone most often came up against in competitions), the label has since been used to describe Saarinen's peers, including Paul Rudolph, Philip Johnson, and of course Stone. However, Stone is the only one who has not previously received objective, scholarly treatment—a crucial step if there is ever to be a thorough appraisal of their collective body of work.

"Colossus." "Visionary." "Giant." These are just some of the superlatives used to describe Stone in his prime in the late 1950s when he emerged as one of the first "celebrity architects" (as they are known today). The diversity and scope of his architecture knew no bounds—from master plans for entire university campuses, urban revitalizations, and foreign government complexes to hospitals, cultural centers, museums, airports, and banks, not to mention extensive residential work. At his peak, Stone was acknowledged as one of the most distinguished and progressive American architects, with a huge and prestigious workload that brought him exceptional prosperity.[4] Recognized by 1966 as the "Man with a Billion on the Drawing Board," as a *Business Week* headline read, Stone had estimated annual commission fees of $5 million.[5] He achieved "phenomenal success on very ambitious projects," as Stone himself explained to a colleague, with buildings on

four continents, in thirteen foreign countries, and in thirty-two states.[6] His contributions to twentieth-century architecture were widely recognized: Among the many professional honors and awards he received are five honorary academic degrees (two masters and three doctorates) and five prestigious Honor Awards from the American Institute of Architects (AIA).

Colleagues considered him exceedingly intelligent, with a remarkable visual memory, great knowledge of history, and enviable artistic talent. When Stone was nominated for an AIA fellowship in 1957, Pietro Belluschi, dean of the School of Architecture and Planning at the Massachusetts Institute of Technology (MIT), called him "the most imaginative designer of his generation."[7] He was also one of the best-liked and most-fair-minded members of the profession, with Gordon Bunshaft admiring his sincerity and thoughtfulness, Philip Johnson his integrity, Max Abramovitz his genius, George Rockwise his thoroughly engaging demeanor, and Frank Lloyd Wright his honesty.[8] Similarly, Stone easily won the admiration of many

Stone and President John F. Kennedy with a model of the National Cultural Center (later the John F. Kennedy Center for the Performing Arts; 1958–71) at a White House luncheon for the Business and Special Gifts Committee, October 8, 1963.

for being able to "draw anything except a sober breath," as *Time* notoriously reported in a 1958 cover story about him, never completely dissipated.[14] In spite of great charm and personal magnetism, Stone could also be deliberate, doggedly pursuing projects he set his sights on—such as the National Cultural Center (memorialized as the Kennedy Center after President Kennedy's death in 1963), for which extant correspondence chronicles his thirteen-month courtship of the key decision makers.[15] He commented in 1959 to Senator Fulbright, cosponsor of the legislation authorizing the building, "It is understood that I will not necessarily be the architect. However, I guarantee that I will make the choice inevitable for them," and he did.[16] As a risk taker in the early part of his career, Stone considered the word security as "cowardly inertia," which helps explain why he had a chronic problem with solvency.[17] Even so, when the odds were stacked against him, his discernable humility and sure optimism could banish apprehension—so much so that one of his clients, Arthur Hanisch, for whom Stone built the Stuart Company (1955–58) in Pasadena, California, admiringly dubbed him the "Arkansas Hillbilly Dalai Lama (see fig. page 101)."[18]

Adept at accommodating the interests and needs of his clients, Stone instilled confidence by giving them a sense of control.[19] He believed that architecture should tell a story about the patron, and so he played to their idiosyncrasies, initially attracting such prominent clients as Nelson Rockefeller, Vincent Astor, Frank Altschul, and A. Conger Goodyear, and then after the war, Robert Dowling, Robert Moses, Sam Spiegel, Victor Borge, Huntington Hartford, and Joyce Hall—in addition to foreign ministers, ambassadors, Congress, and four first families of the United States.

Stone could not have achieved such success without the unremitting support of three key people: an architect, a publisher, and a politician—in that order. During his formative years, his mentor was Henry Richardson Shepley, a Boston architect named after his grandfather, the great Romanesque Revivalist Henry Hobson Richardson. In addition to hiring Stone in 1924 after observing his work at the Boston Architectural Club and then writing a letter of recommendation to study at Harvard University's school of architecture in Cambridge, Massachusetts, Shepley was on the jury in 1927 that awarded Stone the distinguished Rotch Travelling Scholarship. He also served on the committee that, beginning in 1953, oversaw the execution of Stone's masterful American Embassy complex in New Delhi, India.[20] In 1957 Shepley endorsed his nomination for the AIA fellowship and in 1958 proposed him to the National Institute of Arts and Letters (now the American Academy of Arts and Letters), the highest ranking honor society of the arts in the United States.[21]

While Shepley helped Stone refine his architectural skills and make introductions, Howard Myers, publisher of Time Inc.'s *Architectural Forum*, exposed him to the benefits of self-

of those with whom he worked: Octavio Méndez Guardia, his associate architect for the famed El Panama Hotel in Panama City, always maintained that their intimate, midnight talks in the drafting room accelerated Méndez Guardia's professional growth years beyond his actual experience.[9]

Tall and dignified with a slow, strong gait, people described Stone as having a kind face with endearing, bassetlike features. His relaxed style stemmed from a southern upbringing, which was akin, Stone said, to those of Booth Tarkington's Penrod and Mark Twain's Tom Sawyer.[10] One person's opinion of him as "an easy-going, somewhat disorganized embodiment of the old saw that you can take the boy out of the country, but you can't take the country out of the boy," seems on the mark.[11]

Stone never missed an opportunity to generate a laugh, says Ernest E. Jacks, his most loyal employee, in a thoughtful recollection completed in 2000.[12] Ever ready for a party, he was remembered for being a terror of New York City's Greenwich Village, undoubtedly because of his excessive drinking, which lost him jobs until he successfully quit in 1955 (after a number of attempts).[13] Nonetheless, Stone's reputation

Billboard announcing the construction of the El Panama Hotel (1946–51) on Via España, Panama City, Republic of Panama.

Oak lounge chairs with rear legs derived from plow handles made by Fulbright Industries (1949–54), Fayetteville, Arkansas. *George Silk*

promotion and publicity. Sometimes cited as one of Stone's drinking buddies (along with Buckminster Fuller, George Howe, Alfred Shaw, Samuel Marx, Alvar Aalto, and John Fistere), Myers was far more.[22] Stone formed a deep bond with this affable, imaginative man and saw him regularly until his untimely death in 1947.[23] Myers not only found Stone much-needed work (including the redesign of Myers's own East Fifty-seventh Street apartment in New York City) but exposed him to such luminaries as Frank Lloyd Wright—who became a close friend of Stone's—as well as the journalist-entrepreneur Henry Robinson Luce and his wife, Clare, who became important clients.[24]

The third inspiring figure in Stone's life, Senator Fulbright, served as a crucial political catalyst for him.[25] The distinguished statesman was extremely proud of his boyhood friend, praising him to the United States Senate as "one of the most famous and successful architects in the world."[26] He advised the president of the University of Arkansas in Fayetteville that in spite of Stone's student reputation as a loafer and roisterer, he was the only person qualified to undertake the design of its Fine Arts Center, which Stone executed between 1948 and 1951 (see pages 72–75).[27] Their relationship deepened when Fulbright hired Stone to create furniture designs for his family's fledgling lumber and wood-parts company in Fayetteville.[28] But the most important sign of his allegiance was his backing of Stone as the architect of the Kennedy Center.

Museum of Modern
Art (1935–39) by
Stone and Philip
Lippincott Goodwin
(1885–1958), 11
West Fifty-third Street,
New York City.
Herbert Gehr

To a certain extent, the ups and downs of Stone's career reflect the state of his personal life, particularly as it pertained to his three wives. Gordon Bunshaft, one of Stone's first employees, suggested as much in 1957 when he wrote, "Ed's architecture, in many ways, reflects Ed as a person."[29] His first wife was Sarah Orlean Vandiver, a native of Montgomery, Alabama, whom he met in Europe and married in 1930 and by whom he had two children: Edward Durell Jr. and Robert Vandiver. Then in the same month that their divorce was finalized, in June 1954, he married Maria Elena Torch, whom he had met on a transatlantic flight in 1953. With Maria, Stone admitted to being "disgustingly content" and said the marriage was responsible for some of his most significant architecture, implying that the romanticism that appeared in his work emanated from her.[30] Although they had two children together, Benjamin Hicks and Maria Francesca, the marriage ended in a cyclonic, very pubic divorce in 1966. Finally, in 1972, Stone married his secretary of six years, Violet La Stella (née Moffat), with whom he had one more child, Fiona Campbell, two years before he died in 1978.

Born in 1902, Stone liked to remind people that his life spanned "the horse and buggy, the automobile, the air,

the atomic, the jet and the space ages." His exposure to extraordinary economic swings, domestic unrest, and international confrontations as well as remarkable technological advancements and an American cultural renaissance all show in his architecture.[31] Readily apparent as a boy, Stone had exceptional artistic talent that sustained him throughout his life. While attending architecture school at Harvard and then at MIT, he was required to follow programs based on the prestigious École des Beaux-Arts in Paris, which influenced his aesthetic philosophy of finding a clean, elegantly proportioned solution to a complex problem and then, as one of his early associates characterized Stone's method, schmaltzing it up with decoration, often with a profusion of geometric pattern.[32] His persistent fondness for decorative detail (in spite of untold numbers of disapproving critical reviews) was undoubtedly impelled by his own artistic lens. Stone had considerably less inclination for technical matters: he himself admitted, "I am not an Eiffel or a Buckminster Fuller. I am not an inventive engineer."[33] Nor did he have the business acumen of Nathaniel A. Owens, the theory of Robert Venturi, the influence of Ludwig Mies van der Rohe, or the cultural power of Philip

Johnson. Nonetheless, Stone's artistry firmly places him with these modern masters.

His earliest experience as an architect was in New York City when he worked on unprecedented commissions in the luxurious Art Deco style. That reductivist aesthetic, defined by geometric abstraction and streamlined motion, is manifested to varying degrees in the first of Stone's four periods of independent production beginning in 1933. But Stone took his cue even more from the Museum of Modern Art's 1932 International Style exhibition as he experimented with the forms, materials, and spatial arrangements of the European models. He soon was recognized as a pioneer modernist—even as he began to incorporate distinctly American influences in his designs. But while his production, primarily residential, attracted the attention of the print media, it connected Stone to only one major job—the Museum of Modern Art's new building on East Fifty-third Street in New York City. Designed in collaboration with the older, more conservative architect Philip Lippincott Goodwin, Stone's most thoughtful contribution was the front façade, much of which has been preserved in spite of extensive alterations and additions to the museum campus.

During his second period of production, between about 1940 and 1951, Stone utilized the International Style for commercial and public projects, believing that its rigid structural system was well suited for the demands for efficiency and economy. At the same time he experimented, as many others did, with the American vernacular for residential designs—in particular using the indigenous materials and regional inspirations of Frank Lloyd Wright and such California Bay Area Style architects as William Wilson Wurster. Stone's New York City practice was disrupted by a wartime stint in the Army Air Force's Planning and Design Section in which he worked his way up to the rank of major. Afterwards, in 1945, he reopened his practice in Great Neck, New York, building numerous modularly planned horizontal structures of such natural materials as solid lumber, rough brick, and stone.[34] Even though Stone claimed he did not find much satisfaction in what he referred to as this "hair-shirt" period, it did inform his evolving signature aesthetic.[35] His enduring fondness for naturalism, which he began to combine with symbols of luxury, is fully expressed in his Tile Council of America's promotional bathroom mock-up. Pictured in *House Beautiful* in August and September 1953, the bathroom is furnished with an imposing sunken tub and is illuminated by natural light from the circular skylight and through the glazed windows and door to the patio, where a statue by Glen Lux is strikingly offset by greenery, wooden fencing, and an overhead trellis.

Importantly, it was in this third period of production, between about 1951 and 1962, that Stone consolidated his various sources, as seen with two important government commissions: the American Embassy in New Delhi and the United States Pavilion at the Exposition Universelle et Internationale Bruxelles 1958. Both were intended to communicate the nation's political and economic supremacy over other countries, especially those with dangerously conflicting ideologies. But since Modernism had become associated in the United States with political radicalism,

Chancery (1953–59) at the American Embassy, Shantipath, Chanakyapuri, New Delhi, India.

for the embassy Stone had been asked to depart from established modern precedents. As he innovatively combined aspects of the International Style with culturally familiar concepts and forms, Stone conspicuously utilized a rich variety of decoration, much of which carried functional responsibilities as well. The essence of his achievement was captured in the proclamation made by the president of Colby College in Waterville, Maine, in 1959 as he was conferring an honorary doctorate of fine arts on Stone, "You are now a leader in the effort to restore to modern architecture some of the manifestations of elegance and individuality that the machine age prepared to sweep away. . . . You have shown that architecture can be unmistakably modern without sacrificing beauty and spiritual enrichment."[36] Welcomed by those who had become disenchanted with pure functionalism, Stone's "new romanticism," as his aesthetic became known, attracted worldwide acclaim because, in the opinion of many, it revitalized Modernism.[37]

Similar to the late-eighteenth-century Romantics, who revolted against academicism by offering dramatic and radical alternatives, Stone's more versatile variation helped significantly to democratize Modernism.[38] Firmly convinced that an architect's work should "fulfill the fundamental need within the heart of man," he accepted with pride the epithet "rational romantic" tellingly bestowed on him in the April 1959 issue of *Gentlemen's Quarterly*.[39] Accordingly, as Stone refashioned his aesthetic for different types of buildings, and clients, his architecture increasingly took on the role of visual spectacle, often embodying the added dimension of glamour, to indulge the senses and elicit an emotional response. Although the primary feature, the perforated grille, was originally conceived as a functional device to reduce heat and glare and to provide privacy, it came to be part of high architectural fashion with long-term mass appeal.[40]

To claim the larger, more diverse audience for his new approach, Stone relied heavily on Maria—his wife, muse, and publicist between 1957 and 1964.[41] Soon after they were married, "the gorgeous Maria," as Olgivanna Lloyd Wright called her friend, whom some likened physically to Elizabeth Taylor, set out to transform her husband's image from a fun-loving, back-country boy into an elegant, chivalrous gentleman.[42] Possessing a sharp, intuitive mind and keen eye, Maria shrewdly popularized his name as part of her effort to cultivate his celebrity—so much so that friends and colleagues grumbled when, in 1956, she insisted he use his full name, as Wright did, as well as drop the names of the firm's associates from correspondence.[43]

As a duo, Stone was the talent, his wife the glamour; he was a likeable guy who could sell just about anything; she

Bathroom mock-up for the Tile Council of America, illustrated in *House Beautiful*, August and September 1953.

United States Pavilion (1956–58; partially demolished) at the Exposition Universelle et Internationale Bruxelles 1958.

was savvy about publicity, which, for a time, she managed in his office. Stone came to depend on her opinion and unrelenting support—even after their life together came to resemble a soap opera.[44] According to one former employee, Maria was 90 percent of his success.[45] Stone probably would have agreed, since he confessed on numerous occasions: "I was like Rip Van Winkle, asleep in the hills, until I came down and Maria brought me back to life."[46]

With Maria at his side, Stone learned to navigate the diminishing line between traditional artist and pop celebrity.[47] Backed by expanding mass communication systems, he embraced the limelight as a means of introducing his architecture to a popular audience who, prejudiced by the media, equated fame with success. Given that the AIA prohibited advertising, and recognizing that when his name was attached to any form of the media his reputation was instantly bolstered, Stone took advantage of television in addition to the ever-increasing selection of publications—not just the ones related to his profession but those devoted to business, entertainment, fashion, literature, society, and popular culture.[48] He also enthusiastically contributed his own writings in themes accessible to everyone: simple, familiar, and understandable. His articles—among the most memorable, "The Case Against the Tailfin Age" in the *New York Times* (October 18, 1959)—are homiletic yet carry brief, at times punchy, messages that express his ideas and impressions—all devised with an eye toward the greater goal of transforming Modern-

Stone with his second wife, Maria Elena Torch (b. 1925), in the breezeway of the Celanese house (1958–59), Oenoeke Ridge Road, New Canaan, Connecticut.

ism into his own decorative aesthetic, which he hoped would be viewed like Wright's Prairie Style as a formal, long-lasting school of architecture.[49]

When the publishing companies McGraw-Hill and Alfred A. Knopf approached Stone in 1961, he was already at work on two manuscripts for two other publishers.[50] One, "The American Landscape," was a diatribe on the careless despoiling of

America's architectural heritage, for which he offers his remedies (the book was cancelled by E. P. Dutton in 1962).[51] The other was his autobiography, *The Evolution of an Architect*, published in 1962 by Horizon Press (the exclusive publisher of Wright's work since 1953).[52] With more than 470 illustrations, Stone's text comprises less than 20 percent of the book, but it is full of entertaining anecdotes and colorful descriptions of influential family and friends, as well as exquisite student sketches (now closely held by family members). As a biographical narrative rather than a theoretical work, it was intended as a mass-market book and thus, besides being his most ambitious promotional tool, has been the most frequently quoted source about him.[53]

Stone's final period of production, between about 1962 and his retirement in 1974, reflects his awareness of the growing requirements of American capitalism. With proven efficiency, satisfaction, and budget management for clients, he firmly believed that his aesthetic, by then entrenched in contemporary culture, could be adapted for immense projects—skyscrapers, corporations, capitols, and universities. Epitomized by the campus at what is now called the University at Albany in New York, Stone was resolute on unifying all the compo-

nents of the plan—here through colonnaded quadrangles that were boldly modulated and grandly scaled. His progressively classical articulations were targeted at making a statement against the austere glass-and-metal buildings, now rampant across the country, which to Stone not only looked bleak and impotent but had unsolvable problems of glare, difficulties with weather-tightness, excessive mechanical equipment, and costly maintenance.[54]

Stone also consciously set out to make a case against the forests of billboards, honky-tonks, catchpenny tourist developments, and miles of little square boxes emerging along American highways. In response to progressive, unplanned development, he was concerned about the preservation of both natural and urban settings, writing in 1962, "I find that I am not a lone nostalgic sentimentalist, but only one of a highly vocal, anti-progress group."[55] Thus, his lifelong "unabashed search for beauty," as he liked to call it, meshed with Sixties movements.[56]

At the same time, certain critics began to insinuate that his work carried the taint of kitsch (or camp), though the word itself was not applied to Stone's work with regularity until after a contemporary critical apparatus for thinking about

Aerial view of the John F. Kennedy Center for the Performing Arts), F Street N.W., Washington, D.C.

it—provided by Susan Sontag's essay, "Notes on 'Camp'" (1964)—had been sufficiently assimilated, consciously or otherwise, into contemporary thinking. [57] Elusive, complex, and constantly evolving, there is no simple way to define kitsch. While some theorists call it a phenomenon and others a sensibility, all agree that kitsch generally implies an aesthetic inadequacy, usually resulting from its intention to satisfy a wide popular audience through immediate enjoyment or entertainment, ease of access, and quick, predictable effects. Cheap or expensive, kitsch often imitates, duplicates, reproduces, or standardizes, and while it can be deceiving leaves nothing to the imagination. Tiffany lamps, *Swan Lake*, and even the giant Art Nouveau stalks designed by Hector Guimard for Paris Métro entrances (all examples used by Sontag) epitomize the crowd-pleasing nature of kitsch. It cannot, however, be subjected to the traditional measures of "high art" such as uniqueness and rarity, truth and beauty, or, even more, transcendence. Rather, kitsch must be appreciated as an emotionally charged, consumable aesthetic often stylized with richness or superfluity.[58] While Stone may not have been aware of its significance, aspects of kitsch were increasingly interwoven in his architecture—so much so that when completed in 1971, the Kennedy Center—with its form emphatically derived from his embassy in New Delhi and interiors of unmatched theatrical extravagance—became the watershed for thinking about Stone as a representative of the "kitsch school."[59] By then, critical response to his work was more or less turning against Stone in the United States, in large part because his buildings no longer represented current impulses. His production had become so vast that it was impossible for him to be personally involved in all design decisions or to appease each client, as he was so adept at doing. While his New York City and Los Angeles offices plodded on, unremarkably, into the 1980s, Stone's inadequacy at business strategy as well as finance and staff management had also taken an irreversible toll. His final book, *Recent and Future Architecture,* published by Horizon Press in 1967, stands as a sad metaphor for the late period of his career: calculated, impersonal, and banal, the enormous tome (much too large for a coffee table, let alone a bookshelf) is far removed from his earlier book filled with entertaining stories, and, most of all, his romantic genius—the very essence of his being. Reviewing the book, *Progressive Architecture* expressed the growing sentiment in the trade—that the twenty-five-dollar "puff-book" represented the dissolution of an "old-time, unconnected architect."[60] When Stone's moment of creative exuberance faded, so did he.

And yet, on his death in 1978, he was remembered as having once been considered Wright's successor as the nation's greatest living architect.[61] While he has failed to generate the same admiration as Wright with each passing generation,

Quadrangle in the University at Albany (1961–71), State University of New York, Washington Avenue.

his architecture nonetheless deeply permeated the American consciousness. By recovering his architecture and observing what the many critics, peers, and even casual observers had to say, it is patently clear that at one time Stone was immensely popular because he touched widely held cultural preferences. He was able to give form to the aspirations of the emerging consumer culture with a variation of Modernism that was at once rigorous, sensual, and traditional. At his peak, his architecture was open to the future—just as postwar America was supposed to be.

This examination of the emergence of Edward Durell Stone as one of the nation's most celebrated architects reveals how the profession engaged in the exciting process of developing a modernist architecture to suit the dynamism of the age. Stone was in the forefront with an aesthetic committed to certain modernist positions but also advocating the interests of the common man. His work, then, crystallizes the sometimes contradictory but also fascinating material evidence of a world power, a middle class, a cultural elite—all striving to define themselves in an age of unprecedented challenges and opportunities.

1: AN ARTIST'S PATH

FROM PASTORAL OZARKIAN TO COSMOPOLITAN SAVANT

It seems to me that an architect should again think of himself as an artist and confess to himself and to his client and to the world that his objective is to do a beautiful building, in fact, a work of art.[1]

The one outstanding quality about Stone that critics and peers alike have consistently agreed on is that he had extraordinary artistic ability. Indeed, Stone always considered himself a creative artist above all else.[2] His talent opened doors to eastern schools, to extensive international travel, and then, as a neophyte architect, to high-profile jobs. Among his noteworthy early contributions is the imposing foyer in Rockefeller Center's Radio City Music Hall in New York City.

Stone was born and primarily raised in Fayetteville, Arkansas. His mother, Ruth Johnson Stone, recognized his creativity early on and encouraged him by dedicating a large room in the house for his use as a carpentry shop. There he could build furniture and boats, miniature towns and roadways, as well as a playhouse, which the neighborhood boys visited in morning and afternoon shifts.[3] At fourteen he entered a birdhouse-building contest sponsored by the Northwest Arkansas Lumber Company (a Fulbright family concern). He fashioned a bluebird house in the shape of a log cabin out of sassafras branches and won first place, three dollars, and mention in the Fulbright family newspaper, the *Fayetteville Democrat*. Stone reminisced that it was his "undoing" when he discovered that by doing what he liked best he could earn "both glory and money."[4]

But Stone floundered academically, perhaps because his mother died just after he turned seventeen and thereafter he had an unstable home life. He did not have much of a professional role model since his father depended on his inheritance

and worked only intermittently. Stone's grandfather, Stephen Keblinger Stone, who arrived in Fayetteville in 1839, had invested in land and a dry-goods store in the town square, which allegedly was the largest and most successful business in town.[5] Married to Amanda Brodie, a public-spirited woman whose father, Lodowic, was also an early settler, Stephen Stone was said to be a man with a continuity of purpose, business acumen, and gracious personality who left an indelible mark on the community when he died in 1909 as Washington County's richest man.[6]

Between fall of 1918 and spring of 1920, Stone attended a training high school at the University of Arkansas, where he was proficient only in mechanical drawing, a subject that would have utilized his natural abilities.[7] He subsequently attended the university's College of Arts and Sciences for six terms, but his grades hovered in the C and D ranges. He was placed on academic probation in 1921, and most teachers, he said, saw no future for him.[8] But in the winter term of 1921 to 1922, he received an A in Elementary Freehand Drawing, and the teacher, a Miss Galbraith, was so enthusiastic about his rendering of the Parthenon frieze that she apparently took it on herself to write his much older brother, James Hicks Stone (called Hicks), then a practicing architect in Boston, asking him to take his brother under his wing.[9]

Stone visited his brother—who remained a lifelong inspiration even after he died young of cancer in 1928—in the sum-

Foyer in the Radio City Music Hall
(1929–33) by Associated Architects,
1260 Avenue of the Americas,
Rockefeller Center, New York City.

mer of his nineteenth year.[10] Hicks introduced him to the work
of such regional architecture as Henry Hobson Richardson,
and together they visited New York City, where Hicks led his
brother blindfolded onto the Brooklyn Bridge; his first glimpse
of the sublime skyline, Stone recalled, changed him forever.
The same summer, Stone saw the Pan American Union Building (1907–10; now the Main Building [MNB] of the Organization of American States) in Washington, D.C., a classical design
of white marble by the Beaux-Arts–trained architect Paul
Philippe Cret in association with Albert Kelsey. He was awed,
particularly by the interior patio (or atrium), which was paved
in brightly colored tiles, enclosed by a sliding-glass roof, and
adorned with a pink marble fountain, lush tropical vegetation,
and birds.[11] In fact, Stone claimed, in 1966, that he repeated
this classical garden design in every one of his buildings![12]

While Stone recalled that he returned to Fayetteville
motivated to study, in truth he continued to perform poorly
in class.[13] After a semester he gave up and moved to Boston,
where in June 1923 he found a job as an office boy in the
architecture firm where his brother had once worked, Strick-
land, Blodgett & Law (1920–32); during the winters of 1922
to 1924, he studied in the evenings at the Boston Architectural Club, founded in 1889 to provide lectures, exhibitions,
classes, and studio spaces for students and professionals.[14]
There he mastered the classical orders by making analyt-
iques, elevations surrounded by decorative arrangements of

significant details, drawn in ink and then rendered in Chinese washes—technical skills that he considered essential to
developing creative ideas. He later immodestly recalled, "I
must say that when they were done you could hardly believe
that the hand of man could do such beautiful things."[15] Henry
Shepley, president of the Boston Architectural Club between
1922 and 1926, who recognized how gifted Stone was at turning an ordinary design into an object of beauty, invited him to
join his firm, Coolidge, Shepley, Bulfinch and Abbott (1924–
52), as a draftsman in January 1924.[16] Under his direction,
Stone was exposed to the firm's Beaux-Arts tradition of enrich-
ing its structures with classical ornament—working on such
projects as the George Alexander McKinlock Dormitory and
the reconstruction of Massachusetts Hall, both at Harvard, as
well as on the Washington Building in the District of Columbia
and the Fabyan Building in Boston.[17]

With Shepley's endorsement, in May 1925 Stone again followed in his brother's footsteps by applying to the Graduate
School of Design at Harvard. There, he was a special student,
which meant he was not a candidate for a degree but for a cer-

Stone as a student, ca. 1927. *Bachrach*

tificate of accomplishment, and he received one of three $250 scholarships (the full tuition fee) by placing highest in a two-stage design competition based on Beaux-Arts methodology.[18]

At Harvard, Stone did brilliant work, according to George Harold Edgell, dean of the architecture school, and was easily considered the most talented by his peers. Though, surprisingly, he only received a B- in Modelling Architectural Ornament in Clay and in Drawing from the life, Stone did successfully pass the intermediate architectural design course, Study of Elementary Composition, taught by Jean Jacques "Jake" Haffner—the Nelson Robinson Jr., Professor of Architecture, with whom he had become acquainted during the critiques at the Boston Architectural Club.[19] Haffner, who studied at the École des Beaux-Arts between 1907 and 1912 and won the Premier Grand Prix de Rome in 1919, practiced a style of teaching that emphasized individual progress rather than a regimented program. It was well-suited to Stone's temperament, and he became a devoted student.[20]

Though later claiming to be "an architectural history buff" who liked to travel with Sir Banister Fletcher's legendary *History of Architecture* (1896) under his arm, Stone only took two architectural history courses in his life—both at Harvard.[21] He was proficient, receiving Bs in History of Ancient Architecture, taught by Dean Edgell, and in History of Roman, Early Christian, and Byzantine Architecture, taught by Kenneth John Conant, an assistant professor of architecture who would later become a leading medieval archaeologist. Stone benefited from their respective teaching methods: for Edgell, he was required to make sketches from lantern slides and execute complete renderings of reconstructed buildings; from Conant, he learned how to use objective systems of classification to analyze historical structures and objects.[22] While Stone had cordial relationships with both, he kept in touch with Conant and later relayed

to him that his course had had a "profound influence" on him.[23] Significantly, Conant and Edgell had each studied under Herbert Langford Warren, who had established the architecture program at Harvard in 1895 and passed down to his successors—and by extension to Stone, too—his belief that architecture is essentially a fine art.[24] Stone remained steadfast to this vision throughout his life.[25]

While Stone's strong visual memory contributed to his enthusiasm for architectural history, he was less proficient at the technical aspects of construction. Even though he received a C+ on the Construction Problem, presented each year by Charles Wilson Killam, a skilled engineer who taught at Harvard beginning in 1908, Stone failed Killam's exceedingly difficult course, Theory of Building Construction—Statics, Resistance of Materials, and Elementary Structural Design.[26] According to his classmate Walter Harrington Kilham Jr., one afternoon Stone arrived in the drafting room, visibly distressed, and said that he couldn't take it any longer, and as his parting gesture, threw his slide rule on the floor.[27] Extant correspondence indicates Stone's decision was not that impulsive, since his request to be excused from repeating the course, as required, was denied.[28] Attributing his failure to a poor beginning and confident that Stone could obtain the requisite B or better, Dean Edgell appealed to him, "Let us assume that you will be with us next year and that I shall not have the distress of seeing work as fine as yours in design labelled 'M.I.T.' of [sic] 'Yale', 'Columbia', or 'Penn', for the matter of that!"[29]

In spite of Edgell's passionate plea, in the fall of 1926 Stone enrolled at MIT as a Special Student in Architecture—Course IV, which did not require him to study engineering. There he presumably studied under Jacques Carlu, whom he had also encountered at the Boston Architectural Club. Another product of the École des Beaux-Arts and a winner of the Grand Prix de Rome, Carlu espoused the philosophy that an architect's mission is to unite "the memory of the past with the expectation of the future," a point of view that would have resonated with Stone.[30]

As part of the Beaux-Arts method of teaching, both schools encouraged students to participate in design competitions. In the ones sponsored by the Beaux-Arts Institute of Design in New York City (founded in 1916 to extend the activities of the Society of Beaux-Arts Architects in Paris), Stone was required to prepare, within nine consecutive hours, a sketch on a given subject and then complete drawings within six weeks. Although he received a first mention for a railway station in May 1926, he was only awarded a second medal for his picturesque country inn in December, the latter illustrated in the *Bulletin of the Beaux-Arts Institute of Design*.[31] He must have also been disappointed that in March 1927 he narrowly missed a first medal (out of 224 entries) for the summer school of fine arts competition, which included a $500 scholarship to the Fontainebleau School of Fine Arts in France, where Carlu was associated.[32] This submission shows developing themes that would be present in his later work: severe, flat Spartan walls that extend as the building façade; historical and cultural references; geometric-patterned fenestration (here somewhat Secessionist in spirit); water and fountains; interior courtyards with trees and plantings; covered colonnades; and a curvilinear dining room protruding from an otherwise rectilinear form.

In May 1927, Stone finally did win a competition, the coveted Rotch Travelling Scholarship, finding himself "delighted but surprised."[33] Founded in 1883, and based on the Prix de Rome model, the Rotch Travelling Scholarship, as it is still called today, was originally open only to young men with training in the state of Massachusetts. After passing a preliminary examination, Stone was one of sixteen to advance to the second stage and then one of four in the final competition, in which he was required to prepare a preliminary sketch and then drawings for a studio and business establishment for an architecture firm with 250 draftsmen.[34] Illustrated in the periodical *Pencil Points* in July 1927, his idyllic scheme of conference and drafting rooms surrounded by gardens (a concept that would forever be ingrained in his mind) brought him $3,000 for two years of study abroad.[35]

Between September 1927 and October 1929, Stone traveled primarily throughout Europe, recording thousands of years of architecture in his memory as well as in his sketches and watercolors, thirteen of which are illustrated in his book, *The Evolution of an Architect*.[36] He was required to periodically send the scholarship committee sketches, watercolors, and carefully studied drawings—or envois, as they were known in the French system—as evidence of his study and travel, but it is not clear that he always did so. For example, he received permission from the committee to create two envois of Oxford University's Radcliffe Observatory and the restoration of a Pompeian house, the plan for which would be hugely influential in his later work, but there is no record he executed

them.[37] In 1928, however, he did produce envois of the Loggia dei Leoni at the Villa Borghese in Rome and of the Cathédrale Sainte-Cécile d'Albi in southern France.[38] Although Clarence Howard Blackall, the secretary of the scholarship committee, had recommended to Stone that he primarily focus on notes and measurements, these exquisitely rendered drawings attest to his ability to comprehensively examine and illustrate historic structures.

This experience reinforced his belief that a knowledge of history is essential not just to the understanding but also to the creation of architecture. He later explained, "The obsession with monuments of the past may seem sentimental and pedantic, but I believe the inspiration for a building should be in the accumulation of history."[39] While impressed by both the size and scale of the buildings he saw, it was their permanence—expressed in solid, natural materials, a monumental presence, and the rich articulation of past traditions, especially the classical—that most affected him. Immersed as he was in the Beaux-Arts tradition, in which, he explained, it was perfectly respectable to rely on Italian Renaissance palaces, French châteaux, or Georgian country houses for inspiration, Stone referenced in his mature work such masterpieces as the Doge's Palace in Venice, the Parthenon in Athens, and the Coliseum in Rome (see pages 11, 15, 126 bottom).[40]

Although Stone was required to focus on historic buildings, his sketchbooks also include some fifteen pages of renderings of twentieth-century works. In his autobiography Stone retrospectively claimed to have been excited about the modernist architecture in the Netherlands—public buildings by William Dudok in Hilversum; the Van Nelle Tobacco Factory (1926–29) by Johannes A. Brinkman, Leendert Cornelis van der Vlught, and Mart Stam in Rotterdam; and the Zonnestraal Sanatorium (1926–28) by Johannes Duiker and Bernard Bijvoet in Hilversum. In France he admired cubist houses by Robert Mallet Stevens in Paris, projects by Tony Garnier in Lyons, and churches and concrete hangars at the airport in Orly by Auguste Perret. In Germany he liked the

Part of "A Summer School of Fine Arts," competition drawing by Stone, illustrated in the *Bulletin of the Beaux-Arts Institute of Design* 3 (May 1927): 13.

Starlight Roof restaurant, Waldorf-Astoria Hotel (1929–31) by Schultze and Weaver (1921–39), 301 Park Avenue, New York City.

Berlin theaters and other buildings by Eric Mendelsohn and Peter Behrens as well as Gropius's Bauhaus in Dessau, and in Barcelona, the German Pavilion (1929) by Ludwig Mies van der Rohe. Although Stone did not specifically name buildings by Le Corbusier, he voiced his enthusiasm for *Vers une architecture* (1923), which had been translated from French into English in 1927.[41] And yet, tellingly, he did not document the work of these masters on his travels, implying a lack of enthusiasm for modern functional design.

Stone returned to New York City on the S.S. Berengaria, arriving on Black Friday, October 25, 1929, the day the stock market crashed, setting off the Great Depression. The economy notwithstanding, his talent soon brought him work on two remarkably prestigious commissions: the Waldorf-Astoria Hotel and Rockefeller Center, both exemplary of developing stylistic trends, especially the Art Deco or art moderne. For the Waldorf-Astoria—the last but most prestigious, largest, and most expensive hotel designed by Schultze and Weaver— Stone was hired by Leonard Schultze, whom he had met a year earlier in Stockholm, to work on more than six public rooms, including the famed garden restaurant on the eighteenth floor. Called the Starlight Roof, its distinctive trellised ceiling as well as retractable roof had a clear influence on Stone's later work.[42] Schultze was apparently pleased with the quality of his young employee's designs: Stone confided to his fiancée, Sarah Orlean Vandiver, that Schultze was "all hot and both-

ered" over his color study of a ballroom even though Stone had "to sort of hit a compromise between the conservatism of the office and really going wild." Consequently, Stone was told to report directly to Schultze, instead of the head designer (probably Lloyd Morgan), which, as he told Orlean, "tickles me a plenty and gives me a chance for my own decisions."[43]

For Rockefeller Center, a commercial development whose layout and decoration had enormous influence on Stone, he was made director of the drafting room and chief of design for both the 3,600-seat Center Theater, initially a first-run movie house, and the much larger Radio City Music Hall.[44] While he worked alongside Eugene Schoen for the interior design of the theater and Donald Deskey for the design of the music hall (although Deskey's contributions to the grand foyer were limited to lighting and carpeting), Stone reported to Wallace Kirkman Harrison, one of the principals of Associated Architects, who expected much of the young architect as he labored over the boards in his Graybar Building office.[45] Stone absorbed much from these unparalleled examples of American elegance—the theater foyer's nautical-like round, squat columns above sleek curvilinear walls and the auditorium's twinkling ceiling; the music hall's tremendous scale, richly colored and textured surfaces, profusion of repetitive patterns, and ceremonial circulations for spectacle and drama. Stone would have been aware of the amalgamation of stylistic inspirations, from the Beaux-Arts to the machine age—not just with the designers but also with the many independent artists involved, among them Witold Gordon and Gwen Lux (with whom Stone formed an intimate relationship). He would later hire both to work on his own commissions—Gordon three times and Lux four.

Even though his renderings of the Center Theater interior was published in *Pencil Points* in September 1932 and of the music hall proscenium in *Fortune* in January 1933, Stone did not attend the opening night on December 27, 1932.[46] For he had been discharged for accepting a commission to work with another firm, N. W. Hutchings & Sons, on a recreational fishing lodge for William Vincent Astor called Ferry Reach, in St. Georges Parish, Bermuda.[47] Though he had been very disappointed, Stone was obviously forgiven since Harrison hired him again to produce the final drawings for the acclaimed Rockefeller Apartments at 17 West Fifty-fourth and 24 West Fifty-fifth streets, distinguished by the semicircular bays (see page 45).[48] Indeed, his ability could not be ignored: critic Brendan Gill recalled Harrison once remarking, "Ed, the big bear! The lobby of the Music Hall, that was Ed for you—on his scale. What a talent he had!"[49]

It would be some time, however, before Stone's interest in such grand, opulent interiors, complete with historical and decorative embellishments, could become part of his own work. Hungry for opportunity, the young architect was determined to set out on his own independent professional journey (in the midst of the Great Depression, no less), and he found himself swept into the modernist current.

Center Theater (1929–32; demolished 1954; also formerly known as the RKO Roxy Theater and the RKO Center Theater) by Associated Architects with Eugene Schoen (1880–1957), 1236 Sixth Avenue, Rockefeller Center.

Auditorium in the Radio City Music Hall by Associated Architects with Donald Deskey (1894–1989).

2: THE INTERNATIONAL STYLE

PIONEERING EXPERIMENTATION

American architecture, whatever its debt to others,
must find its own solutions in its own way.[1]

As the 1930s gave way, Stone found himself engrossed in the period's sense of adventure, invention, and experimentation. Never a stylistic purist, he was willing to try his hand at new impulses—streamlined curves, naturalistic embellishments, and stripped classicism, among them—with varying success. However, as he makes evident in his book *The Evolution of an Architect*, he was most "enamored of the sleek mechanics of the International Style," first manifested in his architecture in 1933 with the Richard H. Mandel house in Bedford Hills, New York. While aspects of the International Style became irrevocably embedded in his architecture, toward the end of the decade he began to feel, echoing the general public, that he could not altogether embrace Le Corbusier's edict that a house is a machine for living, a key premise of the movement.[2]

Though Stone had observed modern prototypes during his European tour, his interest in the International Style was more specifically prompted by the Museum of Modern Art's first formal presentation of it, *Modern Architecture International Exhibition* of 1932. He was convinced the exhibition did for architecture what the legendary International Exhibition of Modern Art (1913) at the Sixty-ninth Regiment Armory in New York City had done for modern art. And so, at least with regard to his own experience, Stone held that there was "no single event which so profoundly influenced the architecture of the Twentieth Century"—an opinion at odds with that pre-

sented in revisionist histories, including Gwendolyn Wright's *USA: Modern Architectures in History* (2008), in which she contends that it was the 1934 publication *Modern Housing* by Catherine Bauer that exposed Americans to the progressive architecture in Europe.[3]

The goal of the museum's International Style exhibition—conceived in the prosperous 1920s, when a vast supply of land, labor, and raw materials was stimulating capitalist spending and entrepreneurship—was to provide a model for the development and expansion of modern architecture in the United States. In the preface to *International Style: Architecture since 1922*—the book by the exhibition's curators, Henry-Russell Hitchcock Jr. and Philip Johnson, published in 1932—Alfred Hamilton Barr Jr., the founding director of the Museum of Modern Art, clarified that the ideological, political, and sociological implications of the original European examples were not the primary concern of Johnson and Hitchcock, nor were the specific formalistic qualities.[4] Instead, the curators were interested in identifying the three simple principles that connected the canonical works shown in the exhibition: volume (rather than mass), regularity (rather than axial symmetry), and, most consequential to Stone, the avoidance of applied ornament.[5] Touted by the museum as "the first fundamentally original and widely distributed style since the Gothic," the International Style was essentially presented as a prepackaged formula, meant to replace the fashion

2-5. Aerial view of the Richard H. Mandel house (1933–35), Haines Road, Bedford Hills, New York.
© turnervisuals.com

for historical reference that had prevailed since the Industrial Revolution.[6] The museum's exhibition catalog promoted it as such, offering a specific set of guidelines by which, it claimed, Americans could produce aesthetically sound buildings.[7] As others have observed, the museum saw its mission at the time as "super-critic" by determining what was acceptable to be shown; as "tastemaker" by encouraging dramatic changes in the American landscape; and as "fame maker" by doggedly pursuing various forms of media to publicize architecture as a new museum discipline and, moreover, as a stylish commodity for consumption.[8]

Even though Stone did not recognize that previous to the exhibition, Modernism had already begun to be disseminated through publications, competitions, and small exhibitions, it still was not widely understood, much less accepted, in the United States—at least not by the general public to whom his work would eventually appeal.[9] Consequently, there were conflicting reviews, with opponents contending that the skeleton construction techniques—utilizing a combination of steel, aluminum, reinforced concrete, or glass to allow for functional, flexible planning—resulted in unhappy bleakness.[10] What was not foreseen, however, is that the International Style, as presented by Johnson and Hitchcock, would provide a means by which details could be extracted, modified, and dispersed into American domestic traditions. Stone was a central player in this process.

His earliest attempts were for single-family houses, the market for which was beginning a slow recovery from the Great Depression. His thirty-two-room Richard H. Mandel house, situated on 60 acres overlooking the Croton Reservoir in New York's Westchester County, epitomizes the few early interpretations of the International Style by American architects.[11] Led to the commission by Donald Deskey, with whom Stone had collaborated at Radio City Music Hall at Rockefeller Center, their adventurous client was an heir to the fortune of the Chicago-based Mandel Brothers department store and an associate of Deskey's until 1941. Mandel, Stone recalled, was interested in a good business arrangement, and Stone was interested in designing his first house, and so he agreed to a fee of forty dollars a week.[12]

The Mandel house demonstrates that Stone viewed Modernism as a closed stylistic system—an aggregation of fixed forms—rather than as an attitude, an idea, or a cultural expression. In fact, Stone's Beaux-Arts training facilitated his ability to cut and paste many of the aesthetic clichés presented by the European masters he most admired—Le Corbusier, Erich Mendelsohn, Ludwig Mies van der Rohe, and Walter Gropius. For the plan, which essentially consists of three distinct rectangular areas, Stone found inspiration in the pinwheel configurations (fig. 2.1) of Gropius's Bauhaus building of 1926 in Dessau, Germany. Additionally, the Mandel plan shows a reliance on Le Corbusier's "Five Points for a New Architec-

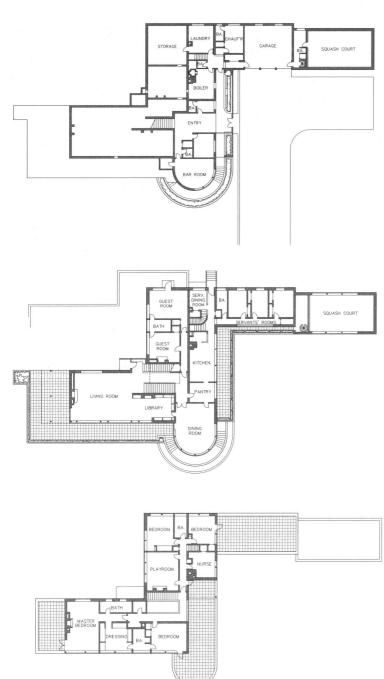

Fig. 2.1. Mandel house first-, second-, and third-floor plans.

mize views of the outdoors. Also consistent with Le Corbusier are the thin lally columns on the western side that elevate the house over a terrace, as well as the three sundecks, or roof gardens, off the bedrooms (which became a textbook feature of the International Style).[14] Inside, the open plan allows for the living room, stair hall, and library to be viewed as a single spacious unit (or be separated with curtains). The dynamic aluminum railings of the staircase between the second and third floors evoke the machine-age symbol of a ship, recalling those in Corbusier's canonical Villa Savoye (1928–29) in Poissy-sur-Seine, France. Moreover, the Mandel house and the Villa Savoye are both proudly situated as blunt, machinelike images on contrasting manicured green lawns, unlike the integrated houses and landscapes of Frank Lloyd Wright, to which Stone would later turn for inspiration.[15] Machine technology was further emphasized by making the car central to the plan; the prominent location of the garage at the end of a winding half-mile-long drive subordinates the main entry to the house at the left.[16]

While the classical axis from the glazed entry up the staircase to the second floor is visually tantalizing, the most distinguished feature of the plan is the curved dining room. The similarly shaped planting bed surrounding the dining room façade emphasizes its vivid juxtaposition to the otherwise rectilinear front façade. The curvilinear form was utilized not just by Le Corbusier and J. J. P. Oud, but also by Mies van der Rohe, in his semicircular dining room in the Tugendhat house (1930) in Brno, Czechoslovakia, for example, and by Mendelsohn, whose drawings for the Schocken department store (1926–28; demolished) in Stuttgart, Germany, show a layering of curves to create a streamlined effect. Significantly, Stone had already experimented with a curved dining room in his 1927 competition drawing for a summer school of fine arts.[17] He was also undoubtedly aware that the increasingly popular form was used by Wallace Harrison (Stone's former employer) in the living and dining rooms at his house of 1931 on Round Swamp Road in Huntington, New York, as well by Norman Bel Geddes for the garage of his House of Tomorrow design, published in *Ladies' Home Journal* in April 1931.[18]

In spite of such precedents, because there were still so few International Style houses in the United States, the Mandel house created much excitement in architectural circles and attracted a good deal of publicity: by 1940 it had been featured in more than fifteen publications, from newspapers and trade journals to mass-market magazines. But unlike the International Style exhibition, which had sparked considerable debate, the reviews of the Mandel house were almost all favorable, indicating that in just three years the polemic against Modernism had become less insistent, at least among critics. In fact, even before it was finished, the house was praised in a *New York Times* article entitled "A $60,000 Dwelling Being Erected at Mount Kisco" (according to a Stone résumé, the

ture"—so much so that in 1935 Johnson recommended that the house be included in the Museum of Modern Art's traveling exhibition on Le Corbusier.[13] Like the buildings of Le Corbusier, the Mandel house is supported on load-bearing columns, and thus the non-supporting walls could be punctuated with long horizontal strip windows of plate glass to maxi-

View from the Mandel house living room into the stair hall and library.

house ended up costing $80,000). Intrigued with the modern features that Stone exploited or modified for his client, the article highlighted the contrasting horizontal lines and single curved surface, the derivation of the exterior form from the interior plan, the contrasting materials of white stucco and flush plate glass, and the absence of ornamentation, all echoing Hitchcock and Johnson's definition of the International Style.[19] Subsequent reviews tended to focus on the integration of the interior and exterior—not only by the terraces and sundecks but also by the windows running the full length of the living room for views and light and by the dining room's glass blocks, or bricks, a material developed in Europe that allows light diffusion but, by preventing people from seeing in, avoids the fishbowl effect.[20] Much has been made of Stone's claim, in his autobiography, that he was the first to use glass block in this country—though, in fact, he was inaccurate since glass block was imported from Europe after World War I and domestic manufacturers began developing it at least by 1931.[21] What is significant, however, is that Stone anticipated a trend that quickly gained momentum in the United States: Owens-Illinois introduced its Insulux glass block at the Century of Progress exhibition of 1933 in Chicago (and by about 1939 had more than 50,000 installations across the country) and Corning introduced its Pyrex glass block in 1935.[22]

Mandel house dining room, illustrated in *House & Garden*, June 1935. *Bodorif*

Mandel house second-floor stair hall serving as a backdrop for a *Vogue* fashion shoot published in 1935. *Edward Steichen*

Mandel house bar room with a mural by Witold Gordon (1885–1965). *Ken Hayden*

Though the media esteemed the Mandel house for being distinctly American in spirit, independent of its European inspiration, surprisingly no correlations have been made between the Mandel house and Rockefeller Center's theater and music hall, which Stone worked on just a few years earlier (see pages 21 and 25). And yet, the house does have a similarly consistent, albeit far more subtle, quality of glamour, visible, for instance, in the elegant second-floor staircase hall, with the crisp, white angles accentuated by the streamlined railing. The legendary photographer Edward Steichen, who had probably been introduced to Stone when he designed a photo mural for the men's lounge in the Center Theater, recognized as much and staged a *Vogue* fashion shoot at the house in 1935.[23] More directly related to the Rockefeller Center projects are the stylized bar room on the first floor of the Mandel house, which is embellished with a mural by Witold Gordon, who had designed lounge murals at the music hall, as well as the curvaceous dining room, which recalls the one in Samuel Lionel ("Roxy") Rothafel's private apartment at the music hall. In fact, both dining rooms featured Deskey-designed tables with a light inserted in the top. Like the music hall, the Mandel house—containing some sixty-five pieces of furniture and lighting devices designed by Deskey—was a rare example of a modern American *gesamt-kunstwerk*, or total work of art.[24] It was the cooperative effort—between architect, designer, and patron—that made the house such a satisfying representation of the new method of building, according to Sheldon and Martha Candler Cheney in *Art and the Machine: An Account of Industrial Design in 20th-Century America* (1936).[25] There had been little opportunity for such collaborations in modern American residences and it obviously influenced Stone's future approach.

A number of critics, including the Cheneys, also considered the Mandel house as a "machine house," harking back to Le Corbusier. The image as such has stuck—with architectural historian Richard Guy Wilson, for example, observing in *Machine Age in America, 1918–1941* that the rounded dining room extrusion and the extended third-floor deck of the Mandel house epitomize the machine in motion.[26] Stone, however, along with the public in general, was still conflicted about glorifying the mechanical (and therefore the impersonally functional) aspects of the house. So even though it was said that the Mandel house would become the standard by which modern architecture and decoration would be measured, it more realistically represents, at least retrospectively, a notable statement about the divergent American responses to the International Style: intrigue and optimism versus apprehension and misunderstanding.[27]

So uneasy were American suburbanites about the International Style that Stone's next commission, the Ulrich and Elizabeth M. Kowalski house, also in Westchester County, sparked a backlash. As Stone recollected, the local zoning ordinances were subsequently changed to protect what he disdainfully

Ulrich and Elizabeth M. Kowalski house (1934–36; redeveloped),
Old Roaring Brick Road, Mt. Kisco, New York. *Bill Maris*

considered "a synthetic colonial community."[28] Now extensively altered, the Kowalski house originally exhibited much of the same vocabulary as the Mandel house—the most prominent feature being the glazed cylinder, containing a staircase, strikingly juxtaposed to the horizontal volume behind it as well as to the front wall enclosing a service yard—a feature Stone would further develop (fig. 2.2). As at the Mandel house, Stone also turned to European precedent for the rear façade; the long rectilinear block with uninterrupted glazing is reminiscent of the south façade of the Tugendhat house by Mies van der Rohe.

Not long after, the local gentry in Moncks Corner, South Carolina, were similarly incensed by the modern guesthouses Stone designed for Henry and Clare Luce on their eighteenth-century rice plantation about 40 miles north of Charleston, which they had purchased in 1936.[29] Clare's response was: "Why should I build an old mansion on the Cooper River?… This is none of my tradition, and it would be false to ape the old ways."[30] Stone's structures here, however, differed from his previous buildings in that he made an effort to incorporate regional influences.

Mepkin Plantation, as it was called before being converted into a Cistercian Trappist monastery in 1949, was adored by both Luces as an occasional oasis from the pressures of New York City. According to one biographer, it

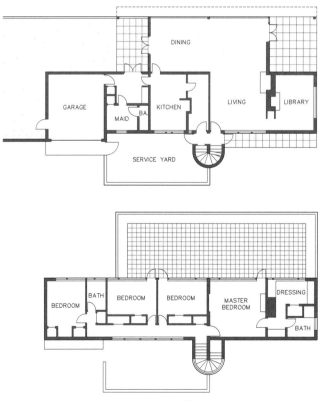

Fig. 2.2. Kowalski house first- and second-floor plans.

Claremont guesthouse (1936–37; demolished) for Henry Robinson (1898–1967) and Clare Boothe (1903–1987) Luce, Mepkin Plantation (now Mepkin Abbey), Mepkin Abbey Road, Moncks Corner, South Carolina, illustrated in *House & Garden*, August 1937. *Samuel H. Gottscho*

was Clare who engaged Stone to survey the site and submit sketches, but Henry must have agreed, since he then owned *Architectural Forum*, whose major purpose was to "dramatize the contribution of modern design to the building of a better America."[31]

Stone arranged the four small guesthouses (Claremont, Strawberry, Tartleberry, and Washington, each named after a plantation) around a pronounced rectangular courtyard, enclosed on the front by a long serpentine perforated-brick wall and on the other three sides by a one-story-high wall that also linked the front of each houses, similar to Le Corbusier's 1919 design for "maisons en béton liquid (fig. 2.3)."[32] The overall organization of buildings positioned in relation to a large open green space, or bowling green, references Thomas Jefferson's classical plan for the "Academical Village" at the University of Virginia in Charlottesville, as does the serpentine wall, which Stone would repeat many times over (see page 53).[33] Also significant to Stone's later development, the plan honored the centuries-old landscape—majestic oak trees covered with Spanish moss complemented by abundant figs, wisteria, bamboo, azaleas, and camellias.[34]

The Luces' residence, Claremont, the largest and only two-story house, was approached along a classical axis from the front entrance of the complex down the length of the pool. Its façade repeated the gesture of the primary axis—a perfectly symmetrical abstracted Regency-style mass broken only by an exaggerated sash window flanked by decorative roundels and by two doors surrounded with quoins. Each of the other three guesthouses was pierced only with a door surrounded with quoins and a small rectangular window. Even though Stone used traditional construction methods and details appropriate to southern living, he complied with modernist principles by whitewashing the brick walls of the guesthouses to resemble stucco and giving them flat roofs, ample metal-framed windows, and spacious terraces. The rear façade of each, visually more exciting than the front, were designed to integrate the house with the Cooper River landscape. Of particular interest is Claremont, in which part of the sundeck was cut away to admit light into the central dining room—a detail reminiscent of Le Corbusier's iconic cubed Esprit Nouveau pavilion at the Paris Exposition des Arts Décoratifs of 1925.[35] Extant drawings also show that some of the outbuildings around the

Claremont rear façade. *Alfred Eisenstaedt*

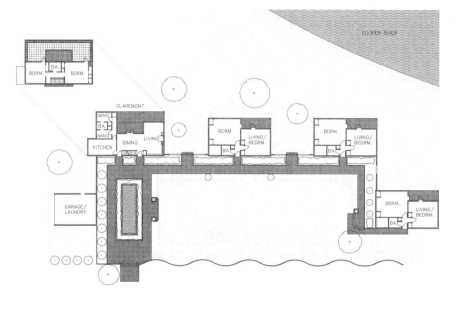

Fig. 2.3. Mepkin Plantation site plan.

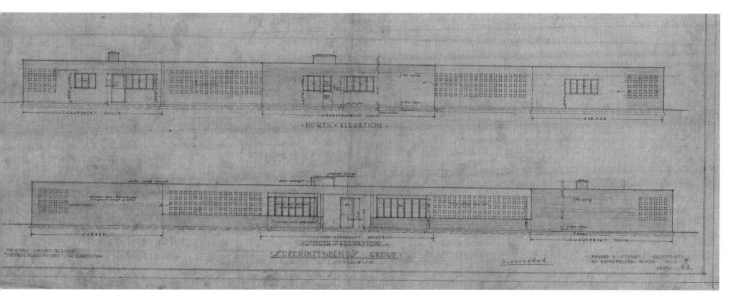

Elevations of Mepkin Plantation outbuildings, 1935.

Frank Altschul Library (ca. 1939), Overbrook Farm, River Bank Road, Stamford, Connecticut. *Ezra Stoller*

Entrance to the George Preston Marshall house (ca. 1938), Rock Creek Drive, Washington, D.C. *Ezra Stoller*

perimeter (which included a stable group, blacksmith shop, servants' house, power plant, and superintendent's group) were detailed with decorative grid patterns on the façades, already a defining characteristic of Stone's architecture.

Because Stone was still relatively inexperienced, however, the guesthouses had structural problems. In addition to chimneys that did not draw properly and a utilities system that he did not fully understand, everything leaked: "Give me a three-act play to write or assign me to war duty in Europe, but don't ask me to solve this one. Help! Help! Help!" Clare exclaimed in frustration in 1941.[36] Consequently, when Henry Luce was considering changes in 1945, he was hesitant to continue with Stone. Howard Myers, Stone's protector, encouraged Luce to work with the architect again, reminding him that he had already created an extraordinarily fine plantation grouping.[37] Stone did his best to alleviate the stream of problems at Mepkin but was certain he shook Luce's trust in him, later concluding, "I stand in evidence that as a client he is a great humanitarian."[38] Though awarded a silver medal in 1937 at the annual exhibition of the Architectural League of New York, some reviews criticized Stone for favoring function over graciousness. Most, however, were positive, highlighting his use of terraces, sundecks, and wide window spans to maximize the entrancing vista and, as *Architectural Forum* (and thus Luce) pointed out, his ability to thoroughly adapt modern design to the traditions of the South.[39]

Stone's interest in harmonizing modern architecture with its environment is further evidenced in the small library (with kitchen, bath, and roof terrace) he completed in 1939 on the Stamford, Connecticut, estate of Frank Altschul, a philanthropist, bibliophile, and authority on international affairs.[40] He integrated the small "hideaway" with its pastoral outdoors by using such natural materials as oak and creating two large sliding glass panels—a challenge to construct, even though similar units had appeared in European houses as well as in Rudolph Schindler's house (1921–22) in West Hollywood, California.[41] The building form, however, composed of two bold brick rectangular volumes, was critically dismissed because the smaller one in front with a protruding streamlined roof looked heavy in comparison with the sculpted rectilinear roofline behind it. While Stone could have been thinking about the canopies at the RCA Building in Rockefeller Center, the Art Deco detail was also popular with other architects, including Walter Dorwin Teague who used it on his standardized Texaco station.[42] Stone again used a streamlined canopy at the entrance of a house he built for George Preston Marshall, owner of the Washington Red Skins. Perhaps Stone chose the theatrical gesture, which looked incongruous with the rest of the design, in deference to Marshall's wife, the silent-screen actress Corinne Mae Griffith.[43]

The plan of Stone's earlier Wayne V. Brown house in Darien, Connecticut, was a more direct expression of the International Style, consisting of two rectilinear concrete-

Wayne V. Brown house (1936–37; redeveloped), Hollow Tree Ridge Road, Darien, Connecticut. *Gottscho-Schleisner*

Brown house rear façade.

block volumes pierced by ribbon windows. Its entrance, originally a breezeway with a gravel floor, recalled similar voided spaces designed by Le Corbusier, such as his Esprit Nouveau pavilion, as did the open plan, configured to include a second-floor dining area overlooking a two-story living room.[44] And yet, the grand neoclassical portico on the rear façade makes a distinct nod to American tradition—simply but firmly.

Stone more competently merged regional influences with a modern vocabulary in the Albert Carl Koch house in Cambridge, Massachusetts, in association with the owners' son, Albert "Carl" Koch Jr., a student at Harvard. The most distinctive feature is the way in which a second-floor bedroom,

Albert Carl Koch house (1936–38), Buckingham Street, Cambridge, Massachusetts. *Ezra Stoller*

View from the Koch house porch into the living and dining areas. *Ezra Stoller*

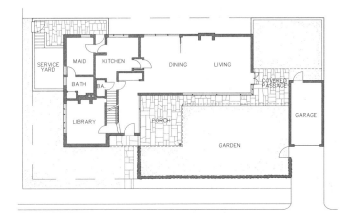

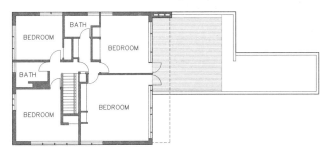

Fig. 2.4. Koch house first- and second-floor plans.

pierced with metal windows, appears to float over a porch that, as part of a larger garden, is enclosed by a 6-foot-high rubble wall (fig. 2.4). Along with the stone walks and terrace, it shows Stone's experimentation with vernacular materials, recalling Le Corbusier's solid rubble walls at the Maison de Mandrot (1931–32) near Toulon, France, and the Pavillon Suisse (1930–31) at the Cité Universitaire in Paris.

For at least ten years, the Koch house—as one of a handful of early modernist houses in Cambridge—held the attention of critics, who admired the plan not only because it effectively maximized a small lot while providing privacy, but also because it applauded the use of natural materials. In 1939 it received *House & Garden*'s first prize for architecture, as well as a grand prize from the Pittsburgh Glass Institute for its window composition: whereas the open-plan living area had large plate-glass windows looking onto the front garden, the dining area facing the rear was given translucent glass for privacy.[45] Then in 1947, citing its practical plan, *House Beautiful* named it one of the twelve best houses of the previous twelve years. It was pictured in two exhibitions organized by the Museum of Modern Art: *Art in Our Time* (1939), which celebrated the tenth anniversary of the museum and the opening of its new building on West Fifty-third Street, and *Three Centuries of American Architecture* (1939–41), which travelled after its opening venue at the Jeu de Paume in Paris. It was also in the most popular compendiums of the day—John McAndrew's *Guide to Modern Architecture: Northeast States* (1940), James and Katherine Morrow Ford's *The Modern House in America*

Approach to the A. Conger Goodyear house (1936–38), Orchard Lane, Old Westbury, Long Island, New York. *Ezra Stoller*

(1940), and George Nelson and Henry Wright's *Tomorrow's House: A Complete Guide for the Home-Builder* (1945).

Despite its critical success, the modest Koch house has not achieved anywhere near the recognition of Stone's house for A. Conger Goodyear, a native of Buffalo, New York, with vast railroad and lumber interests who was also an art collector and founding president of the Museum of Modern Art.[46] In addition to the forthright modern plan, form, and detail, the Goodyear house expressed Stone's enthusiasm for luxury and, even more, the glamour that would characterize his mature style.[47]

As the story goes, Goodyear admired Stone's contributions when working on the Museum of Modern Art building and asked him to create an intimate weekend house for him in Old Westbury, Long Island. Stone gave Goodyear exactly what he wanted, his client remembered with pride some twenty-five years later, "the best-designed small house in the country!"[48] Approached from a long, winding drive, the strikingly low, horizontal, structure of whitewashed brick stood starkly alone on a hilltop, originally with views of the Long Island Sound. Before an addition, the original L-shaped house could be experienced as a series of four primary spaces, with plate-glass windows creating ambiguity between the interior and exterior environments (fig. 2.5). Like other Stone houses, the front entrance is discreet, but the brilliance of the design unfolded upon entering through the wooden doors, treated more as decorative screens than as protective enclosures, to the first of these spaces, a walled courtyard, enclosed on one side by a covered loggia leading to the front door. The large windows in the interior gallery, or hallway, connecting the main rooms, allowed Goodyear's renowned art collection (much of which is now in the Albright-Knox Art Gallery in Buffalo, New York) to be seen by visitors walking to the entrance while the outdoor wall fresco by Pierre Bourdelle could be viewed from the inside.

The second primary space is determined by the circular shape of the dining room, which is progressively repeated from the interior recessed lighted dome (7 feet in diameter), table, carpet, windows, and walls to the exterior roof line, terrace, equally spaced trees, and brick wall. In contrast, the rectilinear-shaped swimming pool in the third space butts up against a wall with plantings outside the two bedrooms. The fourth space comprises the living room with floor-to-ceiling panels of fixed glass and a few awning windows opening to a terrace, where there was a much-photographed small pool—later to become fundamental to Stone's aesthetic—with a robust Henry Moore sculpture on a rising plinth (see the advertisement on page 39).

Unlike Stone's earlier Mandel house, where volume is built upon volume, the horizontal span of the Goodyear house is boldly bisected by a vertical plane with a deep, pronounced cantilevered roof over the living room. Although some critics assume Stone was looking at Wright, it is more likely that at this date he was recalling Mies van der Rohe's German Pavilion at the 1929 International Exhibition in Barcelona, which he had seen as a Rotch Travelling Scholar and later said he admired for its pristine beauty. It would be a lifelong influ-

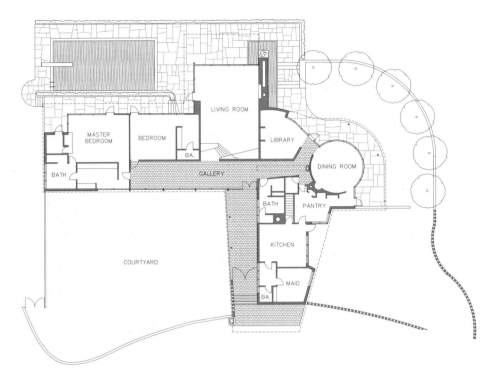

Fig. 2.5. Goodyear house site plan.

Goodyear house dining room.

ence. The description in his autobiography of the pavilion as a "simple rectangular platform and roof, with walls continuing out from the interior to form quadrangles and courts" characterizes the Goodyear house as well. Museum of Modern Art curator Elizabeth Mock, who illustrated the Goodyear house in *Built in USA since 1922* (1945), recognized Stone's effort, noting that the floor and roof slabs seemed incidental to the walls and steel lally columns.[49]

The interiors of the Goodyear house, also departing from Stone's earlier work, are sumptuously decorated with such richly colored woods as teak, textured patterns of brick pavers, and ornately grained marble.[50] In contrast to the Mandel house living room, where contemporary chrome and simply upholstered furniture contributed to a neutral setting, the living room of the Goodyear house was enlivened with period and contemporary decorative arts, including small tables by Alvar Aalto and a coffee table by Isamu Noguchi, which Stone liked a lot.[51] While it is not known how involved Stone was in the decoration of these rooms, for the dining room, which had a pale gray-blue ceiling, travertine floor, and a rug in yellows, greens, and terra-cotta, Stone wanted a mural to adorn one of the walls. So in 1941 he offered it as a competition project for students of mural decoration at the Beaux-Arts Institute of Design in New York City, but the jury (of which Stone was a member) did not find any satisfactory submissions.[52] In 1946, however, during a period in which he showed a marked interest in collaborating with artists, Stone purchased from his friend Alexander Calder a mobile to hang from the dining room dome and thought it "looked wonderful."[53]

Long admired by critics, the Goodyear house almost immediately attracted extensive publicity, from *Architectural Forum* to *House & Garden*.[54] In addition to being shown in the Museum of Modern Art's exhibitions *What Is Modern Architecture?* (1938) and *Built in USA, 1932–44* (1944), photographs of the Goodyear house were featured in the Architectural League's 1940 *Versus* exhibition, which contrasted modern with traditional designs. In 1945 Mary Roche of the *New York Times* even offered the Goodyear house as an answer to the vaunted California prototype—long, low, rambling blocks with overhanging eaves, lots of glass, and outdoor living areas.[55] That same year, six images were published in *Tomorrow's House*. Accolades continued over the next two decades, indicating that the house remained the gold standard for modern residential design: the Architectural League awarded it a silver medal of honor in 1950 and the Museum of Modern Art included it in the 1965 retrospective *Modern Architecture U.S.A.*[56]

No less significant is a 1948 advertisement that compared Oldsmobile's new Futuramic automobile to the Goodyear house—the relationship between the two clearly perceptible in their low modern profiles, evident curves, and sizable windows.[57] It was one of a series of Oldsmobile ads—scheduled for *Life*, *Saturday Evening Post*, *Fortune*, *Time*, and *Collier's*, with architectural vignettes (by Robert Law Weed, George Fred Keck, Vincent Kling, and Frank Lloyd Wright)—that Stone's friend John Cushman Fistere (then in the advertising department at *Fortune*) convinced him to participate in by pointing out that it would educate the public about modern design.[58]

The Goodyear house still stands as an icon of American Modernism, thanks in part to the attention it received in the media when a developer slated it for demolition in 2001. The World Monuments Fund and the Society for the Preservation of Long Island Antiquities stepped in, along with the Barnett and Annalee Newman Foundation, and entered into a partnership to purchase and maintain the house until a sympathetic buyer was found. Although somewhat altered, it is now protected by a preservation easement and since 2003 has been on the National Register of Historic Places.[59]

Even though Stone erected more modern houses than most in the 1930s, he still had limited work due to the lagging economy and so for more exposure was willing to engage in all types of promotional projects for general interest, shelter, and women's magazines in addition to the architecture trade journals already reporting on his work.[60] The plans he produced tended to be for low- to medium-budget houses—some modern, others more traditional, but all with innovative spatial planning, new applications of materials, and the modern interest in capturing the external environment from the inside. Sometimes full-scale demonstration houses were built; at other times only small models were produced and photographed, usually accompanied by specifications, estimates, and complete drawings for purchase. Mass-market consumer magazines were increasingly interested in publishing such designs, often collaborating with department stores, showrooms, galleries, and the Better Houses in America program. These publications were tremendously influential in educating the public about good house design and construction and in raising public awareness about the benefits of architect-designed houses. They also promoted the ideal of homeownership as a symbol of prosperity and security, which corresponded to Herbert Hoover's encouragement at the Conference on Home Building and Ownership in December 1931, when he declared: "To possess one's own home is the hope and ambition of almost every individual in our country."[61] When the Roosevelt Administration took over in March 1933, however, the housing industry was still moribund.[62] Convinced that the production of efficient, moderate-cost, single-family housing could reduce unemployment and stimulate recovery from the Great Depression, the government made this sector of the economy a national priority through tax, banking, and

An outstanding example of "Futuramic" design in the field of architecture is this attractive home in Westbury, Long Island-Edward Stone, Architect.

FUTURAMIC

*Hydra-Matic Drive, white sidewall tires optional at extra cost

"Futuramic" is a brand new word for "The dramatic design of the future"-the finest of functional modern design in any field. Among automobiles, the Futuramic Oldsmobile best exemplifies this trend. There's utility, as well as beauty, in its low modern hood, curved windshield, extra-size windows, and lower, wider body. GM Hydra-Matic Drive* is a Futuramic" feature, too-combining proved dependability and thrilling performance with "no clutch, no shift" driving ease. It's SMART to Own an Olds-the Futuramic "98", or the bright, sparkling Dynamic Oldsmobile in the "60" and "70" Series.

FUTURAMIC OLDSMOBILE

Oldsmobile advertisement with a vignette of the Goodyear house terrace outside the living room, published in *Fortune*, April 1948.

It's Yours to Build

Collier's House, designed for modern living by Architect Edward D. Stone and described in the March 28th issue, scored a direct hit. Complete working plans and specifications for which you would have to pay hundreds of dollars are yours for the cost of reproducing and mailing—$3.

Address COLLIER'S HOUSE

Collier's, 250 Park Avenue, New York City

PLEASE DO NOT SEND CURRENCY

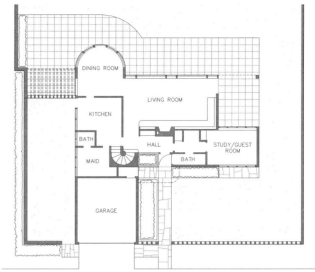

Fig. 2.6. *Collier's house* (1936) first- and second-floor plans.

Front façade of the *Collier's* house model in an advertisement published in *Collier's*, May 16, 1936.

Rear façade of the *Collier's* house model.

Maurice L. Miller house (1938),
Louisville, Kentucky. *Robert Flanders*

insurance programs. Yet modern design was generally not endorsed, exemplified by the small-house designs first published in 1936 by the U.S. Federal Housing Administration (FHA), all of which were stylistically traditional.[63]

Thus, it is surprising that in that same year, the FHA approved Stone's design for an "ideal modern house for a man of moderate means," commissioned by *Collier's*—a literary magazine with a circulation of more than 2.5 million.[64] This "Good Place to Live," as the eight-room house was billed in the first of a series of six articles, was uniquely designed to address the domestic needs of the average American family, taking into consideration comfort, convenience, economy, and attractiveness. Published over a two-month span, the articles focus on the architecture, garden, interior decoration, lighting, and kitchen design as well as the financing of the house.[65] In addition to illustrating Stone's floor plans and model (by his preferred model maker Theodore E. Conrad), working drawings and specifications could readily be purchased for three dollars.[66] The public response was enthusiastic, with some twelve hundred people ordering the Stone plans during the first three months. "That's enough to house a community of six thousand and make a completely modern town," a *Collier's* advertisement triumphantly proclaimed in May 1936.

Even though the FHA specified that a small house could not be reduced from something larger, those close to Stone knew his *Collier's* house was a small version of the Mandel house: Stone simply eliminated the rear rectangular volume and turned the house around so that the more dramatic side with the circular dining room could be enjoyed from the private rear garden (fig. 2.6).[67] While meant to live up to the Mandel house's high standard of design, the *Collier's* house was priced at $12,000 to $16,000, a quarter of the price of the former, and instead of being offered as an example of the International Style, it was presented only as a house for "mod-

ern living," to be considered as one of many stylistic alternatives, including the still prevalent "Colonial, or Spanish or Old English or what-not" variations.[68]

Cognizant of the public's ongoing apprehension about Modernism, the reader was encouraged to think about the revolutionary idea of designing a house from the inside out so that it could meet the day-to-day needs of the entire family. Its modern features were cleverly contrasted with traditional American ones: Among the many modern amenities described are a heated two-car garage attached to the house, as opposed to a converted stable at the back; a walled front courtyard (recalling the Kowalski house) serving as an outdoor extension of the house, as well as an enclosed private garden at the back, instead of open yards; flexible room arrangements, rather than the established plan of a porch and living room in the front with the kitchen in the rear; and maids' rooms near the kitchen and the laundry room near the bedrooms—and not, respectively, in the attic and the cellar. State-of-the-art utilities and technologies (heating and air-conditioning systems, fire- and soundproofing, insulation, and mechanical equipment), contemporary materials (linoleum, glass brick, cork, terrazzo, Formica, and rubber tile), a judicious use of space (closets and storage), and an emphasis on the out-of-doors (terraces, sundecks, and plate-glass windows).

Stone himself was aware of only one house actually erected (and now substantially altered) according to the *Collier's* plan—for Edward Clifford Jones Jr. on a large wooded property on Sylvan Avenue in Fairmont, West Virginia, which received honorable mention in *House Beautiful*'s twelfth annual small-house competition in 1940. To date, however, seven others are known to have been built soon after publication—in 1937 for Doris Dockstader Rooney in Dodge City, Kansas; Charles Augustus Wallace in Columbia, South Carolina; and E. T. and Tom Miller in Downey, California; in 1938

Fig. 2.7. *Collier's* house (1938) floor plan.

for William C. Ilfeld in Las Vegas, New Mexico; Maurice L. Miller in Louisville, Kentucky; and David Armstrong McNeill Sr. in Thomson, Georgia (both the Wallace house, now known as the Wallace-McGee house, and the McNeill house are on the National Register of Historic Places).[69] There is no similarity in the professional backgrounds of the owners, which included clothing and furniture retail, grain farming, banking, mercantilism, and sanitation engineering as well as concrete-pipe and box manufacturing. However, all wanted a more worldly aesthetic indicative of modern culture than local professionals could deliver. Though the cost of each house varied due to regional differences and individual modifications, certain distinctive features were consistent in all of them: white rectangular façades juxtaposed with a curvilinear dining room as well as ribbon windows, flat roofs, and outdoor living spaces with primary rooms opening onto them.[70]

As prototypes in their communities, it was inevitable that the houses attracted media attention, albeit with some anticipated apprehension: The *Hutchinson News* was quick to reassure readers that the ultra-modern Rooney house in Dodge City, Kansas, did not forsake comfort or suitability, whereas, regarding the Miller house, the *Louisville Courier-Journal* emphatically declared: "But People Do Live in Glass Houses." The latter article, however, did not once reference Stone and instead pictured a drawing by Samuel Calvin Molloy, an architect who headed his own firm in Louisville. William Gordon Lyles, a draftsman and designer at Wessinger and Stork, similarly adapted the house in Columbia.[71] Stone's authorship of these houses, which were twice removed from the original prototype, the Mandel house, was no longer meaningful or necessary for them to be well received.

Even further distanced from the original is an eighth house built in Newark, Delaware, in 1948 for Stuart Randall Carswell, an army colonel, and his wife. The couple had seen the *Collier's* plan in 1936 and decided to wait to build their house until Carswell retired. When Stone's office did not respond quickly enough to a letter of inquiry, Carswell hired a local architect, who so loosely interpreted Stone's *Collier's* plan that it is barely recognizable as such. Constructed of brick, this later variation lacks such distinctive characteristics as the curved dining room, terraces and sundecks, and glass-block windows. With the essence of the prototype gone, the desire to stay within the doctrines of the International Style was no longer a requisite consideration.[72]

Thus, the progression of these built *Collier's* houses illustrates the transformation of an avant-garde aesthetic into a popular commodity for the geographically, economically, and culturally diverse middle class. For Stone, his observation of the icons of European Modernism, especially as they were presented in the International Style exhibition, had been the first and necessary step in the design of the Mandel house, after which the *Collier's* plan, even more distant from the original, was sold, and then its variations were appreciated as new.[73]

In 1938 *Collier's* asked Stone to again design a house—this time for weekends, a concept gaining wide appeal thanks to shortened workweeks and improved transportation systems. As one of four magazine projects he did that year, all rigidly limited by the necessity for low cost, Stone's plan utilizes such modern features as overhanging eaves, ample windows, an open plan, and flexible living spaces (the living and dining areas each contain two built-in bunks; fig. 2.7).[74] The magazine made sure to point out that the plan, priced at about $2,500, fell within the FHA's minimum standards and that it was architect designed.[75] But the most interesting aspect of the house is the optional bunk room—with a built-in bunk, dressing table, closet, and space for a small lavatory—which could be added in multiples at any time for $300 apiece. Assembled by a local lumberyard in less than a week and then delivered to the location, hoisted onto a foundation, and covered with a roof, the bunk-room option is perhaps the closest Stone came to prefabrication, which he personally felt was not an answer, but which was of general interest to the building industry in the period.

Stone's weekend houses published in *House & Garden* the same year could also be erected quickly—in just two weeks.[76] While these small structures, priced between $2,000 and $2,500, looked more traditional, with pitched roofs and wood clapboards, their interiors were modern in terms of flexibility (public spaces could be converted into sleeping areas using curtains or partitions) and indoor-outdoor integration (with large windows, screened-in porches, sundecks, and terraces).

The modern Garden House No. 1404, also created by Stone in 1938, for *Ladies' Home Journal*, was one of six house designs the magazine published each year with complete plans available for a dollar.[77] In conjunction with his featured plan, Stone designed a room display that included a miniature model of the house mounted on a revolving column for the Permanent Exhibition of Decorative Arts and Crafts (PEDAC) galleries at Rockefeller Center, giving him additional exposure during an otherwise bleak period of production.[78]

Of all his paper projects that year, Stone's modern house for *Life* best exemplifies the widespread effort to educate the thousands of readers who, it was suggested, really could afford to build houses of their own or even better ones than they had. Partnering with another Luce publication, *Architectural Forum*, for the most extensive home-building promotion the magazine had ever produced, *Life* asked eight architects to design affordable houses for families from the four main regions of the country who had annual incomes ranging from $2,000 to $10,000. For each house, one architect was to provide a traditional design; another, a modern one.[79] Stone's was for a modern house for the $2,000-to-$3,000-income family, which was presented (ironically for Stone) as a superefficient machine for living. Containing no corridors (a feature indicative of Stone's next period of production), the concrete volume has an asymmetrically positioned front door with a decorative bamboo trellis, of the sort traditionally used in gardens to support fruit trees or creepers, to one side (fig. 2.8). A detail that Stone would routinely use and which would evolve into his signature grillwork, the trellis is repeated on the back façade to enclose a porch and garage. Though the design for the living room wall faced with traditional horizontal brick to set off a vertical metal hood over the fireplace is unusual for Stone, the rest of the features were by then standard for him, including an open plan with a curtain that could separate the living from the dining areas.

The magazine's incessant promotions helped to generate interest in these "most talked-about houses." More than 25,000 full-color cutout cardboard models, including the one of Stone's house, which included floor plans and a printed furniture sheet to cut out for fifty cents, sold out in department stores. Even more impressive are the 121 *Life* houses that were erected throughout the country and furnished by cooperating stores; the house by Stone, probably the one located at 43 Buckingham Drive in Albany, was reportedly sponsored by New York Power and Light.[80]

Stone's competition designs received far more critical scrutiny during this period than his magazine projects.[82] In 1938 he submitted an entry for a Festival Theatre and Fine Arts Center at the College of William and Mary in Williamsburg, Virginia, and in 1939 for a Smithsonian Gallery of Art in Washington, D.C. Although neither was built, in the opinion of art historian James D. Kornwolf these competitions—the prize-winning submissions of both exhibited at the Museum of Modern Art—were catalysts in the dissemination of Modernism thanks to their broad circulation, prominent patronage, and quality of the design.[82] The competition for the Festival Theatre and Fine Arts Center, organized by the American National Theatre and Academy (of which Goodyear was president), had 126 entries, with the two submitted jointly by Stone and Philip Goodwin placing second and third (first place went to a design by Eero Saarinen, Ralph Rapson, and Frederick

Model of Garden House No. 1404, designed for and illustrated in *Ladies' Home Journal*, April 1938. *Louis Checkman*

Fig. 2.8. *Life* house floor plan.

Design for a Festival Theatre and Fine Arts Center at the College of William and Mary in Williamsburg, Virginia, submitted by Stone and Philip Lippincott Goodwin (1885–1958) and illustrated in *Architectural Record* 85 (April 1939): 61.

Simon & Schuster offices (ca. 1939; demolished); erected on the roof of the Center Theater, Rockefeller Center. *Ezra Stoller*

New York Museum of Science and Industry (1938; demolished) in the RCA Building (now the General Electric Building), 30 Rockefeller Plaza.

James). The second-place Stone-Goodwin design, more typical of Stone's work, recalls Gropius's Bauhuas building, with the fine arts department connected to the fifteen-hundred-seat theater and exhibition gallery by a long two-story corridor, off of which were the various academic departments.[83] In the Smithsonian competition, promoted as the most important national architectural contest in the last fifteen years by the Museum of Modern Art, Stone was named to the short list of ten out of the 408 entries in the first stage and then was one of eight to receive third prize.[84] Such modern criteria as strict attention to function and maximum spatial flexibility determined the tenor of the program, and Stone responded by uniting the one-thousand-seat auditorium and administration/exhibition spaces (both capable of expansion) with a spacious outdoor loggia, a feature he much preferred. While the jury commended the thoughtful arrangement of buildings, the circulation in the exhibition spaces was considered too inflexible and Stone again lost to Saarinen (this time in collaboration with his father, Eliel), perhaps cementing his general disdain for architectural competitions."[85]

One of the few corporate commissions to come Stone's way at this time was for a glass pavilion for the publishing company Simon & Schuster (and which in 1947 was featured in the film *Gentlemen's Agreement*).[86] Since it was to be erected on top of Center Theater (which Stone had helped design), there were fewer building restrictions, enabling him to repeat some of the features of his houses, the most conspicuous being the sheltering eaves hanging over the fixed-glass walls with views of the roof garden.[87] Stone also designed the birch furniture (made by the Bartos Company

Aerial view of the Museum of Modern Art by Stone and Goodwin, 11 West Fifty-third Street, New York City, and, beyond, of the Rockefeller Apartments (1935–36) by Wallace Kirkman Harrison (1895–1981), 17 West Fifty-fourth Street. *Wurts Brothers*

and W. & J. Sloane), foreshadowing his interest in furniture design in the 1950s.

Also at Rockefeller Center, through Wallace Harrison, Stone was responsible for a $40,000 exhibition space for the New York Museum of Science and Industry, which opened in February 1936 in the lobby of the RCA Building. The three levels of the 60-square-foot exhibition space—which effectively met the challenge of comprehensively presenting the museum's more than two thousand very miscellaneous objects—were connected by a prominent staircase, distinctively modern in its planar severity while at the same time promising traditional Beaux-Arts spectacle for the nearly three-quarters-of-a-million people who would visit by 1938.[88]

While these small commissions are not well documented, nor much remembered, they did contribute to Stone's faculty to resolve the many trying challenges presented by his subsequent and to date most acclaimed building, the Museum of Modern Art. Wedged between nineteenth-century brownstones on the north side of West Fifty-third Street, the design of the façade of crisp lines and sleek surfaces is Stone's most notable contribution and helped locate Modernism in the American context, earning him the appellation "spearhead of Modernism."[89]

It has generally been assumed that Stone was chosen to assist Philip Goodwin in designing the museum by Nelson Aldrich Rockefeller, a trustee of the Museum of Science and Industry and, far more actively, of the Museum of Modern Art (as treasurer, 1935–39 and as president, 1939–41, 1946–53). However, in a 1943 memoir A. Conger Goodyear (who had been president when the museum was designed) recalled that he and Rockefeller each had come to the conclusion that the

best person to work with Goodwin would be Stone because of his growing recognition as a modern architect.[90]

Also of consideration is Goodwin's own influence—as architect, trustee, and benefactor of the museum.[91] He had been opposed to running a competition (for which Stone was not even on the proposed list) and instead was in favor of picking out the architects "best fitted" to handle the job.[92] Goodwin was shocked when Rockefeller named him as one of them, in March 1936, and knew he needed assistance from a modernist. But he did not want to work with one of the iconic European architects, J. J. P. Oud, Mies van der Rohe, or Walter Gropius, as Alfred Barr wanted, probably because when Le Corbusier visited in 1935 Goodwin had a "terrifically trying" experience, as Rockefeller described it, and afterwards Goodwin informed a colleague he would be "off any kind of genius for a long time."[93] While Goodwin considered a number of others recognized for their contemporary work, including Frederick Kiesler, Alfred Kastner, Oskar Gregory Stonorov, and Hamilton Beatty, in addition to Howe and Lescaze, Albert Frey, Alfred Claus, George Nelson, and Walter Peter Baermann (then working on a room in a house designed by Goodwin), Goodwin agreed on the choice of Stone. Although recognized as a modernist, Stone would have also been empathetic to Goodwin's inclination for traditional design since he too had Beaux-Arts training.[94] So, even though an unlikely match—Goodwin an established Ivy League aristocrat and Stone an ambitious rural Ozarkian—the two men nicely complemented each other and became close friends.

According to a cable that Goodwin sent to Barr in July 1936 explaining his opposition to working with a European collabora-

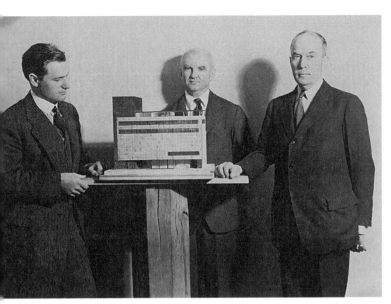

Left to right: Museum of Modern Art board members Nelson Aldrich Rockefeller (1908–1979; treasurer), A. Conger Goodyear (1877–1964; president), and Stephen Carlton Clarke (1882–1960; trustee/chairman of building committee) with a model of the museum, 1937.

tor, Stone was already working with him—though unofficially. His contributions, said Goodwin, had been so "useful and important" that he would consider employing him as a special draftsman. In truth, Stone was already so deeply involved that when Rockefeller was shortly thereafter presented with two design concepts, four or five variations were by Stone, the rest by Goodwin.[95] Although Barr had resigned from the building committee in opposition to the decision to use the Goodwin-Stone team, he would still hold enormous sway over the process. Imagine the pressure put on Stone: not only would he inevitably be compared to the European architects most respected by Barr—who was fast becoming the nation's most powerful taste-maker (and fiercely resisted the appointment of Stone)—but he would also be judged for his ability to offset Goodwin's conservative tendencies.[96] While the stormy and trying planning meetings nearly destroyed Goodwin because of his gentle demeanor, Stone appeared unfettered by the unusual circumstances. His gracious, accommodating manner contributed to an almost unconscious diplomacy, and in addition to being a fountain of ideas, he reportedly agreed to whatever was proposed.[97]

The preliminary plans presented to the trustees in March 1937 reveal that the interior organization of the six-story building was substantially complete: a lecture room, lounge, and storage, packing, and shipping were below street level; the first three floors were primarily given to flexible exhibition galleries, each uniquely posed as an open loftlike space; the fourth floor housed a film department with a projection room and a reading room with stacks; offices occupied the fifth floor; and on the sixth was a members' lounge and terrace along with a trustees' room.[98] Three months later the museum released

its first photographs of a model of the building. The steel and reinforced-concrete main block was to be faced with white Georgian marble intersected with two rows of windows at the top and a half row over the entrance as well as plate-glass windows on the ground floor. A tower faced with dark stone rising 26 feet above the level of the penthouse was to contain a delivery entrance, services, and vertical circulation.

In spite of the collaborative effort among staff, trustees, and architects, as remembered by John McAndrew, then curator of the department of architecture and industrial art, everyone was anxious for the building to be the foremost American example of modern architecture. The trouble was no one could say with certainty what that was.[99] While there was agreement on the general layout, a polemical debate ensued about such issues as the interior lighting (the architects were satisfied with artificial light; Barr was vehemently in favor of natural light), and, moreover, about the expansive marble façade for which, as Stone confirmed, "there was a wide variance of opinion and taste."[100] The two architects struggled with multiple studies, as the scores of extant examples confirm. Goodwin was frustrated, concerned that the various materials, sizes, and shapes would keep the façade from being "restful or monumental," and he told Rockefeller they had restudied the elevation so many times that they were stale on it.[101] At the same time, Goodyear shared his sentiment with Abby Aldrich Rockefeller, informing her that though everyone was doing their best to find the most satisfactory solution, he was not entirely happy about the revised plan.[102]

Although many alterations (including the deletion of the dark tower) were made in the ensuing months, Hitchcock, whose opinion Barr revered, undoubtedly exacerbated the situation when in January 1938 he wrote a lengthy letter to Barr stating that he was "rather horrified" with the white marble front with the pointless windows over the entrance. The barren warehouse effect, he lamented, would surely blemish the city.[103] By this time, however, Goodwin was inclined to consider all major problems settled and in fact was already producing working drawings. Nonetheless, as Gordon Bunshaft (then assisting Stone) recalled, Stone was busily reworking the front elevation.[104] On February 4, 1938, Stone sent Rockefeller four sketches of the façade he had created over the weekend with a note informing him, "I have not discussed these ideas with Phil [Goodwin] as I wanted to make sure that you thought that these represented an improvement over the present elevation, and I would not want him to know that I had prepared these drawings." [105] Stone did admit, however, that he had shown them to Barr and Harrison, both of whom thought they were the finest to date. Accordingly, just five days after receiving the schemes, Rockefeller informed Goodwin that the advisory committee had unanimously selected one of them. Significantly, instead of marble, the façade would primarily utilize for the first time in this country panels of milky-

Museum of Modern Art lobby (redeveloped) on opening night, May 10, 1939.
Eliot Elisofen

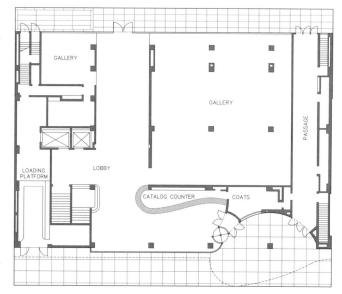

Fig. 2.9. Museum of Modern Art first-floor plan.

white Thermolux—a sandwich of spun glass between sheets of clear glass with hermetically sealed edges.[106]

Prominently delineated on the cover of the building's inaugural exhibition catalog, *Art in Our Time*, the new building was meant to be a living model of the museum's agenda to continue the object lesson set forth in the 1932 International Style exhibition—namely, to shape American architecture by fostering good building with high aesthetic standards and by providing an effective forum for public education in modern architecture.[107] As a consequence of the museum's intention, since opening on May 10, 1939, the building has invited a running critique. The initial reviews, which tend to be conventional formalistic evaluations, commended its refreshing break with conventional museum design to become "America's first great modern museum," as the *Magazine of Art* proclaimed it.[108] Instead of starting with the design of the façade, the plan began with the inside activities, focusing on clear patterns of circulation and the concentration of fixed service elements (stairs, elevators, lavatories) in order to create open gallery spaces with easy access (fig. 2.9).[109] Critics were also impressed with the numerous innovations that allowed for flexibility, including the huge gallery spaces with movable partitions (reportedly Stone's idea), the removable toggle-bolted, or buttoned, lighting fixtures arranged in strips (track lighting), and the white plaster walls that could be penetrated with nails.[110] Another widely praised departure from traditional museums was that visitors entered the lobby, enlivened by a curved reception desk, at street level instead of by a grand flight of stairs. The deep recess of the entrance, accentuated by the curved marquee, which Stone worked out with McAndrew and Barr, was designed to attract passersby and, importantly, symbolize the museum's shift from an institution exclusively for the elite to one that appealed to the larger public. Although some recognized that the concrete roof—cantilevered over the top floor terrace and pierced with eleven circular holes 5 feet in diameter to expand the sky view and create the sense of a pergola—recalled Le Corbusier's Esprit Nouveau pavilion, it was considered novel.[111] In 1938 *Fortune* compared the roof to a piece of Swiss cheese and the metaphor caught on, so that still in 1977 Ada Louise Huxtable (the influential architecture critic most consistently outspoken

Museum of Modern Art sixth-floor members' terrace (redeveloped).
Alexandre George

about Stone's work) commented on "the famous 'cheese hole' "canopy" (see page 14).[112] Publications also highlighted the building's extensive use of glass—a material broadly associated with Modernism—spurred by a press release highlighting its 7,500 square feet of plate glass, 2,222 glass bricks, and 3,300 square feet of Thermolux.[113]

But instead of specifically referring to the International Style exhibition or European prototypes, such as Gropius's Bauhaus, as they well could have, critics were more interested in discussing the building in relation to the most recent developments in architecture. Lewis Mumford, for example, already a self-professed humanist who felt that modern architecture should emerge organically from human needs, climate, and site, did not like the building's white marble, chrome metal, and blue tile because these materials did not complement the lavender-tan brick of the nearby Rockefeller Apartments or the limestone of Rockefeller Center.[114]

The hopeful expectation that the museum building would establish firm criteria for modern architecture in the United States was diminished by such outspoken evaluations, especially those that fueled the ongoing debate about Modernism versus Traditionalism.[115] For instance, whereas Edward Alden Jewell, art critic of the *New York Times*, admired the building's

reserved individuality and cautious restraint from eccentricity, concluding that its adaptable composition appropriately expressed the fluid cultural life of the modern world, Royal Cortissoz, who, had started his career in the office of McKim, Mead and White and was a notorious anti-modernist, considered the façade among the most forbidding in the city.[116]

Opinion about the building has shifted through the years—in part due to its successive alterations and expansions in the early 1950s (by Philip Johnson; demolished), in 1964 (also by Johnson), in 1984 (by Cesar Pelli), and in 2004 (by Yoshio Taniguchi), inviting new interpretations stemming from stylistic and theoretic developments. Equally influential is the museum's own altered mission—from the acquisition of new works and display of representative art of the previous fifty years to the assemblage of a collection without time limits for an increasingly large, diverse audience.

One of the most interesting periods of interpretation was in the late 1970s following the crisis of Modernism. Johnson, who by then had turned to Postmodernism, made an attempt (with Bunshaft, Harrison, and Edward Larrabee Barnes) to replace the front façade altogether during one of the museum's expansion projects and reportedly urged Pelli, the commissioned architect, to create a new, more unified image. Huxtable responded by calling the building "a rare, superb and almost unique" architectural and cultural landmark that had helped put the International Style on the map. Then, after the museum decided to clean and restore the façade, rather than eliminate it, Huxtable deemed it as symbolic an image of early Modernism as Nude Descending a Staircase (1911) by Marcel Duchamp or Meret Oppenheim's archetypal Surrealist fur-lined teacup of 1936.[117] From her postmodern point of view, the concept of modern had become historical and the museum façade its relic. Thus, the meaning of the façade had changed from its radical and experimental position to one that was patently nostalgic.

Others joined in with postmodern reassessments by identifying ideological motives, cultural meanings, and dominant values. Compared to the museum's later additions, some critics perceived the original façade as an inert archive; others considered it a logo, emblem, or sign.[118] But for Paul Goldberger, who lamented in his *New York Times* article "Wistful Ode," the building façade—at once flagrantly modern and historical (because of its classical three-part elevation)—had lost its original heroic, utopian value due to the demolition of the neighborhood's severely contrasting nineteenth-century brownstones.[119]

In this century, the redevelopment of the entire museum complex by Taniguchi set in motion another round of interpretations in which the original façade was relieved of its passive historical role, as explained in the *New York Times* by architecture critic Nicolai Ouroussoff. Instead of sealing the Goodwin-Stone façade in a time capsule, as had previously been done, Taniguchi fused it with the numerous additions—as well as to the urban environment and even to the art itself by creating a vibrant composition

Museum of Modern Art rear façade and Abby Aldrich Rockefeller sculpture garden, 1939–40.
John McAndrew

Museum of Modern Art after its 2004 redevelopment.
© Timothy Hursley

of overlapping images with multiple historical and contextual meanings.[120] No longer pitted against the various additions, the building acquired a harmonious relationship with the structures to which it was united. As a subordinate to the greater whole, however, the authorship of the original seems less meaningful—ironically fulfilling Stone's prophecy that glass buildings lead to "complete impersonal anonymity."[121]

Even though the museum's façade may well have made modern architecture fashionable in contemporary American culture as has been contended, at its completion Stone's attitude about Modernism was ambiguous. Given the realities of the feeble economy and his lack of commissions, along with his discontent with such aspects of the International Style as plain machine-like finishes, blunt articulations of structural techniques, and design standardization, Stone recognized he needed much wider appeal. Thus, going forward the dematerialized expression of the International Style would begin to give way in his architecture to other contemporary currents, and in particular the trend toward what Mumford called in 1939 "The American Tradition."[122] Even though Stone was still willing to open himself up to experimentation and assimilation, he would expand as well on the practices he had already acquired—not just in style but also in his professional affiliations and media savvy.

3: EMBRACING
THE AMERICAN IMPULSE

Machinery is naked . . . . People are not.[1]

Stone was convinced that instead of the utilitarian good taste of the 1930s, a larger vision for architecture was needed, and during the next decade focused on expanding his definition of Modernism showing a keen awareness of current trends and values. His intriguing but little known production in this period, which lasted into the early 1950s, reflects his response to the shift from prewar anxiety and economic distress to a booming postwar recovery. Having now had a taste of successs, he was all the more motivated to work with the media, whose covereage, he undoubtedly hoped, would continue to foster his recognition, clientele, and much–needed remuneration.

Stone's designs, however, reveal his conflicted attitude toward Modernism: like other architects of the time, for houses he became interested in the American vernacular, using indigenous materials and regional variations—inspired by Frank Lloyd Wright and California's Bay Area Style architects; for commercial structures, he continued to employ the abstract functionalism of the International Style because of its promise of economic efficiency. Hence, until later in the 1950s, no single work represents Stone's approach to architecture, and all must be considered together.

The diversity of his commissions, each with widely varying program requirements—ranging from multiple low-budget dwellings and a furniture collection to luxury hotels and large-scale planning projects—was crucial to his maturation

and helped shape his opinions about urban planning and zoning, the fusion of the visual arts with architecture, and the conservation of green spaces. His predilection for decorative patterning—cutouts, trellises, piercings, and the like—was always present, even if at times subtle. Moreover, his tightly organized, inward-facing plans with clear patterns of circulation and centralized atriums yielded lasting conceptual breakthroughs.

Many of Stone's designs in this second period of production, especially for houses, were not met with the same critical success as those of the previous decade. The Museum of Modern Art grew increasingly perplexed by his work, even though it had displayed photographs of his architecture in numerous exhibitions between 1938 and 1946. In the opinion of Arthur Drexler, curator of the department of architecture beginning in 1951, Stone's work did not express the significance of the moment, perhaps because Drexler considered the modular wood houses with which Stone was so involved just too trivial.[2] And yet, intriguingly, and certainly central to Stone's story, it was in his domestic architecture of this period that Stone formulated his ideas about the unique aesthetic he fully developed in the late 1950s.

Stone claimed in his autobiography that when the 1940s commenced he did a complete about-face in his architecture after a cross-country tour during which he absorbed all that he saw, not just buildings but landscapes, too: Yellowstone Park,

Postcard of the front façade of the El Panama Hotel (1946–1951), Via España, Panama City, Republic of Panama.

Atrium of the William Thurnauer house (1949–51), North Forest Drive, Teaneck, New Jersey.

Lake Tahoe, redwood forests, and Pennsylvania countryside settlements.[3] But his professed awakening to the rich American heritage trailed a popular current for vernacular regionalism. As Elizabeth Mock explained in *Built in USA since 1932*, American architects were reconsidering Pennsylvania stone and wood barns, New England white clapboarded structures, and the low rambling ranch houses in the West—not so much because they were picturesque but because of their frank application of indigenous materials and their subtle adaptation to climate and topography.[4] While Stone's interest in the vernacular may well have been kindled by his rural upbringing on the Arkansas frontier, he was more likely compelled by the upward trend for structures of traditional, honest construction, which his revered colleague Howard Myers was calling for in *Architectural Forum*.[5] By joining in the movement to broaden the definition of Modernism, Stone would not only have an opportunity to interest the general public still steeped in American tradition but satisfy his own need for an aesthetic open to embellishment.[6]

Even though most histories take Stone at his word that in the 1940s he repudiated the International Style, many features from his work in that aesthetic persisted.[7] Aspects of the Goodyear house (see page 38), for example, were repeated in countless variations: the centralized outdoor courtyard with a loggia to one side for numerous L- or U-shaped buildings, such as the Frederick L. Maduro house (1947–48) in Great

Dining room in the Bertram N. Linder house (1948–53; demolished), Hickory Hill Farm, Dalton, Pennsylvania. *Maynard L. Parker*

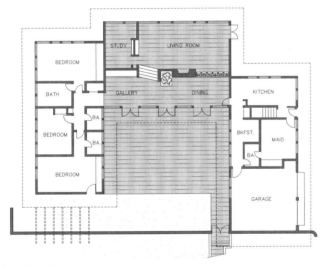

Fig. 3.1. Maduro house ground-floor plan.

Stone and his wife Maria with Frank Lloyd Wright (1867–1959) and his son-in-law William Wesley Peters (1912–1991), December 1957. *Charles Ross*

Neck, New York (fig. 3.1); the circular dining room in the Joseph S. Wohl house (1946) in Lawrence, New York; and the perforated serpentine wall outside the I. H. Kempner Jr. house (1946–47; demolished) in River Oaks, Texas. As the decade progressed, Stone made these details more fanciful or flamboyant: the Bertram N. Linder house in Dalton, Pennsylvania, had a covered loggia with large rhythmic stone columns as well as a circular dining room innovatively defined by a movable grass-cloth screen on a ceiling track. Similarly, for the Bay Roc Hotel in Montego Bay, Jamaica, he not only built his characteristic serpentine wall but also a vibrantly curved metal awning.[8]

Stone himself considered the decade his Frank Lloyd Wright period, his interest in the older architect perhaps reinforced by the exhibition *Frank Lloyd Wright: American Architect*, which premiered at the Museum of Modern Art in November 1940.[9] Unlike most architects, however, he actually became a close friend of Wright's.[10] Personally, the two had much in common: both had tumultuous relationships with women and illicit romantic liaisons, knew how to exploit the media (with the help of their artful wives), had expensive tastes and perpetual financial troubles, put forth a public persona with a contrived personal narrative, and saw themselves as outside the mainstream of their profession.[11]

The initial bond between Stone and Wright must have emerged from their efforts to offer alternatives to the International Style. Their correspondence and Stone's own writings make clear that he developed a holistic understanding of Wright and a deep appreciation for his contribution to architecture. "No modern architect today takes a pencil in hand without subconsciously paying homage to Frank Lloyd Wright," he believed.[12] Inevitably, Stone patterned himself and his architecture after Wright—sometimes consciously, at other times not. But whereas Wright remembered everything but copied nothing, Stone deferred to his Beaux-Arts technique of emulating formalistic detail. He did not assimilate and abstract as Wright did without resorting to some frame of reference.

In his visits to Wright's homes and studios—Taliesen East in Spring Green, Wisconsin, and Taliesin West in Scottsdale, Arizona—Stone took in Wright's synthesis of architecture and landscape, as well as his adeptness at handling such natural materials as redwood—valued for its rot resistance, insulating properties, and low maintenance. Stone's houses demonstrate his enthusiasm for such Prairie Style features as low, horizontal building forms with flat or sloping roofs that seemed to hug the earth; clever outdoor living spaces; indirect approaches to entrances; continuous bands of windows running below broad sheltering eaves; and the stabilizing presence of the hearth. He was also drawn to Wright's cost-efficient, one-story Usonian houses, which had been presented along with Stone's modern house, among others, in the September 26, 1938, issue of *Life*. He recognized that Wright's modular constructions of

Bay Roc Hotel metal awning.

Perforated serpentine wall at the Bay Roc Hotel (1951–53; redeveloped as Sandals Montego Bay), Kent Avenue, Montego Bay, Jamaica.

wood, stone, and brick standing on thin, radiant-heated concrete floors and topped with protruding slab roofs were better organized, easier to maintain, and more economical than traditional houses.[13]

While on his cross-country trip, Stone also visited San Francisco, where he was introduced to the work of the Bay Area Style architects, known for incorporating local landscapes and traditions into modern plans and concepts. Generally small in scale, Bay Area Style houses utilized a vernacular vocabulary that took into consideration lifestyle, climate, and topography, using indigenous methods of construction and materials, particularly wood, which was abundant in the region at the time.[14] Stone responded to many of the finely worked details of this vigorous aesthetic (as the architects themselves liked to describe their work): low-pitched gable roofs, wood surfaces with white trim, and unpretentious open plans that skillfully merged with the landscape.[15] While William Wilson Wurster is generally recognized as the founder of the Bay Area Style, Stone gravitated toward Gardner A. Dailey, with whom he became friends.[16] Unlike Wurster, who had a predilection for pragmatic solutions without ostentation or showmanship, Dailey liked to reference the historical, the exotic, and the Japanese in his more elegant structures. Although Stone certainly did not share the two passions that motivated Dailey—engineering and botany—he took note of the "great finesse and refinement" in Dailey's designs.[17]

An impressive early experiment with the "natural house," as Stone called it, was his 1940 House of Ideas, a full-scale demonstration house—an increasingly popular marketing

technique derived from world's fairs—erected on the second-floor terrace of the International Building, west of Fifth Avenue on Fifty-first Street at Rockefeller Center.[18] The project had been conceived by Stone in collaboration with two of his favorite colleagues, Howard Myers and John Fistere (the "unholy trio," as Stone liked to call them), who had been appointed advisers to the Rockefeller Home Center to provide information on residential planning, construction, equipment, and financing.[19] Sponsored by *Collier's*, the two-story house for four

Fig. 3.2. *Collier's* House of Ideas first- and second-floor plans.

Collier's House of Ideas (1940; demolished), erected on the International Building terrace, 45 Rockefeller Plaza. *Gottscho-Schleisner*

House of Ideas living area with a view of the "combination room" and a terrace. *Mattie E. Hewitt*

set out to show to a broad audience that modern architecture could be adapted to both physical and emotional comfort—a sharp departure from the machine-for-living look of the International Style house that Stone had created for the magazine four years earlier.[20] Designed for the informal lifestyle of the average family, the seven versatile rooms displayed a host of building products and furnishing ideas.[21] Each day the house attracted an average of more than fifteen hundred visitors, who could also purchase a booklet about its features for ten cents.[22]

Corresponding to Stone's new enthusiasm for naturalism, the house was given a woodsy quality: the exterior was sheathed in redwood and accented with white doors and trim, after Bay Area Style examples. Wooden rafters extended from

the cantilevered slab roof (with recessed lights in the soffit) over the larger of two second-floor terraces. The interior walls were of waxed oak plywood, a composite material recently standardized for mass production.[23] Floor-to-ceiling Thermopane glass sliding walls and steel-framed awning windows integrated the interior with the exterior.

Like Wright's houses, it was designed for easy upkeep and economy of space, with the ground-floor open plan essentially one large space with a single permanent wall separating the living area from the kitchen (fig. 3.2). Of note is the combination, or three-purpose, room: exposed to the kitchen by an open service counter, or pass-through, it served as a dining area or, when the dining table was folded into the wall, as an entertainment room for ping pong or movies; the section closest to the bathroom could also transition into a photographic darkroom or be partitioned off to form a guest room. The three upstairs bedrooms were likewise multifunctional as studies, playrooms, dens, or hideaways. Built-in storage and furniture (features also promoted by Wright), some of it dual-purpose, were created in collaboration with the interior decorator Dan Cooper and his Danish employee, Jens Risom (later widely recognized for his furniture designs). The innovative double bunks in the room for boys, staggered so that the ends of each bed were clear, expanded the concept of built-in furniture and received particular media attention.[24] Stone utilized the bamboo trellis—not just outside but inside, too—to distinguish spaces yet allow light to penetrate through in interesting patterns, anticipating the geometric grillwork that would become his signature.[25]

His fondness for trelliswork is also evident in the dining alcove he designed for the annual *Contemporary American Industrial Art* exhibition at the Metropolitan Museum of Art in 1940. There, he took naturalism even further with a split bamboo awning; woven-reed matting covering the floor, wall, and ceiling; and wood furniture, including cane-backed chairs of his own design that were manufactured by the Bartos Company in Brooklyn.[26] A profusion of foliage spilled out of small containers hanging from the trellis and in stepped rectangular boxes secured to the brick wall in such a way that water dripped down from one to another as effectively as a torrent.[27] This predilection for water, a fundamental component of Stone's work going forward, is even explicit in the drawings of his early student days (see page 23).

As the diversity of his projects indicates, Stone was willing to accept just about any invitation that would help sustain his professional survival during this uncertain time. In 1941 he agreed to be a member of the jury for the Museum of Modern Art's Organic Design in Home Furnishings competition. He also designed a model of a modern, two-story doll house (built by Theodore Conrad), which the museum had hoped would be marketed by F.A.O. Schwartz.[28] The same year Stone produced six flexible, low-maintenance weekend cottage plans for *Better Homes & Gardens*, recommending they be adapted to individual site conditions and regional materials. The title of the article, "For Grand and Glorious Weekends," however, hardly reflected the nation's growing preoccupation with war preparations, nor the fact that new construction was being reserved almost exclusively for the government.[29]

Forced to explore alliances more closely related to the wartime effort, Stone found work designing two low-budget defense housing developments. The first was Monongahela Heights in West Mifflin, outside Pittsburgh. As Stone explained in his autobiography, Walter Gropius and Marcel Breuer had previously been asked to design Aluminum City Terrace, a development with 250 units in Kensington, about 25 miles outside

Dining alcove designed for the exhibition, *Contemporary American Industrial Art* (1940), Metropolitan Museum of Art, New York City.
Ezra Stoller

of Pittsburgh, and in 1941 Stone was approached to construct a second group for the short-lived Division of Defense Housing Coordination (1940–42). In actuality, however, a huge program of war housing had been launched in the region, where even before the war there had been insufficient housing near the steel factories.[30] Under the Lanham Act, passed by Congress in October 1940, $150 million had been appropriated for defense housing near military installations and in such urban centers where rural workers were migrating to factories to produce war equipment. Between 1940 and 1941 well over one hundred architectural firms engaged in these projects.[31]

According to *Architectural Forum*, the Pittsburgh area's defense housing was distinctive because its architects were given extraordinary encouragement to find lasting ways to improve housing standards.[32] As Wright was cautioned at about the same time for his (infamously cancelled) Cloverleaf Housing project in Pittsfield, Massachusetts, the government did not want "cracker-boxes" or "skyscrapers laid down on their side," but rather, well-placed, creatively designed housing.[33] Specifically, it called for efficiency through large-scale planning, swift construction, and economy of space, materials, supplies, equipment, and ongoing maintenance—a departure from most traditional housing development specifications.[34]

Although current histories note the leading modern architects involved in defense housing—Oscar Stonorov, Richard Neutra, Louis Kahn, Hugh Stubbins Jr., Antonin Raymond, Eero Saarinen, Clarence Stein, and Frank Lloyd Wright—Stone's Monongahela Heights commission has been largely overlooked, in spite of being illustrated in *Architectural Forum* in May 1942 and again in July 1946.[35] Of the proposed 368 units for families with an average income of about $2,600,

Model of Monongahela Heights (1941–42; now Mon-View Heights) on Midway Drive, West Mifflin, Pennsylvania. *Ezra Stoller*

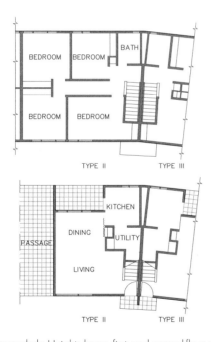

Fig. 3.3. Monongahela Heights house first- and second-floor plans.

only 342 were actually constructed, at a cost of nearly $1.5 million, because the 33-acre sloping site was so irregular.[36] Rather than scarring the hillsides with bulldozers, as was the case in other developments, Stone preserved the terrain with a thoughtful arrangement of forty-seven buildings, all sheathed in redwood, some of which are rectangular, either gently receding or stepping down the hillside.[37] The other buildings (nicknamed "the bent barracks") consist of a 320-foot-long

curve, recalling the mid-eighteenth-century Royal Crescent laid out by John Wood the Younger in Bath, England, an early deliberate historical reference on Stone's part, but far from his last.[38] The four interior plans, ranging from one-story, one-bedroom units to two-story units with two to four bedrooms, all had ground-floor open plans (fig. 3.3). Economy was everything: in the two-story houses, for example, the bathroom and kitchen were above each other and back-to-back to all neighboring units, so that only a single plumbing stack was needed and partitions and closet doors (a feature Stone felt obstructed the flow of space) were used sparingly. The largest plan also had a covered breezeway, a detail he would further develop, running parallel to the living area to facilitate access to the back of the building, creating a voided space reminiscent of Stone's International Style work.

The scheme of his second defense housing development, designed for the Federal Public Housing Authority and built in association with John Judson Rowland at what is now the Marine Corps Air Station Cherry Point in North Carolina, likewise preserved its landscape—here of scrub pines.[39] It was one of the best low-cost solutions to come out of the war, according to *Architectural Forum*: the 270 semidetached one- and two-story dwellings, of four different types, were complemented by various combinations of exposed concrete block, brick, and redwood siding for the exteriors.[40] Covered by low-pitched shed roofs with overhangs and ranging in size from one to four bedrooms, the open plan interiors were fully integrated with the outside through large plate-glass windows. Both of Stone's defense housing developments had important ramifications for him because they demonstrated the advantages of compactly ordered, multiple-family dwellings over sprawling single-family houses—a concept he would return to with zeal.[41]

While Stone never showed much interest in prefabrication—a promising concept for many at the time—he did agree to participate in "The New House of 194X," a theoretical project published in *Architectural Forum* in August 1942. Anticipating postwar recovery, thirty-three professionals were asked to present their ideas for utilizing the vast changes that the war would bring to mass production and everyday life, particularly with regard to prefabrication. Each architect focused on a different aspect; Stone's was on the economic, flexible planning with which he already had success.[42] He accommodated the project's thesis with a prefabricated mechanical core, a popular but as yet largely unproven concept, which contained the kitchen, laundry, and bathroom, and all the plumbing and heating equipment. In addition to pre-attached fixtures on the walls, he proposed that the package include a finished floor and ceiling as well as doors, closets, and a kitchen bar screen. But because Stone believed all designs should be determined by individual desires and site conditions, he recommended that the exterior of the core be left unfinished so that it could be customized after installation.

Recalling the Usonian house concept, for the house itself Stone suggested a modular plan that could be adapted by local carpenters (fig. 3.4). His premise that a house accommodate its occupants' needs and tastes is reflected in his decision to offer a primary plan with three variations for different sleeping, dining, and living, arrangements—including a bedroom wing that could be added as needed. The large open space for living, dining, and sleeping, which could be separated by screens, partitions, or curtains, could also have built-in furniture and storage.[43]

Stone's competence in economic, efficient planning must have served him well when he joined the United States Army Air Force in August 1942. Fortunate to be among only 39 percent of the architects in the armed forces who found work in their profession, Stone was chief of the planning and design section in the engineering and development branch of the Air Installations Division that was responsible for the acquisition, construction, and maintenance of airfields, air bases, and bombing and gunnery ranges.[44] While one source reported that he was more or less an office boy, according to extant résumés, Stone worked on the layout of airfields and the development of new building typologies (operations hangars, air depots, control towers, and crash-truck facilities), and he contributed to master plans of airfields contemplated for retention after the war.[45] Of note was the $30 million Fairfield-Suisun Army Air Base (now called Travis Air Force Base) in California. As the first permanent airfield built for the army in fifteen years, it utilized a system of tangential runways to ferry aircraft and supplies to the Pacific Theater. Stone worked on

Housing (1941–43) by Stone and John Judson Rowland (1903–1963) at what is now the Marine Corps Air Station (MCAS) Cherry Point, Havelock, North Carolina. *Ezra Stoller*

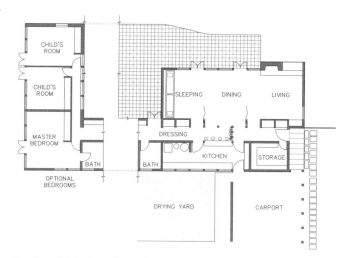

Fig. 3.4. 194X house floor plan.

nine other bases as well, including a $10 million headquarters for the Continental Air Force at Andrews Field in Maryland.[46] Not only did his three-year assignment, ending in November 1945, give Stone experience in large-scale, long-range master planning using specific building types, but it taught him how to maneuver the "frustrating, slow-moving, bureaucratic process."[47]

These skills would not be immediately utilized, however, because after the war there was an urgent need for housing for

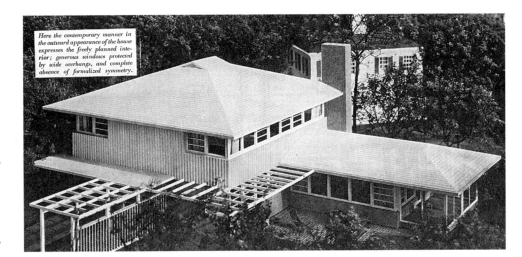

Model house designed for and illustrated in *Ladies' Home Journal*, March 1946.

Dining court and breezeway of a model house designed for and illustrated in *Good Housekeeping*, August 1946. *Ezra Stoller*

Here the contemporary manner in the outward appearance of the house expresses the freely planned interior; generous windows protected by wide overhangs, and complete absence of formalized symmetry.

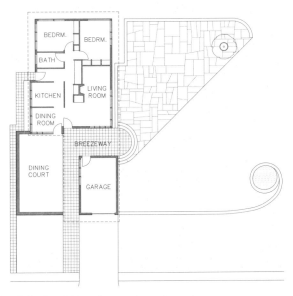

Fig. 3.5. *Good Housekeeping* house floor plan.

both returning veterans and for civilians.[48] A building boom had been set off in August 1944 when Congress passed the G.I. Bill of Rights, which guaranteed home loans to veterans, producing a surge in suburban development for the newly idealized nuclear family.[49] Stone was in the thick of it.

Settling in Great Neck on Long Island, he and his wife, Orlean, rented a seventeen-room house, where he worked, lived, and socialized with his draftsmen until June 1946, when he transferred his residence and business to 50 East Sixty-fourth Street in New York City.[50] "Deluged with commissions," Stone was optimistic, writing to his colleague Victorine DuPont Homsey, "It does look like our day in the sun has arrived … roll out the proper amount of red carpet."[51] By 1951—his most profitable year to date, with income at

$23,500—Stone (along with a staff that had grown from six to twenty) had completed about fifty houses, each generally valued between $30,000 and $200,000.[52]

In this "heyday" for architects, as he referred to the time, Stone continued to turn down few opportunities for self-promotion and participated in a variety of forums, the gallery exhibitions in particular revealing his developing interest in synthesizing decorative and fine arts with his architecture.[53] In 1947 he took part in *Integration* at the Mortimer Levitt Gallery and in *The Modern House Comes to Life* at the Bertha Schaefer Gallery of Contemporary Art, both in New York City.[54] The following year his plan for the George N. Packard house (1947–48; unrealized) in Bernardsville, New Jersey, was featured in another *Modern House* exhibition at Schaefer's gallery, along with a 1-inch-scale model of its living/dining area.[55] But his most entertaining design was the mazelike circular boudoir at the Fifth Annual Home Furnishings Show (1953) in New York City, where, *Time* reported, one could relax on a fur-covered sofa while gazing at a muted abstract painting on the wall and a sculpture of a tubby ceramic pig suspended from the ceiling. Playful, theatrical, even outlandish, this rare conscious piece of kitsch successfully vied for attention with the twenty-five rooms by other leading designers.[56]

Though such forums often promoted hypothetical, even idealistic, designs, those that Stone produced between 1946 and 1950 for four magazines—*Good Housekeeping*, *Ladies' Home Journal*, *Woman's Home Companion*, and *Life*—were far more practical. While considered modern, they were aimed at the conventional and still apprehensive reader, anticipating the long-range trend noted in the *Kiplinger Washington Letter* of February 28, 1953:

> Modern is outrunning traditional in both houses and furnishings, and [the] gap will widen in future years. Not extreme modern, not the stark, but a mixture of the two, an adaptation, with emphasis on simple lines. Practicality and comfort, without regard to any special current style.[57]

In spite of the conservative nature of Stone's promotional paper projects, interesting details stood out as new or experimental in 1946: the vertical log siding above brick on the façade of the *Ladies' Home Journal* house and the brickwork of the *Good Housekeeping* house that was left dark red instead of whitewashed (as he previously did to conform to the International Style), which was offset by clean white trim and covered with a low-pitched roof in the manner of the Bay Area Style.[58] Designed with the landscape architect Janet Darling, the latter house maximized privacy, in much the same way Wright had done in the Usonian house, by positioning the garage and a high-walled court on the street front (fig. 3.5). Stone also utilized a covered breezeway, between the garage and house, a feature he had already used and would continue to privilege. The design received more exposure than most as a result of the model being shown at the National Modern Homes Exposition at the Grand Central Palace in May, and in such department stores as Macy's and Wanamaker's. Consequently, more than 100,000 copies of the Stone plan were requested in a single year.[59]

Another innovative publicity project, illustrated in the April 1950 issue of *Ladies' Home Journal*, was targeted for the hundreds of thousands of newly married couples who wanted better houses than they thought they could afford. The mission, to show readers how to erect their own homes for half the expected price, was demonstrated by David and Virginia Stech, who spent their free time over twenty-five weeks building a three-bedroom ranch house for $8,000 in Armonk, New York.[60] Designed by Stone, the modular post-and-panel house

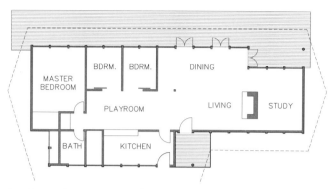

Fig. 3.6. *Ladies' Home Journal*/Stech house floor plan.

View from the playroom into the dining and living areas in the David and Virginia Stech house (1947–50), Whippoorwill Road East, Armonk, New York, designed for and illustrated in *Ladies' Home Journal*, April 1950. *Ezra Stoller*

had a simple but expandable informal open plan of exposed wood construction (fig. 3.6). Floor-to-ceiling windows thoroughly integrated the interiors with the natural surroundings. Carefully pre-engineered and laid out with precut or standardized materials wherever possible, the step-by-step building instructions (Ranch House Pattern No. 501) were offered for sale for five dollars by the Easi-Bild Pattern Company in Pleasantville, New York.[61]

Critically well received, such direct and simple plans were the standard for all of Stone's promotional houses, including those designed for manufacturers to showcase their products.

Fig. 3.7. Ingersoll house first- and second-floor plans.

Of note is the demonstration house he built between 1945 and 1946 for Borg-Warner's Ingersoll Steel and Disc Division. In 1945 the company converted its plant in Kalamazoo, Michigan (where amphibious tanks had been manufactured) into a facility for the production of a patented utility core—a single, 9½-foot-square assembly organized in three principal sections: the mechanics; bathroom with preattached fixtures; and kitchen and laundry.[62] Based on a prototype designed by architect Joel Fletcher Lankton of Peoria, Illinois, the design, production, and promotion of the utility core were managed by Donald Deskey. It was his idea to hire eight big-name modern architects to demonstrate its flexibility in twelve different houses to be located on 10 acres named Ingersoll Village.[63] Promoted as "the World's Fair of postwar housing," this small homes show was considered the most ambitious since the war.[64]

According to architect Harwell Hamilton Harris, who had worked on the project in Deskey's office and also built one of the houses, Stone was assigned the smallest house at 1034 Crown Street (now altered), which he intended to put on stilts. Well along in construction, Harwell recalled, Stone said, "Look, it's a waste. Let's fill it in."[65] Apocryphal or not, the ground floor of the house had originally been conceived as a half-protected space suitable for recreation in southern climates (fig. 3.7). But because it was to be located in Michigan, according to Stone, he enclosed the ground floor with brick and removable sash.[66] Significant to Stone's quest for hall-less architecture, the stairs ascending to the second-floor living space ended in the dining area, which, in turn, led to both kitchen and living room.

Stone's skillful planning is even more evident in the diminutive single-story house (one of two) he designed in 1949 in Garrison, New York, to showcase the Durisol company's new lightweight, pressure-molded blocks of chemically treated wood shavings and Portland cement. Published in *Architectural Forum*, *Today's Woman*, and *Good Housekeeping*, Stone

effectively maximized the compact space by opening the entrance hall to the living area with a floor-to-ceiling wood grille (originally with plants hanging in some of the openings), and cleverly tucking a built-in, 8-foot-long settle beside the grille on the living area side (fig. 3.8).[67] Stone also wrapped the raised ledge of the centrally positioned redbrick hearth around the corner to the dining area as well as placed rows of continuous windows along the opposite wall for natural light. The house is further integrated with the outside by a sheltering cantilever over the terrace, which extends almost the full length of the building, and by a breezeway between the house and the garage. Despite having to use the industrial Durisol blocks (for the exterior walls, interior partitions, roof decks, and floor slabs), Stone's preferred vernacular treatment is articulated in the simple beauty of the exposed post-and-beam wood construction throughout the interior.

In another instance of complying with specific client demands, Stone was one of forty-nine architects commissioned by the Libby-Owens Ford Glass Company to design a solar house for a publication called *Your Solar House* (1947). For his three-bedroom house designed for New York State, Stone effectively followed the requirements of providing a plan inspired by locality, lifestyle, climate, and topography by facing all major rooms south and then giving them ample fixed and awning windows for light and warmth while also providing a sheltering, low-pitched roof with long overhangs—all details he had presented before.[68]

Even though Stone's privately commissioned small houses exhibit characteristics similar to the promotional ones, they generally did not garner the same media attention. An exception was three small houses illustrated in the December 1951 issue of *Progressive Architecture*, one of the few trade publications to acknowledge Stone's ability at planning small houses (overall far more imaginative than his larger ones).[69] These New York houses were all of simple modulated construction and shared such features as natural wood siding, pronounced wooden eaves, large windows, and exterior louvered partitions or patterned fences for visual privacy. "House 1," the one-bedroom Robert Popper house in White Plains is an example of this extreme simplicity. A tribute to the Bay Area Style, the meticulously detailed, long rectangular structure, clad

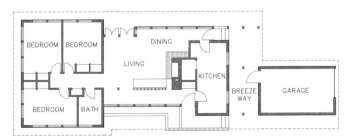

Fig. 3.8. Durisol house floor plan.

Robert Popper house (1948–49), Rosedale Avenue, White Plains, New York. *Lionel Freedman*

View from the living room up to the dining room of the William S. Rayburn house (1947–48), Windward Avenue, White Plains, New York. *Lionel Freedman*

Fig. 3.9. Rayburn house floor plan.

in cypress and topped with a gravel-surfaced flat roof with crisp white projecting eaves and trim, has large windows on both front and back to capture the view of the wooded site. "House 2," for William S. Rayburn, also in White Plains, and "House 3," for Seymour Kimmel in New Rochelle, both of them L-shaped, have exposed wood framing to give them a rural, rugged character, with the interior double-beamed ceiling of the Rayburn house especially effective (fig. 3.9).[70] Stone's associate (and nephew) Karl Holzinger Jr. enthusiastically told Stone that the simple, old barn-framing construction system of the Kimmel house was so conventional that it produced a radical effect of a very thin slab raised on a forest of slender posts.[71] Simple planning and construction strategies would persist in Stone's mature work—even though it seemed less obvious because of the visual impact of his decoration.

As a few of these houses have already illustrated, Stone was intent on eliminating the nonfunctional hallway, which he considered dull, depressing, and ominous.[72] The six different house plans dating from 1947 to 1956 shown on page 98 of his *Evolution of an Architect* track a progression from the traditional "hallway type" of the Rayburn house to the Stech house (see page 59), in which a larger, more functional space (called the dining room on the book's drawing but actually the playroom) replaces the hallway. But it was the top-lighted atrium plan of the William Thurnauer house in Teaneck, New Jersey, that propitiously achieved the hall-less space and from which his subsequent plans evolved. In fact, the atrium feature became as central to Stone's planning as the hearth was to Wright's.

Fig. 3.10. *Woman's Home Companion* house floor plan.

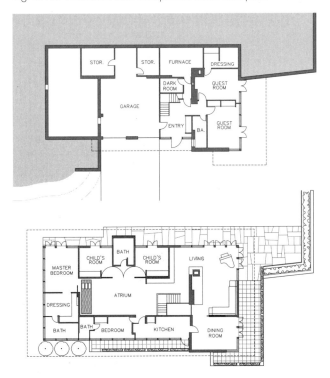

Fig. 3.11. Thurnauer house first- and second-floor plans.

Stone acknowledged that he derived the concept of the atrium from the houses of Pompeii, which had interested him as a Rotch scholar, as well as the Pan American Union building in Washington, D.C., but it also represents a logical progression for him. As the Goodyear house and its many successors reveal, Stone had been wrapping L- and U-shaped houses around a prominent exterior garden courtyard for years, so, in effect, he brought it inside as an atrium. His first experiment with a glazed-roof atrium, published in *Woman's Home Companion* in November 1948, probably helped him see how efficiently it could organize interior circulation (fig. 3.10).[73] The concept, however, was not new to modern architecture: Stone was surely familiar with the open atrium plan by Wurster that had been published—along with Stone's own modern house—in the November 1938 issue of *Life*; and he may have been aware of Wurster's Saxton Pope house #2 (1940) in Orinda, California, where the central open atrium informed the whole design, as noted by *California Arts and Architecture*.[74]

Like Stone's earlier Ingersoll house, the Thurnauer house is entered on the ground floor, where the guestrooms are located (fig. 3.11). An open staircase leads directly into a second-floor atrium (used by the Thurnauers as a playroom; see page 51) that provides access to the family's living quarters. Recognized at the time by Katherine Morrow Ford for its "outdoor living inside," the atrium exudes the naturalistic theme that now permeated Stone's work.[75] A nearly 12-foot-high gabled skylight—partially shaded by bamboo blinds but still nourishing greenery on the wood-paneled soffit—was complemented by red flagstone floors, Hudson River common brick walls, and burlap-covered lighting valances and ceilings. These earthy materials offset the blue-green tiled pool with three stepping stones, suggestive of an outdoor stream, leading to the master bedroom. Although Stone had designed two buildings with exterior pools a year earlier (the Maduro house and the Stranaham Stable Group in Toledo, Ohio), this was his first attempt at making water a main attraction inside.

Naturalism is further expressed on the exterior itself, where red brick is strikingly juxtaposed with horizontal panels of Tidewater Red Cypress and redwood window trim. Copper planters along the balcony railings frame the second level, which also has low, rectangular windows with a distinctive grille pattern tightly wrapped under a 7-foot sheltering overhang. When the rays of the setting sun strike the façade, giving it a warm reddish brown glow, the wood itself becomes the subject of the design.[76]

William Thurnauer, co-owner of Julius Blum and Co., a distributor of ornamental architectural metalwork, and his wife, Maria, a concert singer, had hired Stone to build their split-level dream house after seeing one of his Long Island houses in *Architectural Forum* (probably the Walter Janney house of 1946, published in September 1947, which is similarly covered with brick and cypress siding) as well as those

Southeastern view of the Thurnauer house, North Forest Drivek, Teaneck, New Jersey.

Detail of the Thurnauer house.

Redwood grille at the top of the Thurnauer house staircase.

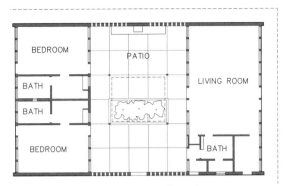

Fig. 3.12. Bay Roc Hotel guest cottage floor plan.

published in George Nelson and Henry Wright's *How To Plan Your Post-War Home Now* (1945).[77] While the Thurnauer family's initial criteria was primarily comfortable living and easy maintenance—still a radical bit of thinking in the region—the unimposing, casual elegance of their $80,000 house ended up providing a suitable backdrop for the many classical music concerts and receptions they hosted for such luminaries as Frederica von Stade, Claude Frank, and Rudolf Serkin.[78] "If ever a home was geared to the personality of its occupant the awesome American split-level home at 628 North Forest Drive, Teaneck, is!" exclaimed a local reporter in 1956.[79]

Far different from the other houses in the neighborhood, the reviews, mostly local, conservatively focused on the softly modern and refreshingly individual appeal of the house. And yet, of all of Stone's houses, this one best shows the direct influence of Wright—for example, in his George Sturges house (1939–40) in Brentwood Heights, California, or his first scheme for the Malcolm Willey house (1932–34) in Minneapolis.[80] Andrew Thurnauer, the son of the owners, recalled:

> I was probably in college when I saw a picture of one of Wright's houses for the first time. I can remember the shock that I felt. What had seemed so original about our house was not so original after all. Looking back to that time, I have to wonder how I could have grown up in a house so clearly inspired by Wright without being aware of it.[81]

While the Thurnauer house was not exactly a *gesamtkunstwerk*, or total work of art, Stone, like Wright, did try to exercise control over its interior design. Andrew Thurnauer ruefully remembered that his small bedroom, or alcove, as he referred to it, had to disappear during the day—by sliding the retracting shojilike screens (a Stone favorite) behind the walls—so it could become part of the atrium. Similarly, although the Thurnauers' baby grand piano was the heart of family life, Stone instructed them, "Throw it out into the garden. It doesn't suit the house." But of course they did not.[82]

Retrospectively, Stone said, his "very eventful" atrium "spelled the doom of the corridor" in his succeeding buildings.[83] While he at once repeated the concept for the guest cottages of the Bay Roc Hotel, he expanded it in the Harold N. Rosenberg house in Englewood, New Jersey (figs. 3.12 and 13). Divided front to rear into three equal parts, the house is centered by an open two-story atrium living room, traversed by a second-floor balcony, where the front entry is located, which connects the parallel bedroom areas.

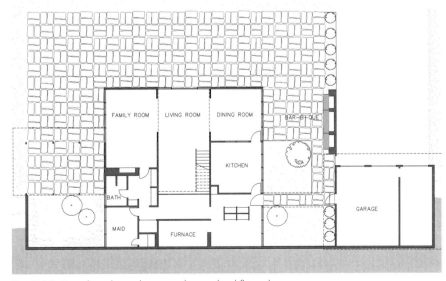

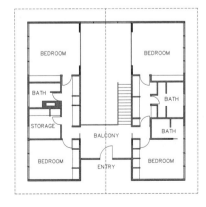

Fig. 3.13. Rosenberg house lower- and upper-level floor plans.

Stone remembered that by the end of the 1940s his approach to wood, brick, and stone houses was pretty well crystallized.[84] In truth, he still had much uncertainty because his W. T. Grant house makes explicit his continued search for a broader definition of Modernism. Prominently positioned on 1,200 feet of water frontage in Greenwich, Connecticut, the $350,000 L-shaped house is centered on an exterior front garden (like the Goodyear house)—dramatically cloistered from the five-car carport by a 5-foot-high serpentine perforated-brick wall, by now a characteristic detail that even Peter Blake of *Architectural Forum* recognized as "so handsome in Ed Stone's kind of vocabulary" (fig. 3.14).[85] The house itself assimilates the modern and the vernacular with modulated spans of steel-framed glazed windows as well as red cypress and brick walls, all covered by a flat cantilevered roof.[86] Even so, Stone's correspondence reveals his enduring preoccupation with the austerity of the International Style, and his effort to create more enrichment signals his forthcoming aesthetic: He suggested the use of cream or yellow paint to enhance

Living room of the Harold N. Rosenberg house (1950–54), Montana Avenue, Englewood, New Jersey.

Aerial view of the W. T. Grant house (1948–49), Field Point Circle, Greenwich, Connecticut.

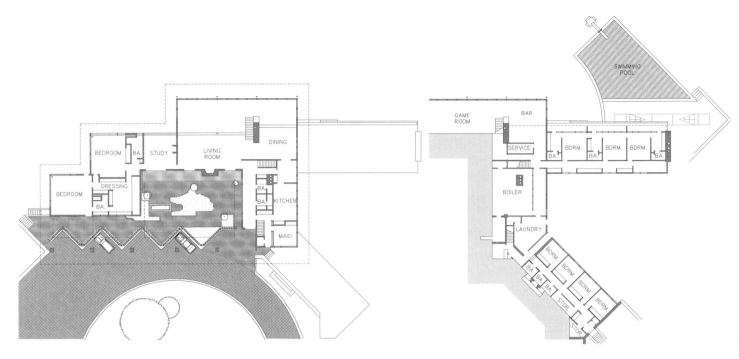

Fig. 3.14. Grant house lower- and upper-level floor plans.

Grant house
western façade.

the warmth of the wood instead of cold white overhangs; a rich wooden grille to cover one of the barren glass windows; diamond-patterned wiring for climbing plants to add interest to an eastern wall; and a cheerful built-up planting bed with hanging ivy outside a bedroom window. Stone also wanted aluminum-disc meshwork to be hung over the deck off the dining area as well as a sculpture by Gwen Lux for the garden.[87]

These last two ideas came from a project he was working on concurrently: the renovation of the Victoria Theater on Broadway and Forty-sixth Street in New York City, which incorporated two wall sculptures by Lux, *Night* and *Day*, along with smaller sculptures used as candelabra. In addition, an aluminum fabric, or mesh, was draped floor to ceiling on the side walls, primarily to hide the remains of the shoddy old theater.[88] Perhaps inspired by Stone's early European travels, when he sketched a tentlike ceiling hung in folds like a textile, or even the Center Theater's sparkling ceiling at Rockefeller Center, the meshwork was composed of aluminum stampings, punched from the sides of motion-picture reels, threaded and clipped to braided lines of aluminum tape, then assembled to create a flowing design— similar to a woman's mesh handbag or a suit of armor.[89]

Though the glistening meshwork was initially conceived for a theatrical setting, Stone used it in vastly different situations, even quite utilitarian ones such as the dining room in one of the three buildings he designed in the initial phase of development at the State University of New York's Mohawk

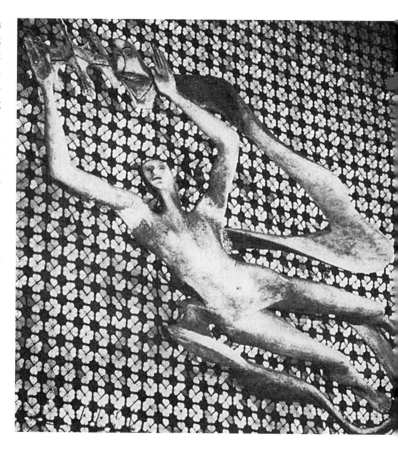

Meshwork wall by Stone, embellished with the sculpture *Day* by Gwen Lux (1908–2001), in the Victoria Theater (1947–49; formerly the Gaiety Theatre), 1547 Broadway/200–204 West Forty-sixth Street, New York City, illustrated in *Progressive Architecture* 31 (May 1950): 62. *Lionel Freedman—Pictor*

Student Union dining room (1956–60; redeveloped), Mohawk Valley Technical Institute (now Mohawk Valley Community College), Sherman Drive, Utica, New York. *Bill Maris*

Morosani house patio. *Paul Rocheleau*

Fig. 3.15. Morosani house floor plan.

Valley Technical Institute in Utica. He even obtained a patent for this "Flexible fabric for use as a ceiling, wall drape, divider or the like" in 1960.[90]

Stone's mounting enthusiasm for theatricality is also evident throughout the Rémy and Virginia Morosani house in Litchfield, Connecticut, the planning phase of which had started before being interrupted by the Korean War. The house is grounded by a large indoor atrium, or "patio," as he called it out on the plan, of Bluestone pavers and Tidewater Red Cypress panels and details, from which most of the other public rooms are interestingly revealed through grilles, three-quarter-high walls, and pass-throughs (fig. 3.15). The patio itself is invigorated with flickering movement both day and night: shadows from the skylights and reflections from the long, narrow pool running along one side of the room are cast on the adjacent red-burned common brick wall of alternating stretchers and headers.

The private bedroom quarters foretell the glamorous interiors Stone would make in his prime period of production. The master bedroom, with a white marble floor, fireplace, and floor-to-ceiling windows capturing sweeping views, is enhanced by a spectacular bathroom. The only published room in the house, it contains a fireplace, an idea with which Stone experimented in an early drawing for his Tile Council of America bathroom mock-up of 1953, and an oval-shaped sunken tub in a pinkish white marble.[91] Although the plaster dome with zodiac signs (labeled as such on one of the extant plans) was never realized, luminescent kappa shells, offset by textured grass-cloth walls, cover multiple doors to create a shimmering effect.[92]

At Stone's suggestion, San Francisco landscape architect Thomas Dolliver Church produced a study of the garden, road, and garage. While the tripartite planted area just outside the back of the house complements the glazed gable at the rear, the large swimming pool is characteristic of Church's iconic biomorphic forms. By working with Church—on twelve projects, seven of them houses—Stone stayed connected to the Bay Area architects for whom Church worked extensively.[93]

Stone's penchant for integrating naturalism with modern features is also present in the line of indoor-outdoor hardwood furniture he developed between 1949 and 1954 for Senator Fulbright, president of the J. H. Phipps Lumber Company.[94] At its peak, the company is said to have been the largest industrial concern in northwest Arkansas, with more than two hundred employees making wagon and plow stock.[95] However, mechanization of farm equipment had forced the senator to find new products, and deeply proud of the accomplishments of his long-time family friend, he asked Stone to create some furniture designs for the company to manufacture.[96]

The original idea was to use the existing labor and equipment to produce a line of five or six items of the "more or less rugged hit-and-miss variety," according to Frank G. Lee,

View from the kitchen into the interior "patio" of the Rémy and Virginia Morosani house (1948–54), Wigwam Road, Litchfield, Connecticut. *Paul Rocheleau*

Morosani house master bath, illustrated in *House & Garden*, February 1957. *Tom Leonard*

who was head of Fulbright Industries, as the new furniture division was called. Stone, however, envisioned some twenty pieces, all made of common natural materials (oak, hickory, and cherry) and requiring skilled workmen (for fine joining, finishing, and weaving) as well as new machinery.[97] Though admittedly nervous about the endeavor, Fulbright was fully committed, asking Stone not only to prepare drawings but also to criticize preliminary models and pass judgment on product development.[98]

On March 21, 1951, Fulbright Industries' modern furniture collection—consisting of seven different types of seating pieces, a three-fold screen, and five sizes of tables with open-slat concentric tops—was introduced at the showroom of Waldron Associates in New York City. The solid wood frames of the seating pieces were adorned with double-woven oak pads produced in the basket-making shop of George Harrison Gibson in Springdale, Arkansas, whose family had been the premier split-oak basket maker in the Ozarks since the 1880s.[99] Although Stone adapted the Phipps Company's plow handles for some furniture legs (see page 13) and wheel segments (called *felloes*), for stools, he was not sentimental about the rural craft origin of these elements. In fact, for inspiration he was more apt to have looked at the contemporary designs of George Nelson, Florence Knoll, Jens Risom, Pierre Jeanneret, and Mies van der Rohe, and even the examples he had

Exhibition of furniture made by Fulbright Industries (1949–54) in the gallery of the Fine Arts Center (1948–51), University of Arkansas, Fayetteville. *George Silk*

observed as a juror in the *Organic Design in Home Furnishings* competition exhibition, such as Martin Craig and Ann Hatfield's dressing table bench, which resembles Stone's stool.[100]

Like the multifunctional spaces in Stone's houses, the furniture was designed to satisfy the compound demands of the new mass consumer by being adaptable to all rooms in every type of dwelling: "We believe you will find it *answers all basic needs*," stated the catalog, titled *Modern by Edward Stone*.[101] Instead of highlighting its vernacular origin, the furniture was marketed for its versatile, comfortable, resilient, and practical qualities, all reflecting modern domestic trends. Reviews similarly valued the modern over the traditional: its quiet elegance, it was noted, made the furniture seem quite unrelated to its humble, home-spun origin.[102]

By spring 1951 the collection had received much fanfare, factory operations were exceeding expectations, and the beginning of a sales infrastructure was in place.[103] The summer was disappointing, however, and by year-end the furniture venture had lost approximately $30,000.[104] When Stone was asked to revise the collection to be marketed only for indoor use, he kept the same essential lines but reduced the scale, and price, while increasing the options.[105] Reintroduced in March 1952, some pieces had been eliminated and others reworked using such new materials as cotton webbing, muslin, natural cane, and even black lacquer. In keeping with his growing enthusiasm for artistic collaboration, Stone had suggested brightly colored printed upholstery by

Joan Miró and his friend Alexander Calder but, disappointingly, he did not get his way.[106]

In addition to hiring a marketing consultant, Stone himself promoted the furniture in the interiors he designed—including a patio setting for the *Art in Interiors* exhibition in 1952 at the Midtown Galleries in New York City and his own office, recognized for its "artful rusticity."[107] Despite his effort, the venture failed in little more than three years, with Stone conceding: "I was not a Twentieth Century Chippendale."[108]

Although his autobiography does not highlight the fact, at the same time Stone was going through this "hairshirt period" of solid lumber, rough brick, and stone, for his larger, often commercial, projects, he still utilized the International Style, believing that its rigid structural system was well suited to the demands for efficiency and economy.[109] A project that never materialized but undoubtedly influenced his own ideas was for the redevelopment of Sixth Avenue (renamed Avenue of the Americas in 1945), with which Stone was involved at various times between 1941 and 1949. Prompted by the dismantling of the Sixth Avenue El (the elevated railroad erected in 1878), the Sixth Avenue Association—incorporated to protect and promote the interests of its property owners and businesses—established two committees to spearhead redevelopment of the avenue. The first was a short-lived rehabilitation advisory committee, chaired by Thomas White Lamb, to modernize the aging buildings and grimy storefronts; the second was an architecture committee chaired by Harvey Wiley Corbett, an ardent supporter of the skyscraper who was determined to transform the avenue into a glass boulevard.[110]

For the latter committee, Stone created a unified plan for twenty-seven midtown blocks as part of what Lewis Mumford considered a magnificent opportunity for a new kind of urban design.[111] *Time* reported that Stone enthusiastically involved his students at the School of Architecture and Allied Arts at New York University, where between 1937 and 1942 he was an instructor of design.[112] Their study of the section between Thirtieth and Fifty-seventh streets was published as a five-page advertisement in the August 1941 issue of *Architectural Forum*.[113] Guided by the Sixth Avenue Association, the plan is divided into three zones: the first, up to Forty-second Street, has stores as well as garment and style centers; the second, up to Fifty-first Street, has primarily consular offices and travel bureaus as well as trade and exhibition spaces for the twenty-one Pan American countries to which the avenue was later dedicated; and the third, up to Fifty-seventh Street, has residences, cultural buildings (concert hall and studio, museums, and art center), and a health and recreation center. While the glass-and-steel buildings followed the six-story height restriction, with higher setbacks behind them, the original concept of a boulevard with a center strip for trees was abandoned, as were the building arcades that had previously been suggested (a feature that, ironically, would be standard for Stone in the 1960s), in favor of tree-lined sidewalks. Stone and his students advocated open areas, some with pools or fountains, positioned in front of the buildings for light and greenery every couple of blocks. Conscious of traffic congestion, they also suggested ample garages placed at intervals along the avenue, with all deliveries to be made inside them.[114]

Even though their somewhat utopian vision was not further developed, Stone tackled the problem again in 1947 with his advanced design students at Yale University, where he was an associate professor between 1946 and 1952. Their model of a typical unit between Central Park South and Forty-second Street was exhibited by the Architectural League of New York and published. Stone's influence is especially seen in the proposed below-grade pedestrian promenade, lined with shops, cafés, theaters, and exhibition spaces—reminiscent of the plaza at Rockefeller Center and anticipating his own General Motors building in the 1960s (see pages 139–41).[115]

While nothing more became of this effort, Stone nevertheless achieved his goal of providing "a framework sufficiently flexible" on which future studies could be based and at the same time obtained additional exposure to the complex issues of urban planning.[116] Aspects of his vision persevered, however, when a decade later skyscrapers were erected on the avenue, mostly by independent developers. Yet he disliked the fact that commercial gain had overruled the association's conception, and he later referred to it as a "cheap, commercial avenue." This experience may well have strengthened Stone's belief that a government-appointed cabinet official was needed to educate the public about the advantages of advanced planning over material expediency.[117]

In 1946, Stone was given another opportunity to demonstrate his competence at unified, controlled planning at Vanderbilt University in Nashville, Tennessee. Convinced that the layout of the 79-acre-campus was poorly organized and too small for anticipated growth, Harvie Branscomb, the chancellor, selected Stone from a number of names recommended by editors to devise a master plan to guide all future development. Stone's boldly conceived plan was enthusiastically received and led to his appointment as the university's consulting and supervising architect for the next ten years, with varying degrees of involvement in site improvements as well as with design and construction, for such buildings as the student union, gymnasium, engineering building, and various dormitories.[118]

"STUDY FOR AN AVENUE OF THE AMERICAS BY EDWARD D. STONE FOR THE UNITED STATES GYPSUM COMPANY," advertisement in *Architectural Forum* 75 (August 1941):1.

Master plan of
Vanderbilt University
(1946–47),
Nashville, Tennessee.

Northern façade
of the Fine Arts
Center (1948–51),
University of
Arkansas.
Lionel Freedman

Fine Arts Center gallery with the El Panama Hotel model and a mobile by Alexander Calder (1898–1976) in the foreground.

Stone was unable to obtain a similar long-standing contractual relationship at his own alma mater, the University of Arkansas—even though in 1957 the university considered it.[119] But there he did build his most celebrated academic building, the Fine Arts Center, finding that the International Style could satisfy the school's specifications for flexibility, simplicity, and an expression of the building's utility and arrangement—all cornerstones of modern planning.[120]

The university's pioneering mission had been for the Division of the Fine Arts to be placed under one roof and to strengthen the role of the arts on the campus as well as in the region.[121] Although Stone was concerned that the million-dollar allocation would be insufficient and force him to make omissions, in actuality it motivated him to create an extremely lucid design, in which, echoing Gropius's Bauhaus plan, the four primary departments are each clearly articulated.[122]

At completion, the Fine Arts Center—a building of reinforced-concrete column-and-slab construction with exterior walls of light-buff brick punctuated by painted steel-framed windows—was the pride of the school, the State of Arkansas, and Stone himself, who remained satisfied with the design throughout his life.[123] Just as Senator Fulbright (who had been president of the university between 1939 and 1941) had hoped, it was a campus monument to Stone's talent. The

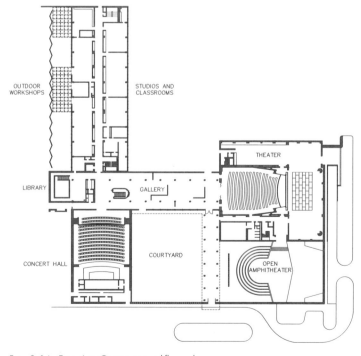

Fig. 3.16. Fine Arts Center ground-floor plan.

Fine Arts Center outdoor workshops.

extensive publicity recognized his now mature ease at handling Modernism, with *Architectural Forum* even declaring it one of the country's best collegiate buildings, on a par with any at Harvard or MIT.[124]

As Stone had done at the Goodyear house (see fig. 2.5), among many others, here he had visitors travel along an extended covered loggia with a courtyard to one side (enclosed from the street by a perforated wall; fig. 3.16).[125] Inside, he struck a fine balance between spaciousness and intimacy as he thoughtfully united the different functions. The first primary space, the exhibition gallery is the building's spine, illuminated by windows (which could be covered by cloth louvers designed by Henry Wright) running around the courtyard side and adjustable ceiling track lights. The artwork was mounted on burlap-covered Haydite blocks or on panels spanning movable floor-to-ceiling aluminum poles. At the end of the gallery is a library with a periodical reading room tucked in an open well below. The second primary space, devoted to the 250-seat concert hall, was furnished with folding canvas director's chairs that could be removed for receptions, dances, and other social functions. Its mesh ceiling (the only bit of Stone-designed glitz), described in the press as a spangled fishnet, was suspended beneath bar joists and lights, obviating the need for furring and plastering, as well as baffling the lights, and also improving the acoustics. The professionally equipped, 335-seat theater, the third space, which was designed in consul-

tation with Norman Bel Geddes, could be converted from a conventional proscenium to a theater-in-the-round.[126] It is complemented by the outdoor amphitheater, with a sunken concrete stage and concentric birch-lined seats for about two hundred, which is separated from the entrance loggia by another perforated brick wall. The fourth space, a three-story studio and classroom block—for music, architecture, and art (sculpture, photography, ceramics, printing, drawing, and painting)—opens to a ground-floor terrace for outdoor painting and sculpture workshops, delineated by a woven-oak zigzag screen and a bold, metal framework above.

While the reviews did not say as much, the interiors showed Stone's interest in synthesizing the arts with architecture—a concept of which Le Corbusier was a proponent and promoted in 1947 at the sixth Congrès Internationaux d'Architecture Moderne (CIAM). Stone not only specified furniture by Charles Eames, George Nelson, Henry Wright, Le Corbusier, George Nakashima, Hans Bellman, Eero Saarinen, and himself, but also eight mobiles by Calder intended for the concert hall.[127] Moreover, for the theater he commissioned two pairs of 11-foot long, irregularly shaped, gouache-painted plaster panels by Lux to flank the proscenium walls. Their theme—scenes from the plays of Shakespeare—are appropriate to the room's purpose, which, architecture critic Paul Goldberger contends was unusual at the time.[128]

Stone's enthusiasm for artistic collaboration is vivid in another one of his major modernist buildings: the El Panama

Hotel. In fact, in 1950, well before the luxury hotel in Panama City was finished, the Architectural League of New York named it the year's "outstanding example of collaborative design"—in architecture, engineering, landscape architecture, interior decoration, and furnishings—and even mounted a two-week exhibition about it.[129]

To be built on 15 acres near the Bay of Panama and the Pacific entrance to the Panama Canal, the $6 million, 271-room hotel was commissioned by the recently formed conglomerate Hoteles Interamericanos, S.A. in anticipation of a postwar tourist rush to South America—Panama in particular, since it was a crossroads for passenger airlines and ships (see page 13). Although sent by management to Havana to study the ten-story Beaux-Arts Hotel Nacional de Cuba, completed in 1930 by McKim, Mead and White, Stone's conception was unlike that or any other.[130] Stone's was a monolithic 450-foot-long white slab structure of reinforced concrete. Its end walls and stairs as well as the two elevator shafts on either side of the center section serve as rigid diaphragms and, together with steel piles driven into the bedrock (causing untold construction delays), ensure stability against earthquakes.[131] The multiple rows of 9-foot-long cantilevered balconies on the most imposing rear side, which shade the guestrooms underneath, create a severe grid pattern resembling a honeycomb, or egg crate. Perhaps uncomfortable with the extreme simplicity, Stone, it was said, wanted to embellish the cantilevers with color-

ful bowers of flowers, which indeed would have been more characteristic of his penchant for ornamentation.[132] Stone had experimented with repetitive cantilevers for shade with his 1941 addition to the Freiderica Hotel (later called the Sam Peck Hotel and now the Legacy Hotel) at 625 Capitol Avenue in Little Rock, Arkansas.[133] Also reminiscent of his earlier work, particularly the Mandel house, on the El Panama's expansive roof is a small circular bar jutting out from a larger rectangular form, both covered with protruding eaves.

To take advantage of the trade winds for cross ventilation (and in place of air-conditioning), most guest rooms functioned like breezeways (fig. 3.17). Mahogany jalousies open onto a full-width private balcony on one side and an open-air public corridor (looking something like a streamlined ship deck) is on the other, a concept he developed in 1937 for an (unrealized) hotel in Hawaii.[134] In the flexibly designed, well-proportioned rooms, a mahogany-framed Lucite screen (manufactured by E. I. du Pont de Nemours) provided privacy between the living/bedroom and foyer/dressing areas, furnished with mahogany case pieces (chest, wardrobe, and dressing table) designed by Stone.

The public areas on the ground floor were divided into zones, sometimes with screens (by now a favorite device) rather than walls. Encased in glass so it could be air-conditioned, the space was ornamented with large tropical plants, a native-themed mural by Witold Gorden, and a louvered

El Panama Hotel rear façade. *Ralph Crane*

El Panama Hotel corridor outside guest rooms.

screen with strips of moss dripping with water and sprouting orchids.[135] Filled with more than two hundred pieces of Stone's Fulbright furniture, its tropical garden atmosphere was amplified outside by Thomas Church, whose organic forms complemented Stone's curved ceilings and sweeping canopies on the terraces.[136]

Upon completion, the El Panama Hotel attracted such a broad range of international coverage that it soon became a forerunner of hotel design for tropical leisure.[137] Even the art critic Aline B. Louchheim (later the wife of Eero Saarinen and one of Stone's main detractors) proclaimed it outstanding for its modern sleek look, tasteful proportions, and sensitively handled mass.[138] After a ten-page article, "Beehive in the Tropics," appeared in *Life* on January 27, 1952, the hotel was quickly filled to capacity. As the project's associate architect Octavo Méndez Guardia informed Stone, it was so in demand that the private dining rooms were being used for men and women's dormitories and people were glad to sleep on cots in the unfinished cabanas in spite of no plumbing or door locks.[139] Indeed, the prestigious international hostelry had an enormous impact by increasing neighborhood real estate values and boosting the local economy; portraying the Canal Zone's image of modern progress; providing local entertainment; and instilling regional pride.[140]

So inspirational was the El Panama hotel that it compelled those involved with the building of the Cadet Chapel (1956–61) at the United States Air Force Academy in Colorado Springs to consider a broader definition of Modernism. In response to a letter from his lieutenant general suggesting that a similar style of architecture be considered, the brigadier general agreed that it certainly could be modified to suit their requirements.[141] Even though Walter A. Netsch of Skidmore, Owings, and Merrill received the commission, the Panama hotel may well have spurred the Air Force's willingness to accept a modern agenda.

While Stone's next hotel project in San Salvador was never realized, he had intended it to take his interest in artistic collaboration even further. In an attempt to make the best client presentation possible, Stone, along with Méndez Guardia, obtained the commitment of a number of artists at the onset, hoping that their program could then not be eliminated. Calder proposed a spectacular mobile garden, with oddly sized, differently colored elliptical metal boxes for plants to be hung at varied levels in an elliptical open well between the ground-floor lounge and the second-floor dining and bar areas. Max Spivak was to design an abstract mosaic terrace floor and mural for the grillroom; and Church, the grounds and swimming pool—with an island containing a spherical sculpture by José de Rivera. In addition to a lighted hanging sculpture to illuminate a reception desk by de Rivera, Lux was to design a construction of baked-enamel sculptured

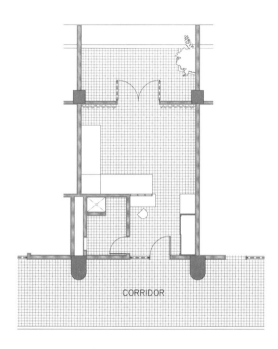

Fig. 3.17. El Panama Hotel guest room floor plan.

El Panama Hotel garden patio. *Ralph Crane*

objects suggestive of Mayan stone carvings; Mexican painter Rufino Tamayo, a mural; Isamu Noguchi, the lighting fixtures; and, of course, Stone was to provide the Fulbright furniture.[142] Though the hotel was to be remotely located, the collaborative effort had critical appeal. It was featured in the *New York Herald Tribune*, where the art critic Emily Genauer called it "the most extensive art-in-architecture project yet conceived in the Western Hemisphere."[143] Stone never lost his enthusiasm for such collaborations, recognizing from his earliest days at Rockefeller Center that they were loaded with infinite creative possibilities.

As all this work illustrates, Stone's second period of production was one of preparation and anticipation. Guided by two lasting mantras—simplicity and beauty—for both residential and commercial work, Stone was remarkably proficient at fusing his own experiences and practices with popular traits of Americanism.

His effort to reduce houses "top-heavy with overindulgences," as he referred to traditional design, to ones that more imaginatively combined comfortable, pleasurable living with economy and function became part of his own philosophy.[144] This emphasis on efficiency suggests the ongoing influence of modernist principles in his work—although Stone was clearly transforming them into new ideas. Realizing that it was important to respond to the requirements of popular culture, he formed a lasting relationship with the print media by consistently supplying editors with the kinds of designs that would appeal to their readers. At the same time, he never forgot the client, who, he believed, ought to have a personalized expression. In his next period of work, these exposures would fully come together and metamorphose into a singular, uniquely decorative modern aesthetic that would bring him tremendous international acclaim and, equally meaningful, great personal satisfaction.

4: A PROVOCATIVE
NEW AESTHETIC
NEW ROMANTICISM

If architecture does not give you an exaltation and lift your
spirit and inspire you, and this is possible even in the smallest
undertakings, then it is not rightfully great architecture.[1]

During the 1950s, as the expansion of middle-class consumerism and mass communications progressively defined American culture, two public commissions brought Stone into his own as a celebrity architect: the American Embassy in New Delhi, India, and the United States Pavilion at the Exposition Universelle et Internationale Bruxelles 1958. Together they helped to bring about a major transformation of Modernism with Stone's tremendously popular aesthetic of "new romanticism"

Stone set to work, using the guidelines determined by the respective committee of advisers for each project. Since the nation was fully entrenched in the cold war—a war being fought with ideas rather than arms—he recognized that these two government commissions would be evaluated with respect to how well they conveyed American ideologies, and that they must manifest such intangibles as stability and openness while appealing both intellectually and emotionally to a global audience.[2] Greeting the challenge not only with imagination and ingenuity but with substantial daring, he strove to bypass dogmatic modernist principles and let cultural and regional traditions determine the tenor of the architectural programs—all part of his greater effort to reconceptualize Modernism. "It was my own and it was unique," Stone said about his simple, ordered classical arrangements embellished with a profusion of textured and patterned decoration. He was proud of his singularity, explaining in an article entitled "Words to Live By:

'Break the Rules!' ": "We are only beginning to understand the power of individuals to shape their own characters by their selection among models and experiences."[3]

Since both commissions were situated abroad, the media was instrumental in introducing them to the world, making it possible for Stone to observe just how quickly his architecture could be circulated and absorbed at home. He learned to promote his own image to reinforce his newfound reputation—with the help of his second wife, Maria Elena Torch, the first of a succession of publicity directors, beginning in1957. She left an indelible mark on Stone's style and widespread appeal not only by ordering his life and inspiring his creativity but by being unfailingly devoted, fiercely protective, and utterly ambitious for her husband (and for herself).[4] In fact, after Frank Lloyd Wright nicknamed the American Embassy in New Delhi the "Taj Maria," she so successfully promoted the piece of personality advertising—illustrated by Alan Cantwell Dunn in a cartoon for *Architectural Record*—that even today Maria remains closely tied to the embassy's official history: the 2004 listing on the Secretary of State's Register of Culturally Significant Property states that the chancery is called the " 'Taj Maria' to give credit to Stone's wife and muse."[5] The tag seems appropriate since, according to a much-publicized anecdote (which also brought Stone extensive press), Maria chose the New Delhi chancery design by rescuing her husband's sketch on a stained manila envelope from a wastebasket.[6]

Chancery
(1953–59) at
the American
Embassy,
Shantipath,
Chanakyapuri,
New Delhi, India,
ca. 1963.

United States
Pavilion (1956–
58; partially
demolished) at
the Exposition
Universelle et
International
Bruxelles 1958.
James Kavallines

"This is the end for us, boys–the tourists go to Ed Stone's 'Taj Maria' now–", cartoon by Alan Cantwell Dunn (1900–1974) drawn for and illustrated in *Architectural Record* 44 (March 1959): 25.

Stone first became engaged with the prestigious commission in the spring of 1953, when asked by the State Department's Office of Foreign Building Operations (FBO; now the Bureau of Overseas Building Operations) to make some design studies.[7] Although an American ambassador had been positioned in India since 1947 (following independence from Great Britain), better housing for staff and their families was badly needed.[8] Also anxious that an embassy be built to both symbolize United States commitment to India and encourage friendly relations, before his departure in 1951, Loy Wesley Henderson, the second ambassador to India, convinced the American government to buy property in the Chanakyapuri (Diplomatic Enclave) area of the new democracy's capital city.[9]

At the same time, however, mounting congressional criticism, public debate, and financial cutbacks were beginning to hamper the entire embassy building program.[10] Fueled by McCarthyism, a faction of right-wing Americans alleged that fears of Communists and other leftists could be allayed by eliminating foreign influences in design and reviving time-honored traditions and values.[11] Their movement against Modernism as it specifically pertained to the embassy program was outlined in a letter that architectural writer and photographer G[eorge] E[verard] Kidder Smith sent in October 1953 to Philip Johnson, then director of the architecture and design department at the Museum of Modern Art, which was actively involved on the cultural front of the cold war and was mounting the exhibition *Architecture of the State Department*.[12] Fearful that colonial columns would sprout not just in New Delhi but all over the world, as Smith fingered the two State Department officials who wanted to disconnect the embassy

building program from Modernism he explained that the director of the FBO, Leland Wiggins King, had been caught in a political crossfire and dismissed. Smith was markedly concerned that because Stone had not yet signed his embassy contract and his design would never materialize.[13] As it turned out however, the foreign embassy architecture program continued in the modern vein, owing, in part, to King's final act of initiating an advisory committee, which included independent architects, to review all proposed embassy designs.[14] It is today believed to be responsible for protecting the government's modern design policy and, in effect, taking Modernism to its next level of development.[15]

Although the State Department representatives on this committee wanted its three architect advisers—Henry Shepley, Ralph Walker, and Pietro Belluschi—to firmly establish a building style, the architect advisers insisted a quality design could only be obtained by granting free rein.[16] And so a policy manifesto was drawn up by Belluschi that invited embassy architects to experiment with alternatives that could be fused with modern planning and technologies. Sensitive to the negative association of Modernism with the left, however, the manifesto was careful not to actually use the word *modern*, instead referring to "new" techniques and materials and "freshness" of approach.[17] It cautioned against using obsolete or sterile formulas and creating undistinguished structures (perhaps in response to the ambiguous International Style glass-and-steel buildings multiplying throughout the country, which Stone himself disliked). It also discouraged conventional past solutions for not reflecting current cultural values. Instead, the architects were asked to creatively apply vernacular traditions—in terms of people and customs, topography and climate (as Le Corbusier was doing at the capitol complex in Chandigarh, where he blended rich Indian references and associations with classical traditions and his own innovative forms).[18] This emphasis on the local situation, which Stone was already adept at assimilating into his designs, was a sharp departure from the original modernist concept that shunned overt iconographic content, historical reference, and decoration.[19] Though the manifesto was only loosely incorporated into the State Department architectural policy of creating goodwill in foreign countries through appropriate architecture, it nonetheless prevailed, and as the first architect to work under its directive, Stone was essentially given a mandate to create a new prototype for embassy architecture.[20] After he signed the contract in March 1954, in a thank-you note to Shepley, he wrote, "I am elated and grateful to you for your efforts in my behalf. I assure you that your vote of confidence will be justified and I look forward to working for you again. I like very much the idea that you, Ralph, and Pietro will review the preliminary ideas. It should prove to be a busman's holiday."[21]

In retrospect, it seems that few architects could have been more ideally suited than Stone for the unprecedented program since it coincided with his own desire to find a more satisfying aesthetic. The clear instruction as well as the surveillance and input of the architect advisers (in addition to the reassurance and inspiration from Maria) allowed Stone to pursue a unique solution within the modernist framework that possessed the dignity and formality commonly associated with government buildings but without the traditional presentation of monumentality resented by modernists.[22]

In April 1954 Stone made a two-week survey trip to India, and four months later he presented to the committee two preliminary schemes for a master site plan. Upon discussing it at length, Stone was asked to restudy and submit a revised plan and specification outlines. In September he provided a considerably reduced scheme and although positively received, judging by the minutes of the subsequent monthly meetings, going forward the architect advisers were thoroughly involved with virtually every detail and made numerous suggestions with regard to layout, proportion, design, and construction.[23] Their contribution to Stone's maturation cannot be overestimated.

The model Stone presented in March 1955 instigated a heated discussion that ultimately affected the entire embassy program. William Pulaski Hughes, director of the FBO (until 1961), was worried that the chancery design was too extreme and not in keeping with local architectural traditions. He particularly disliked the sculptured grilles, or screens, flanking the entrance, preferring the benches in the original scheme. He was joined by other non-architect committee members concerned that modern architecture was faddish or even freakish. But the architect advisers stood firm, reassuring everyone that modern design was indeed in keeping with contemporary American culture and that the embassy would be the outstanding architectural achievement of the century.[24]

In a show of support, Shepley and Belluschi traveled to India to canvas the site and to visit such seventeenth-century monuments as the Taj Mahal in Agra, the building most inspiring to Stone; Shah Jahan's reconstruction of the Red Fort in Delhi; and Akbar's tomb at Sikandra near Agra. The tour reinforced their high opinion that Stone had created a distinguished modern design in the American spirit by using the best from the local tradition—especially the pierced masonry screens of brick or stone and overhanging roof slabs for protection from sun and heat. While Walker had not made the trip, he agreed with the other two architect advisers, further explaining to the committee that while sensitive to the Indian culture, the embassy would achieve a new look expressive of the power and richness of American life.[25]

For the plan, Stone arranged the chancery and the ambassador's house on one half of the rectangular site; on the other half is staff housing of clustered units arranged around open squares, servants' housing, and other service areas (fig. 4.1). The most notable feature of the staff housing is the woven teak

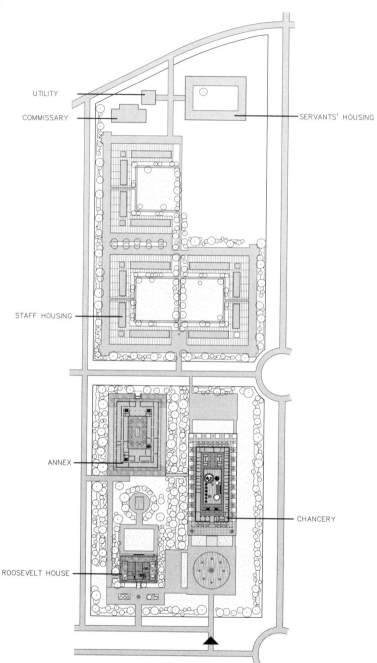

Fig. 4.1. American Embassy, New Delhi, site plan, showing ground-floor plans.

Staff housing at the American Embassy, New Delhi.

lattices on steel columns outside each unit, which produce dramatic striated patterns of light and shade. Said to be reminiscent of the lath roofing over the Estufa Fria ("cold greenhouse"; 1926–30), created by the architect Raul Carapinha in the Parque Eduardo VII in Lisbon, which Stone once sent some of his associates to visit, it also recalls his earlier simple bamboo trelliswork.[26]

According to Stone, the chancery design evolved from the concept of a simple temple, not unlike the classical ones of Greece and Rome (see page 15).[27] Its majestic, single-span rectangular volume hovers between the podium raised 7 feet above ground (for shaded, accessible automobile parking underneath) and the pronounced roof, extending 20-feet beyond the wall plane and supported by delicate, slender gilded columns (recalling those of Ludwig Mies van der Rohe). At the foot of the grand staircase, paved with strips of marble and smooth pebbles from the sacred Ganges River, is a 39-foot circular pool with fountains, a refreshing oasis to induce repose and serenity and to reflect the chancery—as at the Taj Mahal.[28]

The interior is arranged around a two-story central atrium surrounded by air-conditioned offices, one bay deep on both floors with open balconies on the second floor. The lush water garden in the middle of the atrium has a fantastic display of fountain jets, stepping stones, and islands of various shapes, which, as one of the plans indicated, were to be lushly planted with yellow silk cotton, palm, bamboo, and ferns as well as myrtle, iris, and ginger. Though unfortunately not hired to collaborate on this integral aspect of the interior, the sculptor Isamu Noguchi understood better than anyone Stone's intention to transform the visitor through a multisensory experience. He wrote to Stone, "Birds, trees, water—their sound—the

Atrium in the American Embassy chancery.

play of shadow and of sculpture of which it is all a part—the possibilities are immense and challenging."[29]

As was true with much of Stone's architecture, the decorative had a functional responsibility as well, with many elements arising from his deep concern about the extreme heat. Thus, the water garden was to provide evaporative cooling; the deep overhangs, sun protection; and the space between the double roofs over the office areas, air-circulation. Using the cooling principle of the Estufa Fria, where wooden lath roofing protects plants from the inclemency of the winter and heat of the summer, Stone covered the opening over the atrium with a suspended mesh sunshade of anodized aluminum stampings strung on cables for shade, heat dispersal, and ventilation (but not, unfortunately, for protection from high winds or birds).[30]

While the design of the atrium is undeniably sensational, the most noted feature of the chancery for both environmental and decorative reasons was, and is still, the exterior pierced grillwork wrapped around the entire building, which (as at the Museum of Modern Art) conceals the two-story height. Made of molded concrete and marble aggregate tiles strung on rods and finished with gilt-aluminum studs, it stands about 19 inches away from the curtain wall and appears to float between the floor and roof slabs, recalling the polished stone walls of Mies van der Rohe's German Pavilion at the Barcelona exposition of 1929. Although the grille in his first model and plans is perforated with simple circles, the drawings of November 15, 1955, show the final, more complex design consisting of four counterposed tiles that create a pattern of circles containing squares.[31] Stone once acknowledged that he had been working up to the grille, at least subconsciously, from as far back as 1938, but his two-dimensional perforated grid patterns are present in his designs from his earliest student days.

Stone's grillwork concept, patented as "Wall block" in 1959, shows his awareness of Le Corbusier's innovative brise-soleil for his Unité d'Habitation (1947–52) in Marseilles and, more specifically, Wright's California houses of textile blocks of 1923 and 1925. But where Wright had used 16-inch-square tiles, Stone used a 12-inch-square module of four 6-inch tiles, and the methods of attachment were different.[32] Moreover, Wright's intent was to emphasize each tile, whereas Stone's was to create a potentially infinite abstract pattern more typical of the East.[33]

Also unique to Stone is how he split the traditional function of the wall: the curtain-wall frame is filled in with repetitive modules of transparent glass for light and insulation; the grille reduces heat and glare, provides visual privacy, and avoids monotony through its decorative patterning. Striking a harmony between the two, the grille completes the structure by revealing it and at the same time compensating for what it lacks. Thus, while the grille

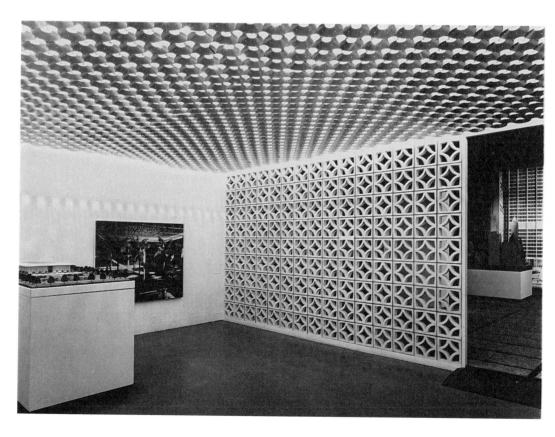

American Embassy exhibit in *Buildings for Business and Government* (1957) at the Museum of Modern Art.
Rollie McKenna

is largely recognized for its decorative effect, it is as essential as the structure itself.[34]

As Stone explained, "Obviously it was no place to build a glass building with the heat; so enclosing the building with a veil, as the ancient buildings of India were, was a very natural solution."[35] His concept of the nonstructural grille recalls the wall veil that John Ruskin, with whom Stone shared a passion for Venetian architecture, wrote about in *The Stones of Venice* (1851–53).[36] It might also have been through Ruskin that Stone developed a deep appreciation for richly veneered surfaces, producing intricate patterns of light and shade that hereafter would become even more visible in his work. Stone could have been introduced to Ruskin's thinking by way of his Harvard professor Kenneth John Conant, who, Stone said, had a "profound influence" on his work. In the foreword to his book *Carolingian and Romanesque Architecture, 800 to 1200* (1959), Conant proclaimed himself to be the academic heir of Herbert Langford Warren and, in turn, his teachers Henry Hobson Richardson and Charles Eliot Norton, the latter an intimate friend of John Ruskin's.[37] As one of the most influential art and architecture critics of the nineteenth-century, Ruskin had a profound impact on American culture and, presumably, on the minds of the men under whom Stone trained.

Yet whereas handcraftsmanship carried a moral value for Ruskin and other nineteenth-century revivalists (and much later Le Corbusier at Chandigarh), for Stone it was simply the most economical means to accomplish the task. Though some of the eighteen hundred workers on the embassy grounds were employed to cast, fire, polish, and assemble the grille tiles by hand, traditional craftsmanship—where the uniqueness of each piece and the pride of the creator is honored—was irrelevant to Stone.[38] Thus, even though such publications as *Architectural Forum* considered the "loving hand workmanship" an implication of the decoration, Stone had every intention of giving the embassy a modern finish.[39]

Well before it was completed, the embassy created a stir in architectural circles, with Eero Saarinen, for example, proclaiming it a marvelous structure, indicative of its typology, a compliment perhaps spurred by the embassy's coverage in *Architectural Record* and *Architectural Forum* in May and June 1955, respectively.[40] Maria Stone did her part to spark interest, too, informing editors that during a visit with Wright on July 28, 1955, he had raved to Stone about the embassy, deeming it the most beautiful building he had ever seen, including the Taj Mahal.[41] Her story first appeared in the *Palo Alto Times* in an article headlined "It's News When Wright Lauds an Architect" and thereafter in other publications.[42]

The Museum of Modern Art surely contributed to the excitement as well by featuring the embassy (along with five other examples of "the best recent modern architecture") in its 1957 exhibition *Buildings for Business and Government*. Illustrated with photographs and a model of the chancery—along with full-scale mock-ups of the grille and the mesh ceiling in the atrium—the embassy design demonstrated, in the opinion of the curator Arthur Drexler, that the United States government was at last rightfully recognizing modern architecture. Positioning Stone's embassy as an alternative to the more luxurious formalism of New York City's Seagram Building (1954–58) by Mies van der Rohe (also featured in the exhibition), Drexler endorsed Stone's aesthetic by highlighting the transformation of many of the structural elements into decoration.[43] Subsequently, as the show was discussed in various publications, Stone was commended for successfully merging such polarities as the conservative and the experimental, the classic and the romantic, and the austere and the highly decorative.[44] He had, in effect, penetrated the barriers of Modernism.

The dedication ceremony in early January 1959 helped to bring about a deluge of interest.[45] On the first day the embassy was open to the public, 6,500 people visited in three hours; on the second day, 8,500, with another thousand or more still in line at closing; and on the third day, more than 15,000 in five hours.[46] Jawaharlal Nehru, India's first prime minister, proclaimed himself to be enchanted with the embassy's "dreamlike, haunting beauty and an atmosphere of romance"—a pronouncement that flashed all over the world.[47] Impressed with the integration of western and eastern elements, it was the building's sense of fantasy to which the Indians seemed to respond strongly, with one staff reporter from the country's most prestigious newspaper, the *Statesman*, remarking that it was like entering a tale from the *Arabian Nights*.[48]

Awarded the AIA's highest honor in 1961, for articulating "srenity and power in government in terms appropriate to the country in which it is guest," the embassy in due course obtained legendary status.[49] Its reputation as one of the best-known examples of American architecture in the 1950s still prevailed at the time of Stone's death in 1978.[50] It had become a symbol of its epoch, a monument to the ideas and aims of the United States.[51]

In spite of this widespread acclaim, however, the embassy, and thus Stone's aesthetic, exposed the complex, often contentious relationship between the modernist format and more conventional themes and elements. While some understood that the grillwork offered a practical solution to the dilemma of how to minimize heat and glare, modernist proponents feared that its patterning could easily distract the eye from the building's true function.[52] And then in the hands of imitators, critics feared, it could be manipulated into a highly predictable package and in the process be made banal, as the curtain wall was by then.[53] Stone was well aware of the apprehension—even commenting on more than one occasion that his textured and patterned grille was considered in some circles "as vulgar as tattooing." His choice of words harkens back to Adolf Loos's still influential essay "Ornament and Crime" (1908), in which the Papuan, who tattooed his whole body because he was not yet fully evolved, was famously compared to modern man on whom tattoos signaled criminality or degeneracy.[54]

The polemic about the embassy's decorative effect was also imbued with past arguments against historical recollection. The historian William H. Jordy, for example, contended that its grillwork (weighty and static, he thought) was derived from the perforated concrete panels of multicolored glass at Notre-Dame du Raincy (1922–24) in France by the rational classicist Auguste Perret, and that the embassy's Beaux-Arts formalism was revived from Henry Bacon's Abraham Lincoln Memorial (1911–22) in Washington, D.C. [55] The classicism of Stone's embassy, however, was most often considered in relation to the work of Mies van der Rohe.[56] But whereas he reduced classicism to a radical skin-and-bones framework, Stone's bold statements of grand scale, strict symmetry, axial definition, centralized space, and hierarchical organization are all archetypal classical features that violate much of what was thought to be modern. Not surprisingly, then, when Spiro Kostof compared the embassy to Crown Hall (1952–56) at the Illinois Institute of Technology in Chicago in his *History of Architecture* (1985), he concluded that Stone vitiated the Mies paradigm.[57]

Importantly, such criticisms fail to explore how established biases have affected the reception of the Stone aesthetic—the ultimate example being the (often stigmatized) feminine reading of his architecture, in particular his grillwork, as "delicate," "lacy," "saccharine," "dainty," "prissy," and so forth. As opposed to the fine or high arts that are typically gendered masculine, decoration is commonly associated with the lower arts, which, historically, have been marginalized or demeaned for having evolved from utilitarian domestic crafts.[58] This distinction is strikingly illustrated in the widely known proclamation by Le Corbusier and Amédée Ozenfant in *Aprés le cubisme* of 1918: "There is a hierarchy in the arts: decorative art at the bottom, and the human form at the top. Because we are men!"[59] Many still remain under the sway of this binary model and thus (consciously or otherwise) dismiss Stone's architecture for not representing the emphatically male figure of Modernism.[60]

Correspondingly, Stone's architecture has also been measured against the exaggeratedly masculine variation of Modernism called Brutalism (exemplified in Le Corbusier's Chandigarh).[61] Stone understood that Brutalism's strain—an exploitation of the raw, crude properties of reinforced concrete to extend the heroic masculine image of technical prowess— was blatantly antagonistic to his effort to obtain a romantic, decorative splendor, which he believed could be accomplished through the delicate refinement of concrete.[62]

Although Stone unquestionably turned to the great Mogul monuments for inspiration in accordance with the program manifesto, his sure hand enabled him to effectively synthesize regional details, as he had learned to do in the previous

View of the chancery at the American Embassy, New Delhi.

decade, in response to climate, site, and culture.[63] While many admired Stone's artistry, others thought it impossible to incorporate a foreign place into western design and that it could only result in meaningless formalism.[64] The distinguished Indian author Patwant Singh objected to the embassy's derivation from the Taj Mahal in Stone's strict bilateral symmetry, white massing, patterns of filtered sunlight, and reflecting pool and also thought it inappropriate to combine the intricately patterned decoration of traditional Indian design with such

Aerial view of the United States and Russian pavilions during construction at the Exposition Universelle et International Bruxelles 1958. *Michael Rougier*

modern features as the flat cantilevered roof and curtain wall. He was perhaps influenced by the Delhi architecture of Edwin Lutyens, who had been accused of grafting regional details onto a thoroughly monumental western image in order to reinforce British colonial rule.[65] Regardless, accusations reflecting a growing concern for cultural imperialism would continue in Stone's Middle Eastern work.

The embassy also agitated Modernism's uneasy relationship with monumentality. Though in the 1940s the Swiss historian Sigfried Giedion had led a great debate about how best to achieve monumentality and at the same time be loyal to the tenets of Modernism, there still was no consensus on how to do so.[66] Thus, it was a bold statement in March 1958 when *Time* announced that Stone had managed in the embassy "to reintroduce into modern architecture the quality of monumentality."[67] Other reviews followed suit, observing that in addition to giving the building the requisite power and dignity, Stone achieved a truly democratic expression through grace and romance. This "new public architecture," as labeled in the title of an *Architectural Forum* article, not only demonstrated that monumentality no longer had to be articulated in a specific format but that together with Modernism it could express the American conscience while symbolizing the nation's heritage.[68]

In many respects the embassy shared a formal vocabulary with the United States Pavilion by Stone at the Exposition Universelle et Internationale Bruxelles 1958 (see pages 17 and 79). But the pavilion invited even more imagination and adventuresomeness too. Stone well knew that it would have to elicit a poignant response, not only from the thirty million people who would visit the building during the six-month exposition but also from the millions of Americans who would know it only through the media.[69] He also recognized that the exposition would provide a forum in which the two superpowers, the United States and the Soviet Union, could be examined and compared by the rest of the world. In fact, the face-off between their two pavilions ended up as one of the fair's most powerful attractions: "It took no deep vision to see Brussels as a battlefield of propaganda, a priceless chance to pit the American culture against the Red slave system," a reporter shrewdly commented.[70]

While the United States government had agreed in principle to participate in the exposition by October 1954, it was not until May 1955 that Paul Cushing Child (Julia Child's husband), an exhibits officer for the United States Information Agency (USIA), was sent to Brussels to evaluate American participation.[71] He recommended that the government select a prestigious architect who could create an impressively beautiful pavilion that would make a lasting impression, as Mies van der Rohe's German Pavilion at Barcelona had done in the past twenty-five years.[72] But government officials vacillated and did not commit for another seven months to the magnificent plot of a little more than 6 acres being held in reserve.[73] Two more months passed before Edmund R. Purves, executive director of the AIA, formed an advisory committee to select the project architect.[74] While the committee of architects, under the chairmanship of Earl Theodore Heitschmidt of Los Angeles, considered some seventeen candidates, Stone's was the only name on which they could all agree.[75]

Traveling to Brussels in April 1956, Stone reportedly sketched the design on the spot, winning the praise of Heitschmidt, who concluded that Stone's ability far exceeded that of any man he had known in recent years.[76] Seizing on the natural contours of the irregular triangle shape of the site (as he had done for his defense housing projects), Stone also took into consideration that a streetcar tunnel underneath would preclude a multistory building and that accommodations had to be made for the eleven willow trees that King Baudouin I of Belgium wanted preserved.

Even though the American government was bitterly divided over the extent of its involvement in the exposition, Stone proceeded to work in good faith and at the end of July reported that the pavilion was "all designed and ready for a presentation." When he was finally given an opportunity to show the plan three months later it was enthusiastically received and unanimously praised. The "brilliant" solution, it was recorded in the minutes, was "practical, structurally sound, and flexible enough to be adapted to any type of arrangement of exhibits," and he was directed to proceed with very few modifications.[77]

Having decided that the composition warranted an imposing setting, half of the site was devoted to a compelling outdoor oasis, the only one at the exposition; the rest went to a 340-foot, two-story free-span pavilion inspired by the Roman Coliseum (fig. 4.2). It was complemented by two smaller structures: a building wrapped in a trellislike grille and containing a multipurpose theater and offices, which was discreetly joined underground to the main pavilion; and a 65-foot-wide cylinder, called the Circarama, in which a nineteen-minute pictorial tour of the United States produced by Walt Disney Productions was continuously displayed on a 360-degree screen.[78] The plaza itself, emulating magnificent European examples, was paved with rose-colored concrete in a radial grid pattern and featured more than one hundred equally spaced apple trees and state flags. An elliptical reflecting pool, 224 feet long, contained submerged lighting, about fifty fountains, and a large black-sheet-metal rotating sculpture by Alexander Calder called *The Whirling Ear* (now at the Palais des Congrès in Brussels).[79]

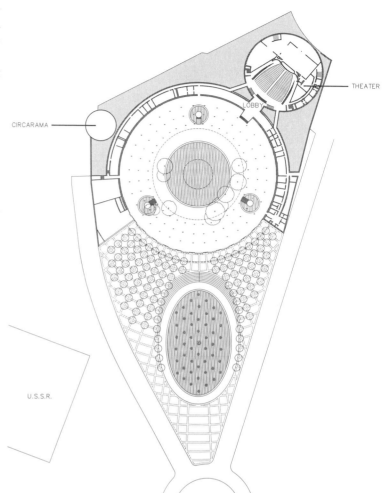

Fig. 4.2. United States Pavilion site plan.

United States Pavilion (left) and its multipurpose theater (right).

As for the main pavilion, to obtain the desired light-and-airy quality, Stone used a suspension system consisting of a roof framed in the manner of a bicycle wheel—an outer steel rim connected to an inner steel ring with radial high-tension steel cables. The vertical load was carried by double rows of gold-colored steel columns—all light and slender because they did not have to hold the lateral force. Although cables under tension had been employed as structural members in tents and other temporary buildings for centuries, they were rarely used in such buildings until after 1950, when Matthew Nowicki designed the State Fair Arena (later renamed the J. S. Dorton Arena) in Raleigh, North Carolina. His building quickly made it apparent that the concept was one of the most economical ways to span large spaces.[80] Stone's was the largest of the tension structures at the 1958 exposition but less flamboyant structurally than the others—the French Pavilion by Guillaume Gillet with Jean Prouvé and René Sarger or the hyperbolic-parabolic pavilion by Le Corbusier for the Dutch electrical manufacturer Philips Company.[81]

As he explained in a radio address, Stone viewed the United States Pavilion as an updated version of Joseph Paxton's Crystal Palace at the Great Exhibition of 1851 in London, where a tradition of using exhibition architecture to articulate the spirit of progress in science and technology had been established.[82] Even though Stone's first obligation was to the functional plan in accordance with modern principles and experimental materials, the innovative engineering of his pavilion, highly unusual for Stone, did not draw attention to itself, primarily because the excitement was in the decorative effect.[83]

Understanding the pavilion to be a symbol of democracy, Stone astutely made transparency one of its key features: the interior was illuminated through the extremely simple gold, crystalline, and white exterior walls constructed of plastic laminated sheets held in tension with a light-steel lattice system secured by gold-colored escutcheons at the intersection of the diagonals. The cantilevered outer roof was covered with 2,100 translucent panels (each about 4 feet by 12 feet) made of two layers of plastic laminate on aluminum frames.[84] As was typical of Stone, here the functional and the decorative became one.

Although Stone's first inclination was to place a plastic dome in the roof, he created an aperture to allow sunlight and rain to collect in the circular pool located in the center of the pavilion. Intent on artistic collaborations for works expressive of the program, Stone had hoped to place a dynamic vertical fountain by Richard Lippold in the pool to represent "the unfolding golden flowering of American culture" (a rendering is illustrated in Architectural Record in July 1957), which would have made explicit the inherent message of the pavilion, but it did not materialize.[85]

Much of the pavilion's luminous interior was produced by its gracefully swagged, glittering mesh canopy made of thousands of gold-anodized aluminum disks, through which both daylight and artificial illumination filtered from above.[86] Stone said the concept was from a print of the restored interior of the Roman Coliseum covered with a velarium in A History of Architecture by Sir Banister Fletcher, which was illustrated in the pavilion's promotional materials.[87] But the prototype for the meshwork itself was his Victoria Theater in New York City (see page 67).

During the building phase, Americans kept a close eye on the Russian scheme, concerned that the formidable neighbor's mammoth classical pavilion—a monolithic rectangular structure rumored to have cost $50 million—would give a propaganda advantage over the more economy-minded American one.[88] Both European and American critics agreed, however, that the frosted-glass building, prefabricated in Russia and shipped over in sections, resembled a factory or hangar—cold and unimaginative.[89] Compared almost exclusively to the United States Pavilion in the press, its massiveness accentuated the more welcoming Stone building.[90]

In spite of Stone's request to design or coordinate the exhibits themselves, the job was given to James Sachs Plaut, a consultant to the State Department, and his team.[91] While there was little enthusiasm for what looked like a "hotchpotch" presentation, Stone's architecture was almost always exempt from the relentless criticism. In fact, when the White House sent George Allen, director of the USIA, to Brussels for an inspection, he felt, as most others did, that the United States Pavilion stood alone for its superior design.[92] Other political dignitaries agreed: Adlai Stevenson thought it serene and beautiful; Herbert Hoover, a stroke of genius.[93] Letters sent to the President of the United States from fair visitors (as requested) illustrate that nearly everyone understood that together the transparent walls, festive atmosphere, and abundant landscape symbolized American ideals.[94]

Even though a few critics were troubled by the pavilion's monumentality—expressed in its large scale, classical references, and grand layout—for the most part the idyllic, dreamlike effect it produced dissipated the objections.[95] The pavilion as fantasy played into the contemporary enthusiasm for extravagantly contrived display—visible, for example, at Disneyland (founded 1955) in Anaheim, California, or in the "Miami Baroque" hotels of Morris Lapidus.[96] By being consistent with existing popular tastes, Stone was more easily able to transgress modernist tenets. It did not go unnoticed: In the middle of the exhibition, Douglas Haskell, editor of Architectural Forum, questioned, "Is modern architecture molded by popular taste?" After identifying three new trends in architecture—decoration (to which he related Stone's work), drama, and free improvisation—Haskell had to agree that by incorporating such pleasures of consumption as pools with lighted fountains, latticed plastic screens, and sparkling ceiling mesh into functional design, Stone's pavil-

United States Pavilion interior.

ion represented a rapprochement between modern architecture and popular taste.[97]

A month later, however, Haskell returned to his modernist allegiance, circulating a memorandum to his staff explaining that although the pavilion was a great modern building, the media had failed to adequately consider Stone's rational structural approach: in its site plan; extraordinary functionalism; novel engineering of the suspension roof; magnificent interior space (with which no amount of bungling of the exhibits could interfere); easy yet exhilarating circulation pattern; wiring and lighting systems cleverly tucked under the meshwork; and theater, an architectural gem that operated beautifully.[98] The consequent five-page article, titled "A Final Look at Brussels,"

reclaimed the pavilion from populist fantasy architecture and returned it to mainstream Modernism.[99] There was not one comment about the decoration, reflecting the editor's inability to comfortably locate it within the modernist framework.

Going forward, Stone would seek to resolve this inherent conflict between Modernism and popular culture by seizing on the opportunities created by the widespread endorsement of his stylistic direction, due in part to the unprecedented media coverage of both the Brussels pavilion and the New Delhi embassy. While also honoring a basic modernist format, Stone's mission, enabled by the period's extraordinarily optimism and growth, was to make an architecture that would fully represent and satisfy great numbers of people.[100]

5: ARCHITECTURE AS COMMODITY

*And I want to make it clear from the beginning that I am
a romantic, pure and simple. I like economy of line but not starkness.
I like generosity of proportion but not giantism. I like a certain
amount of lushness in the setting but not over-dressed vulgarity.*[1]

Stone continued to create enormous excitement in the late 1950s as he reformulated his "new romanticism" in imaginative reiterations for an increasingly diverse clientele. Accordingly, *Time*'s 1958 cover story about Stone declared him "one of the profession's freest spirits and by general consensus the most versatile designer and draftsman of his generation."[2] With unprecedented endorsement by the mass media, his architecture became appreciated as a fashionable commodity. It gave a jolt to the age-old covenant of exclusive, highbrow patronage of art and for the first time, at least for Stone, was integral to popular culture.

Even before the New Delhi embassy and Brussels pavilion were finished, their worldwide publicity gave Stone the opportunity to apply his aesthetic to a broad range of typologies—from an expansive medical center to a small gas station. In so doing, he extended the definition of modern architecture to include historical references, regional influences, natural elements, and of course, decoration, in order to fulfill the demands of mass consumption. By this process, he in effect hastened the arrival of Postmodernism.[3]

Distributed primarily across the United States, rather than overseas, the greater accessibility of his projects to the media both reinforced and furthered public interest. In contrast to the International Style, where simple but severe forms were generated by programmatic requirements and structural capabilities, his designs now had a vibrant communicative power.

They were lauded for their humanistic considerations and, even more, for giving decoration back to the people—albeit in a modern package. Although the critics' focus on decorative effect tended to obscure Stone's adeptness at planning, at the core of his approach was his ability to turn even the most challenging architectural problem into an elegant solution. His plans are symmetrically ordered and generally arranged around a centralized atrium—for clear circulation and avoidance of corridors—with the primary rooms often accessing outside cloistered gardens or courtyards, an idea Stone cherished.[4] Equally important to Stone was his desire to engage viewers in drama and sensory delight. He insisted on certain traditional symbols of luxury characteristic of theater design or other opulent spaces, including metallic (especially gold) surfaces, white marble, dark wood, and royal-red textiles—all very seductive and sumptuous.[5] Though no longer working primarily with indigenous construction methods and materials, Stone continued to infuse his architecture with naturalism—filtered patterns of sunlight, pools of water, and hanging plants—contributing to what he considered an exhilaration of the spirit.

The detail for which Stone was still best known, however, was his grillwork, which quickly became his trademark after its initial success at the New Delhi embassy.[6] Subsequently, as noted in 1959 in *House & Garden*, "the grille look" was everywhere—fashionable not just in architecture but also in fab-

Stanford Medical Center
(1954–59), Pasteur Drive,
Palo Alto, California.

Gulf gas station (1957–60;
demolished), New York
International Airport (also known
as Idlewild; now John F. Kennedy
International Airport), Queens,
New York.

ric, paper, and appliances.[7] So ubiquitous had it become that one American ambassador to India publicly voiced concern that the embassy's stature was being debased by Stone's succeeding work.[8] While Stone later admitted that he might have overindulged his own enthusiasm, he continued to recycle or reconfigure his grillwork into innumerable, often clever, formulations of circles, stars, hexagons, octagons, quadrilaterals, and so forth until about 1967.[9] Consequently, the architecture critic Ada Louise Huxtable still remembered in 2004, that people could not get enough of the signature gimmick.[10] As a form of pop architecture, the mass consumption of the grillwork implied a democratization of a culture previously determined only by the elite.[11]

A close examination of Stone's publicity demonstrates how the media helped to establish his aesthetic in the mass culture and utterly exalt the architect himself. Television was especially responsible for disseminating (and dramatizing) his architecture as a form of entertainment. By producing a common experience among viewers, television encouraged

View of the *Form Givers at Mid-Century* installation at the Virginia Museum of Fine Arts, Richmond, February 26–March 20, 1960, showing work by Stone, including models of the American Embassy (1953–59) in New Delhi and the Gallery of Modern Art (1958–64) in New York City.

ongoing dialogue and thus familiarity with Stone and his work among members of the mass audience—an essential component to popular acceptance.[12] Stone's momentum built steadily after his Brussels pavilion was first introduced on Ed Sullivan's Sunday night variety show on February 2, 1958 (see pages 86–89). Not only did Sullivan proclaim his great pride that Stone's United States Pavilion was the most magnificent at the exposition, but he also put in a plug for the New Delhi embassy (still under construction), noting that Frank Lloyd Wright had lavishly praised the plans (see pages 78–87).[13] Less than two weeks later, Stone became the first architect ever to be interviewed on Edward R. Murrow's *Person to Person*, a television series with an estimated weekly audience of twenty million viewers. As Stone and his wife, Maria (who understood that in the world of celebrity, their private life was consumable merchandise), gave a tour of their recently redesigned town house in New York City (see page 103), the interviewer, Gary Moore, proclaimed Stone one of America's foremost architects.[14] Six months later, Stone made a guest appearance on the game show *What's My Line?* Although the celebrities on the panel failed to establish the identity of "Mr. E. D. S.," after being told he was the architect of the Brussels pavilion, Arlene Francis rhapsodized: "It's the most beautiful building there, Mr. Stone. Everyone says that it is absolutely glorious to look at." The host, John Daly, added that he considered it the most beautiful building he'd ever laid eyes on.[15]

In addition to the enormous advantages of television, Stone received "potent propaganda," as he explained, from the print media, both popular and trade, whose extensive coverage of his work also helped to swiftly spread his name to a larger public: in February 1958 his New York City town house was featured in *Vogue*; in March, *Time* ran its cover story on him, which illustrated seven of his current projects.[16] A month later Stone was named one of thirteen "Form Givers" whose most significant statements in architecture were to be surveyed in *Form Givers at Mid-Century*, a two-year traveling exhibition, organized by *Time* in cooperation with the American Federation of Arts.[17] Curated by Cranston Jones, the *Time* associate editor who had written the Stone cover story, the show opened in April 1959 at the Corcoran Gallery of Art in Washington, D.C., and then traveled to more than fifteen other prominent venues, ranging from the Metropolitan Museum of Art in New York City to the Seattle Art Museum. Stone was also one of seven architects featured in *The New Age of Architecture*, a forty-minute film created by the editors of *Architectural Forum* to accompany the exhibition.[18]

His achievements garnered attention within his own profession, too. In February 1958 Stone was elected to the National Institute of Arts and Letters; in March he was named a fellow of the AIA for his achievements in design; and in May he received from the AIA two awards—an Honor Award for his Stuart Company in Pasadena, California (see page 101), and an Award of Merit for the Brussels pavilion.[19] Stone's own promotional efforts generated further familiarity in the public realm. He gave talks at Lion's Clubs, Rotary Clubs, and Chamber of Commerce groups, often juxtaposing great historic structures with cheap and transitory contemporary places (and in so doing promoted his own decorative aesthetic).[20] Another favorite approach was to open his talks with his Nine Rules:

1. Don't work too hard
2. Beware of progress
3. Don't be modern
4. Go to bat for beauty
5. Don't fall in love with your first idea
6. Don't get into trouble
7. Don't be a money changer in the temple
8. Don't talk back to your wife
9. Don't be too worthwhile

Although not a sophisticated aesthetic program on the order of Le Corbusier's "Five Points" or even Wright's criteria for Prairie School architecture, his presentations—entertaining and anecdotal, quotable and memorable—were perfectly attuned to the postwar ethos.[21] His efforts paid off: after hearing him speak at a Rockefeller Planning Conference about the importance of preserving land around building sites, one listener offered to donate 40 acres in Little Rock to the University of Arkansas for a new hospital, with one stipulation: that Stone design it—and he did.[22] Pasadena client Ludwig Lauerhass, for whom Stone had created an intriguing, but unrealized, house design, exclaimed in a letter, "Scarcely a publication appears without a story or pictures or both about you and your great work."[23] As his name became a household word and his aesthetic a cultural object of desire, Stone's reputation soared, as did his confidence, which is apparent in his unabashed self-promotion: "The best in architecture has shifted from Western Europe to the United States, and I don't doubt that I share part of the responsibility," he boasted to the *New York Times* in 1958.[24]

Accordingly, on more than one occasion Stone said that Henry Luce and his wife, Clare, helped make him "so worthy in the eyes of the world."[25] In addition to being continuously featured in the Luce publications, *Fortune, Time, Life, Architectural Forum,* and *House & Home,* in this period of production Stone produced preliminary plans for two sizable projects for the Luces, one of them a Cistercian monastery to be built on their Mepkin Plantation property in South Carolina. As Clare Luce appealed to Stone to produce the drawings at no charge, she promised a permanent legacy, "You are doing a splendid and generous thing in contributing your great architectural skill—no genius—to this wonderful cause. . . . Most surely in the final analysis it must also be for the greater glory of Stone, and one which will endure, as monasteries have a habit of doing, throughout the centuries."[26]

Model of Our Lady of Mepkin Abbey (1958; unrealized).

He was enticed to reply: "The ingredients are here—an idealistic cause and your confidence. I will try."[27] The design for Our Lady of Mepkin Abbey illustrates Stone at his most imaginative and, importantly, anticipates his 1960s production. Even though the monks intended to build it themselves using their own homemade pattern concrete blocks, the plan is elaborate, with a colonnaded quadrangle containing four open courtyards, one of them with a domed campanile, and twelve hemispherical domes on top of the flat roof.

Although never built, the monastery design was published in Luce's *Architectural Forum,* as was Stone's design for the University of Arkansas hospital—a vertical plan with clear patterns of circulation, centrally grouped services, and efficient placement of departments.[28] Stone was sure that the publication's "masterful" presentation of the Arkansas hospital landed him the commission for the Hospital del Seguro Social del Empleado (Central Hospital of Social Security for Employees) in Lima, Peru. Built in association with Alfred Lewis Aydelott of Memphis, Tennessee, the axially organized

Western view of what is now the University of Arkansas for Medical Sciences (1949–56), West Markham, Little Rock.

Hospital del Seguro Social del Empleado (1950–58; now Hospital Edgardo Rebagliati Martins), Av. Edgardo Rebaglati, Av. Jesus Maria, Lima, Peru.

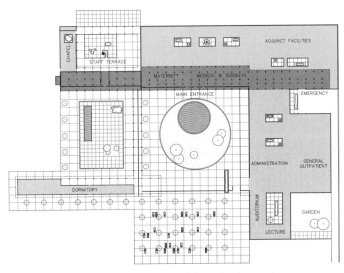

Fig. 5.1. Hospital del Seguro Social del Empleado site plan, showing ground-floor plan.

complex features a fourteen-story concrete main building that efficiently joined two separate functions: a 350-bed maternity unit and a 500-bed medical and surgical unit (fig. 5.1).[29] Facing a large central plaza, the high-rise is juxtaposed with lower-story components, and, similar to Stone's Arkansas hospital design, the plan includes landscaped terraces and gardens along with a central courtyard with a large circular pool.[30] Stone was pleased with the results, writing to a colleague, "The fact that we have been able to consolidate all services for these varying functions in one simple compact building we feel is an accomplishment."[31] Critics heartily agreed that Stone fulfilled with elegant simplicity the hospital's tremendously complex requirements.[32]

The Peru hospital prepared Stone for another great undertaking: a state-of-the-art 715,321-square-foot medical center encompassing a hospital and medical school for Stanford University and a hospital for the City of Palo Alto, California, all situated on a 56-acre site at the university (fig. 5.2).[33] Although Stone believed there was no more difficult or complicated architectural project than a hospital, he saw the commission as a "marvelous opportunity" and after being compellingly endorsed by such clients as the chancellor of Vanderbilt University, he opened an office in 1955 in Palo Alto to begin work, establishing a steady long-term presence in California.[34] For the plan, Stone initially was guided by a preliminary study by Zachary and Isadore Rosenfield, which had concluded that a horizontal structure would be more efficient and economical than the more typical vertical one; and by a 1947 "Memorandum on Planning" by Lewis Mumford,

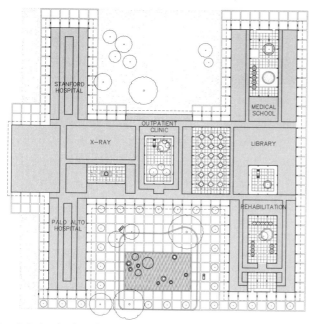

Fig. 5.2. Stanford Medical Center site plan, showing ground-floor plan.

Stanford Medical Center interior courtyard. *Jon Brenneis*

Stanford Medical Center entrance courtyard by Stone and Thomas Dolliver Church (1902–78).

which recommended that all new construction at Stanford privilege the late-nineteenth-century site plan by Frederick Law Olmsted and the university's main quadrangle buildings by Shepley, Rutan, and Coolidge.[35]

Even though bureaucratic dissension existed between the university and the city, Stone's logical, functional plan, with clear circulation and economy of construction, reportedly quieted both sides.[36] Based on a 22-foot module, the plan is classical in inspiration, with the central axis disciplined by the symmetry of its H-shape, in which seven large, three-story pavilions were distributed. Reminiscent of Wright's Imperial Hotel (1912–38; demolished) in Tokyo, also an H-shaped structure of interlocking masses with covered colonnades defining open courts, it surpassed his previous hospital designs in its integration of the various functions by means of gracious loggias with lofty colonnades—scaled, textured, and colored to harmonize with the rusticated sandstone-block surfaces of the quadrangle buildings.[37] The result was a radically new concept—a hospital of restful beauty with almost every part related to garden courts, a feature applauded for its humanistic consideration.[38] Stately, gnarled oaks and towering eucalyptus trees, complemented by the mountainous background, enhanced the landscaping, designed in conjunction with California landscape architect Thomas Church. The entrance courtyard, again recalling Europe's public squares, had a striking rectangular pool with vibrantly illuminated fountains. Appealing to both visual and auditory senses, it produced an immediate synergistic effect on patients and visitors alike.[39]

Stanford Medical Center exterior colonnade. *Jon Brenneis*

The structure itself features all-encompassing concrete grillwork blocks 44 inches square, each with a bold waffle-like pattern. Referencing Wright's 1920s textile-block houses, where patterned columns and spandrels contribute to a similarly assertive stance, the grillwork pattern is repeated on the walls, columns, spandrels, mullions, and plant boxes and is echoed in the Roman coffers incised under the large roof overhangs (see page 91). The massive scale of the façade is relieved with golden saucer-shaped hanging planters with lights underneath them, which at night, it was said, helped to make the medical center look like a palace of maple sugar.[40] The epithet—"a little Versailles for the sick"—suitably connotes its image of majestic, monumental splendor.[41] Recognizing as much, *Architectural Forum* titled its feature story "Medicine's New 'Taj Mahal,'" an unmistakable reference to Stone's former sensation, the New Delhi embassy.[42]

Although his success was founded on large commissions, Stone was able to fluently adapt his style to the domestic scale as well, the outstanding example being a house he designed for Josephine Graf and her husband, Bruno, between 1955 and 1958. Articulating the requisite aspirations of upward social mobility and affluence, it offered a dream world rife with sensual pleasure and magical illusion—just as the Brussels pavilion did. Even more, the house is a compelling demonstration of what the historian Alice T. Friedman has labeled "American Glamour," echoing the contemporary visual cultures of Hollywood cinema and Madison Avenue advertising.[43] It fact, it can even be considered an example of the "gorgeous kitsch" of the privileged, described by Matei Călinescu in *Five Faces of Modernity* (1987).[44]

Josephine Graf, who had become president of the Herbert Oil Company after her first husband died in World War II and left her plenty of Texas money, was clear she wanted a white two-story house with marble floors built around a swimming pool.[45] The rest she left up to Stone, making the commission for him "the thing dreams are made of" because it offered the rare opportunity to freely elaborate on his ideas.[46] Built in Dallas (and not in Southampton, on Long Island, where *Progressive Architecture* announced it would be located when it gave the plan a commendation in January 1956), the five-bedroom, 15,000-square-foot house was designed in collaboration with Church for the exterior landscape and T. H. Robsjohn-Gibbings for the interior decoration (fig. 5.3).[47]

In many respects the culmination of Stone's earlier residential concepts, the house shows a reliance on simple geometric shapes; a minimum separation between the indoor and outdoor areas; a human scale for the structural elements; and a profusion of patterned detail, often organic.[48] More specifically, the first-floor plan recalls the atrium-planned Thurnauer house as well as the tripartite division of the Rosenberg house. The central atrium features a foyer delineated by a floor-to-ceiling open-patterned walnut screen that veils the most theatrical space beyond—a 40-by-20-foot illuminated rectangular pool with a round marble island in the center, on which stands a dining table and chairs. A bridge traversing the pool leads to a living room distinguished by two walnut screens. Beyond the northern one is a 25-foot-long oval swimming pool, accented by a golden fountain on a marble plinth. A glazed wall joins the swimming area to an outdoor terrace with a decorative pool and fountain. Flanking the central atrium are the library, music room, bedrooms, and baths, which were connected to outdoor gardens and terraces cloistered by walls—a favorite Stone theme. Upstairs, the large master bedroom looks out onto two covered terraces, the larger one conceived as an eye-catching peristyle with golden columns and an overhead aluminum trellis complementing the exterior grillwork.

While the interior was an exceptional demonstration of conspicuous display, the exterior was derived from the modernist principles with which Stone had experimented in the 1930s. The lower portion of the horizontal front façade of plain white stucco has only a glazed entrance; the second floor façade, encased in Stone's New Delhi–patterned grille in grayish white terrazzo (a material he considered "almost as

Bruno and Josephine Graf house (1955–58), Park Lane, Dallas, Texas. *Vincent Lisanti*

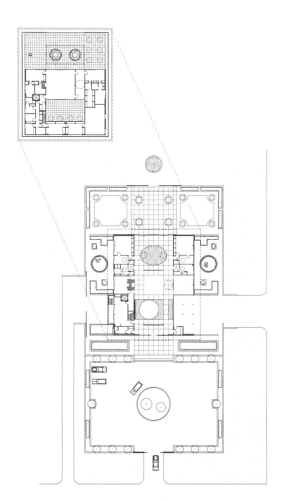

Fig. 5.3. Graf house first- and second-floor plans.

Graf house dining room.

Graf house second-floor terrace.

elegant as marble"), is boldly finished with a protruding flat roof.[49] It is almost as if the house is a Villa Savoye, inclusive of Corbusian voided spaces and framed vistas, but standing on a thin Miesian wall instead of pilotis—its free plan patently clear nonetheless. Unlike its International Style antecedents, however, the "out of this world" house, as Stone called it, was recognized by the media for offering a new type of environment that harmoniously combined the past and the present with gracious formality and luxurious hospitality.[50]

Stone obviously believed that an "ornamental house" with "poetic space" of "astonishing virtuosity," as the Graf house was described in various reviews, would be fitting for an official governmental residence as well, and so he expanded on the scheme when commissioned to design Roosevelt House, the residence of the American ambassador to India, situated west of the chancery's circular pool on the New Delhi campus (see fig. 4.1).[51] From the start in 1956, however, the commission was problematic primarily because Stone's conception was far grander than the State Department envisioned—not just in expense but in extravagance.[52] Although thoroughly revised between 1957 and 1960, his final plan did not consider the simple day-to-day needs of its occupants but instead focused on anticipated diplomatic gatherings served by a large staff.

Centered by a lavish two-story atrium, the plan again utilizes tripartite zoning, here with the balcony of the Rosenberg house (fig. 5.4). An open sculptured spiral staircase (altered during the Moynihan ambassadorship) just underneath the balcony ceremoniously winds around a small circular pool with a multijet fountain. In an effort to harmonize visually with the neighboring chancery, instead of partitioned walls, Stone utilized open grillwork for the front-to-rear division of the ground floor and to enclose the family and guest sitting rooms upstairs. While grillwork was also positioned on both sides of the front entrance, for reasons of economy Stone merely used L-shaped grille panels at each exterior corner of the single-span rectangular structure.

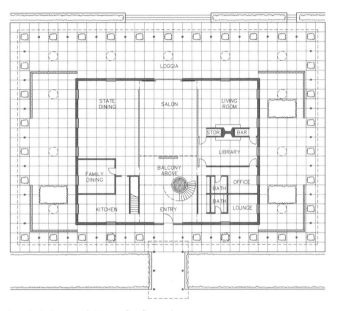

Fig. 5.4. Roosevelt House first-floor plan.

Rear façade of Roosevelt House (1956–63) at the American Embassy, New Delhi. *James Burke*

Catherine "Kitty" Galbraith (1913–2008) with servant working in the Roosevelt House loggia, ca. 1963. *James Burke*

Elizabeth Brennan Moynihan descending the renovated staircase in the Roosevelt House salon, ca. 1974.

Published reviews and comments by residents recognized that the $700,000 house lacked the creative edge that had generated such excitement over the chancery. Ambassador John Kenneth Galbraith, its first tenant, noted in his diary that the staterooms, which could comfortably hold a party of five hundred to one thousand, were a bit too grand, with the balcony traversing the salon reminding him of the main concourse of Grand Central Station.[53] But more troublesome than the lack of warmth and coziness was that the interior open grillwork provided little acoustical or visual privacy.

Amusing anecdotes proliferated: children clambered over the grilles, and a secretary of state reported that the Galbraiths' Siamese cat had climbed through one of them to join him in bed.[54] But whereas the Galbraiths chose to ignore the inconveniences and take advantage of the opportunity to elegantly entertain, when Chester Bowles returned to India for a second ambassadorship in 1963, he and his wife flat out refused to reside in the house. Even though by then the interior grillwork had been modified with plaster fiberboard and curtains, they believed the "White Elephant," as the house

City of Palo Alto Main Library
(1956–58), Newell Road.
Phil Fein

Main Library reading room. *Phil Fein*

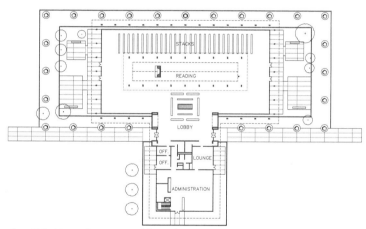

Fig. 5.5. Main Library ground-floor plan.

was dubbed in the *San Francisco Chronicle*, was essentially unlivable.[55]

Equally provocative was the reiteration of the New Delhi embassy for the Gulf gas station (see page 91). Located at New York International Airport, Stone had been retained by the Port of New York Authority (where Howard Cullman, under whom Stone built the Brussels pavilion, was honorary chairman).[56] Assuming that familiarity would encourage marketability, Gulf Oil Company boasted about the building's use, on a reduced scale, of the features that won acclaim in both New Delhi and Brussels.[57] But this effort to mimic previous success for profit—without regard for time, place, or function—opened Stone to charges of architectural kitsch since here elements of his style were blatantly condensed to a reproducible commodity.

More suitable, and certainly better received, were his mixed applications or expanded variations of previously worked elements, which could not only be modified to the local situation but be cost effective, too. For his two Palo Alto libraries, Stone successfully gave them a strong vernacular flair (recalling his earlier "hairshirt period" of production). Modern in conception, the Main Library is a glass-and-steel structure protected by deep eaves with an open plan inside (fig. 5.5). However, the New Delhi–patterned grillwork that wraps around the building and extends to form outdoor reading rooms on two sides is of terra-cotta. The vernacular spirit was further achieved with exterior steel columns sheathed in redwood and with the double-pitched roof (with operable-sash gabled ends) covered with wood shingles and pierced by a chimney of reddish-orange brick. Inside, the grille pattern is recalled in the luminous ceiling of molded-plastic panels framed in redwood. The gabled ceiling in the central reading area is enhanced by a bold redwood soffit, with plants on top,

Stuart Company (1955–58; redeveloped as the Stuart at Sierra Madre Villa), East Foothill Boulevard, Pasadena, California.

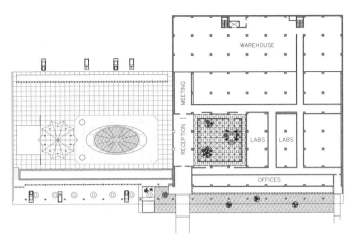

Fig. 5.6. Stuart Company floor plan, with view of lower-level atrium.

Stuart Company atrium.

supported on continuous redwood columns and by a prominent brick fireplace. Domestic in both scale and mood, the Main Library, along with the Mitchell Park branch, was completely functional in the modern sense but warm and intimate as well—its atmosphere of a club, or even of a private home, contributing to community pride and praise.[58]

Stone's interest in creating pleasurable but productive work spaces is also visible in the overall program for what was called the "pill palace"—the new headquarters of the Stuart Company, a pharmaceutical manufacturer in Pasadena, California.[59] Although the owner and president, Arthur Hanisch, considered four other architects, he chose Stone after being introduced to him by Church, who had landscaped the grounds of his Pasadena home.[60] Haunted by childhood memories of working in an unsightly pea-canning factory, Hanisch knew he wanted a building that would maximize employee morale, increase efficiency, and promote social interaction.[61] So successful was Stone in accomplishing these goals that Hanisch led him to three other projects: the Hallmark Gallery (1963–64; redeveloped) in New York City; the Beckman Auditorium 1960–64; see pages 130–31) at the California Institute of Technology in Pasadena; and the Carmelita Cultural Center (1960–62; unrealized), also in Pasadena.[62]

The design of the Stuart Company building is dominated by its nearly 400-foot-long front façade (fig. 5.6). Supported on a gold-colored colonnade, with metal decorations, the building was clad in a New Delhi–patterned grille of milk-white concrete studded with gold knobs. Half the grille ran along the carport, sheltered by a cantilevered roof with gold saucer-shaped planters hanging from square skylights; the other half shielded private terraces for managers.[63] The grillwork, brilliantly illuminated from behind at night, was surrounded by a black-bottomed pool dotted with islands of ferns and palms, well-lit fountains, and a bridge leading to the entry, all of which gave the sense that the building was floating. So satisfied was Stone with the result that soon after he adapted the concept for All Souls Unitarian Church on Wendell Avenue in Schenectady, New York.[64]

The interior of the Stuart building was organized around a central two-story atrium surrounded on the lower level at the rear grade by the manufacturing areas, and on the upper level with the reception and meeting areas, offices, and warehouse as well as clean, white labs. Large circular planters, thoughtfully positioned in relation to the open staircase in the atrium, were complemented by golden saucer-shaped hanging planters and mother-of-pearl bubble lamps, the latter suspended at varying heights (a Stone favorite) from the plaster coffered ceiling pierced by eighty-one clear plastic skylights. The exterior grillwork was repeated as a spatial divider at the top of the stairs, but lower-level and entrance walls were made of concrete block cast with a large oval pill pattern—a kitschy reference to the multivitamins the company produced. The spacious site also encompassed a recreational area behind the carport, landscaped by Church. In addition to game areas and a barbeque, it featured one of Church's signature elliptical swimming pools adjacent to a whimsical folly—a gold-lacquered hyperbolic paraboloid supported on ten metal columns.

As with much of his other work, the entire campus connoted imagination and fantasy, the unreal and the fabulous. Even more, as Hanisch had hoped, production increased more than 107 percent during the first seven months of operation, with almost no employee turnover.[65] Receiving a first-honor award from the AIA and named one of the ten top plants of 1959 by the McGraw-Hill publication *Factory*, the building was thought of as "an architectural marvel of the twentieth century."[66] While the crisp white spaces recalled the International Style, most reviews (thirty-seven articles were published in just eighteen months) were preoccupied with the use of lush, decorative details in a corporate setting.[67]

At the same time, however, *Architectural Forum* issued a note of warning about the grillwork: that if used as stock decoration without a functional purpose (and thus no longer justifiable on modernist grounds) it would quickly cloy.[68] Indeed, even Stone demonstrated that its increasingly diverse role was becoming ambiguous: describing Carlson Terrace, the two-story married-students housing blocks at the University of Arkansas, Stone explained that he employed the New Delhi–patterned grillwork to veil "any irresponsible student housekeeping."[69]

The New Delhi–patterned grillwork in front of the curtain-wall of the seven-story "honeycomb" dormitories (as they were commonly called) at the University of South Carolina in Columbia was all the more encompassing, concealing, as it did, every function.[70] Also now demolished, each set of two buildings (completed in 1958, 1962, and 1965, respectively)

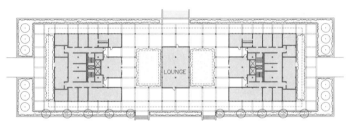

Fig. 5.7. University of South Carolina dormitories site plan, showing ground floor plans.

Carlson Terrace dormitory (1956–64; demolished) at the University of Arkansas.

Two of six dormitories (1956–65; demolished) at the University of South Carolina, Columbia.
Joseph W. Molitor

Design for the Alpha Gamma Rho fraternity house (1958; unrealized), University of Arkansas.

was connected on the ground floor by a one-story pavilion of concrete block (containing a common lounge between two outdoor patios) with the grille carried from the second floor to above the roof utilities (fig. 5.7).[71] Though Stone only worked as a consultant with the local architect, George Thomas Harmon III, he succeeded in giving the dormitories his signature stamp in spite of university authorities balking at the "veil" over the curtain wall.[72] While some critics admired the bold and uncompromising form, others objected that the grillwork was the only architectural detail. Instead of revealing the structure, following modernist principles, the buildings resembled nothing more than platforms for wedding cakes, architecture critic Allan Temko complained.[73] Later, in the retrospective exhibition *Modern Architecture U.S.A.* (1965) at the Museum of Modern Art, the catalog maintained that the featureless grille of the dormitories had been carried to its logical conclusion and could be taken no further in development.[74] But Stone did not see it that way and continued to wrap entire buildings with grilled variations—the Alpha Gamma Rho fraternity house at the University of Arkansas, and more forcefully, the International Cooperative Administration Building (1961–65), an annex on the New Delhi embassy campus (see fig. 4.1).[75] Dressed in a mannerist cloak, the articulation of the plan of these buildings, and others by Stone for Tulsa, Chicago, and New Orleans, seems secondary to the grille, which evoked an immediate association with their maker.

Stone's own town house in Manhattan, likewise prodigiously covered with grillwork, again in the New Delhi pattern, is his most pronounced statement of self-assertion—though arrogantly out of step with the streetscape. Allegedly, Stone sat down one Saturday afternoon and drew a set of sketches (inclusive of furnishings) for remodeling his recently purchased late-nineteenth-century brownstone. He removed all the surface treatments, including the bay, widened the windows on the 15-foot front façade, and covered the upper

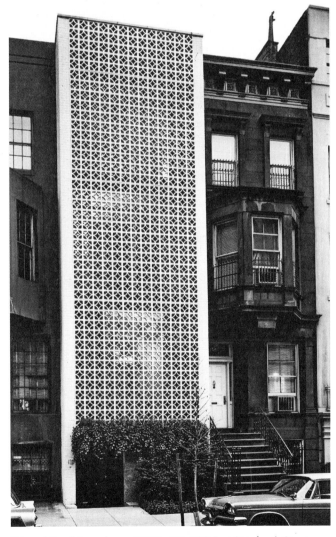

Edward Durell Stone house (1956–58), 130 East Sixty-fourth Street, New York City. *Pedro E. Guerrero*

Fig. 5.8. Stone house second-floor plan.

View from the dining area into the Stone house kitchen.
Pedro E. Guerrero

View from the Stone house second-floor gallery into the drawing room.

three floors with the grille, which he also repeated on the back porch wall and even for the dining table supports.[76] As his front façade for the Museum of Modern Art had done almost twenty years earlier, the house still stands in startling contrast (or contemptuous opposition) to its brownstone neighbors.[77] When completed, it was criticized for essentially being a pocket edition of the collection of Stone, with the mannered grille representing the architect's highly personal style more than anything else.[78] More theoretically, because the grille serves as a billboard, or sign, independent of the structure itself, the Stone house represents what Robert Venturi, Denise Scott Brown, and Steven Izenour would later call a "decorated shed."[79] As a transparently commercial, built-in advertisement, the grille is also subject to the accusation of kitsch.

Beyond the flagrant grillwork, Stone's enthusiasm for textured pattern ("the filigree look," as it was sometimes called) infused the town-house interiors (partially restored in 2005): the porch ceiling covered with his signature metal mesh; the artificially lit plywood grilled ceiling in the third-floor study (see page 147); the plastic-filled shoji screens at the kitchen

entrance; and curtains of gilt-aluminum half globes hung in the first-floor entry and at the second-floor wall between the gallery and drawing room (fig. 5.8).[80] In addition to a gold-and-white color scheme, Stone showed a fixation on the color red, particularly for the plush and carpeting, which especially complemented the mahogany paneling in the drawing room that Maria insisted on preserving.[81] In fact, the interiors embodied, as Stone frequently claimed, Maria's fine Italian features that reminded him of the Medici and Borgia families, both happiest, he said, "in rich colors and the accumulated elegance of years."[82] Embellished with an amalgam of art, ranging from works by Isamu Noguchi, Alexander Calder, and Harry Bertoia to such pedestrian pieces as a mosaic table and pillows by Maria herself, its thoroughly voluptuous air contradicted the modern mandate for simplicity, directness, and austerity.[83]

Nonetheless, according to several media sources, the Stone house was the most talked-about in the city—even by Wright, who reputedly raved about it.[84] In fact, it received so much publicity—the standout feature being in *Vogue*—that when the Jewett Arts Center (1958) at Wellesley College in Mas-

Library–study in the Sam Spiegel duplex penthouse (1959), 474 Park Avenue, New York City, illustrated in *Interior Design*, August 1960.

Design of the summer amphitheater in Central Park, New York City, illustrated on *Playbill*, July 1959.

sachusetts was in its conceptual stage, one building committee member sent its architect, Paul Rudolph, a photograph of Stone's house clipped from *Time*, recommending that he employ similar grillwork.[85]

Even more, the Oscar-winning film producer Sam Spiegel insisted that Stone, with Maria's assistance, duplicate their interior in his Park Avenue duplex penthouse, resulting in "a never-never land," as *Time* described it, of white marble, platinum-gold silk walls, opulent chandeliers, Turkish lamps, and Spanish Renaissance–style chairs—all of which were in the boundaries of what was then considered tasteful.[86] The trappings of Stone were also exhibited, although more subtly, in the outdoor amphitheater he designed in 1959, temporarily located for ten summer weeks at the Wollman Skating Rink in Central Park: the saucer-shaped stage, surrounded by red canvas directors' chairs, was illuminated by four symmetrically positioned gold lighting towers, each 80 feet high, with white trelliswork around their edges.[87]

Though his aesthetic was mainstream, Stone did not lose his capacity for innovative planning. His far-in-the-future downtown plan (1957–58; unrealized), developed with Robert Dowling, for Akron, Ohio, included a garden-type pedestrian mall enclosed in glass with moving sidewalks and air-conditioning.[88] Also visionary is the model for an Ideal Theater that he designed in 1959 in collaboration with Eldon Elder as part of a two-year traveling exhibition initiated by the Ford Foundation to inspire new staging concepts. Conceived with Joseph Papp's New York Shakespeare Festival in Central Park in mind, the theater succeeded in imparting a festive ambience—to such an extent that at the opening night venue the most popular feature was the model's roof, comprising six dia-

Ideal Theater model designed by Stone and Eldon J. Elder (1921–2000) for a traveling exhibition beginning in 1962. *J. Alex Langley*

Rear façade and terrace of the Celanese house (1958–59), Oenoeke Ridge Road, New Canaan, Connecticut.
Pedro E. Guerrero

Fig. 5.9. Celanese house ground-floor plan.

mond-shaped steel sections that never stopped opening and closing somewhat like the lens of a camera.[89]

Regardless of the type of project, Stone appeared to have the golden touch—his ability to attract public applause with no equivalent. For this reason the Celanese Corporation of America sought him out to design a demonstration house (purchased in 1960 by a family who lived there until 2005) to show off its products.[90] Strategically located in New Canaan, Connecticut, where there is an enclave of modernist houses, including Philip Johnson's Glass House (1947–49), the Celanese house received extensive publicity (with no negative criticism whatsoever) both during its three-month open house in 1959 and when the interiors were duplicated at the established home furnishings store, W. & J. Sloan (1852–1987) in New York City.[91]

Using a number of his previous ideas, in some places to an extreme, Stone's plan consisted of two separate structures united under a single roof (fig. 5.9). The larger one, with living quarters, evolved from Stone's customary tripartite zoning further divided into nine distinct square modules—like a tic-tac-toe board—with his customary atrium space just inside the entrance.[92] Joining the two structures is a breezeway, functioning as an outdoor dining room, topped with a wooden trellis inset with translucent plastic panels for light (see page 17). In keeping with the project's "American Idea" theme, the twelve steeply pitched shingled and glazed pyramidal skylights on the roof were allegedly derived from the Native American tepee. The gray cedar-shingle exterior walls are wrapped in places with extreme white latticework (think Colonial Revival) and are extended at one end to enclose a small courtyard (as Stone did at the Main Library in Palo Alto). Though the severely symmetrical plan and self-conscious application of historical details are awkward, the house so impressed the millionaire real estate investor Carlo Paterno that he commissioned Stone to build him a similar one in nearby North Salem, New York, distinguished from the former by the pattern of its latticework.[93]

Given Stone's great workload in the late 1950s, it is somewhat surprising he agreed to participate in such publicity-oriented domestic projects as the Celanese house, especially since he had no control over its profuse interior decoration, with which he was dissatisfied. It is perhaps more understandable that he agreed to submit a plan for row houses to *Life* magazine's "U.S. Need for More Livable Homes" feature because it provided him with the opportunity to pres-

Celanese house atrium.
Pedro E. Guerrero

Celanese house breezeway.
Pedro E. Guerrero

Carlo Paterno house (1959–61; demolished), June Road, North Salem, New York.

Row houses designed for and illustrated in *Life*, September 22, 1958.

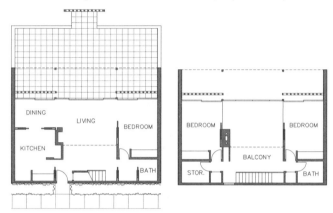

DINING

LIVING

BEDROOM

KITCHEN

BATH

BEDROOM

BEDROOM

BALCONY

STOR.

BATH

Fig. 5.10. *Life* row house first- and second-floor plans.

ent his burgeoning ideas about controlled urban planning.[94] His primary interest was to answer the question succinctly posed in the article: "Can't we finally abandon the illusion of the isolated dwelling, and not let our heritage of a beautiful land be dissipated by miles and miles of little houses with no parks, no open countryside, no beauty?"[95] He articulated his concern about the depletion of the natural landscape by sprawling American developments in his plan of neat, compact row houses for 864 families clustered around U-shaped courts—akin to the Carlson Terrace housing blocks that were arranged in U-shaped quadrangles.[96] Inspired, he said, by the interwar garden suburb of Radburn, New Jersey, designed by Clarence Stein and Henry Wright, Stone's tightly organized plan conserved 50 acres of green space that otherwise would be taken up by traditional houses on individual plots. The row houses themselves—anonymous on the outside but containing a dramatic two-story atrium living area inside—reflected his enthusiasm for the wall-to-wall houses of Pompeii. Each row house had an elegant but practical interior, again utilizing his tripartite plan with a balcony over the living area (fig. 5.10). The sense of spaciousness is enhanced by shoji screens

(instead of the doors he disdained) and a 16-foot-high curtain wall that faces a private patio delineated by a brick wall.[97] A New Delhi–patterned grille is at both ends of the glass and at the park entrance to the patio. As Stone had hoped, the design sparked extensive dialogue about housing development, especially in such regional publications as the *Tampa Tribune*, where one writer commented that while row housing might seem a radical idea, he was drawn to the elegant and gracious family living style offered at affordable prices ($16,000–$20,000).[98]

These projects all suggest that Stone was convinced his aesthetic could satisfactorily be adapted to any situation, including ones deeply steeped in tradition. In spite of his ability to think out of the box in terms of design, his personal philosophy was informed by the more conventional concept of an artist's development: "In the last ten years I feel that I have found my own personal style.... Just as a painter has his own style, so it is with an architect," he said.[99] He promoted his aesthetic as a lasting architectural solution instead of a passing fashion, informing audiences, "We should not be carried away by the latest avant-garde enthusiasms.... Architecture is not millinery."[100]

Consequently, as he spun out ever more versions, many for prestigious or high-profile clients, Stone began to engender criticism as well as rejection. The stakes for public recognition were high, for example, when he was asked by Henry Luce in 1959 to produce a preliminary plan for the National Presbyterian Church in Washington, D.C., which was to be reviewed not just by Vice President Nixon and J. Edgar Hoover but also by President Eisenhower.[101] His plan comprised a two-story podium (with parking underneath), with an arched sanctuary complemented by an adjacent administration building, a circular chapel, and a campanile wrapped in a glistening multicolored metallic screen to be made by Bertoia (fig. 5.11).[102] Inside the sanctuary, slender columns flower at the ceiling to support elliptical domes, each pierced around the sides for filtered light and embedded with colored-glass medallions.[103] While the building committee agreed that the interior was plainly beautiful, one and all said the exterior needed further study.[104] However, Stone could not change the exterior enough to satisfy them because, as explained by Francis Edwin "Hank" Brennan (an art adviser to Luce who became Stone's publicity director in 1964), the design was too fanciful, too delicate, too decorative (i.e., too feminine) and lacked the requisite architectural authority. He continued, "Our dear old friend has gone 'sweet.'" In short, Stone's idea of ecclesiastic architecture as a dramatic luminous spectacle instead of a force of strength and integrity did not fulfill the church's mission.[105]

Though Stone's design for the American Embassy on Grosvenor Square in London received a special accommodation in a limited competition of eight architects, it also was not built.[106] Widely published in trade journals, his plan, in

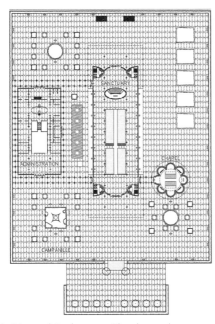

Fig. 5.11. National Presbyterian Church site plan.

Rendering of the interior of the National Presbyterian Church (1959; unrealized), Washington, D.C.

many ways following his established format, is centered by a ground-floor atrium illuminated through the sixth-floor deep-well skylights and embellished with a pool, fountains, trees, and hanging gardens at varying levels. (fig. 5.12)[107] Although both Pietro Belluschi and Ralph Walker, who had advised Stone on the New Delhi embassy, were on the jury, their presence did not give Stone an edge and he lost to Eero Saarinen.

At about the same time, he was also considered for the repertory theater at New York City's Lincoln Center for the Performing Arts. At a meeting in June 1958 to discuss his candidacy, Alfred Reginald Allen asked Stone for reassurance that he was able to make a building without the grillwork.[108] But Stone again lost out to Saarinen, who, as opposed to Stone, was recognized for his interest in seeking a unique, individual approach to each and every project.[109] So for the very reason that the commodification of his "new romanticism" had made Stone "a leading oracle in the eyes of the public," as *Fortune* would recognize, it was also working against him—especially with the highbrow.[110]

In spite of the mounting critical censure about his aesthetic as well as occasional lost projects with big billings, Stone was still exceedingly busy with newly prosperous Americans lusting after his work as a status symbol. The popular culture, organized by the mass media around consumerism, had come to rely on his decorative manner, perhaps as an escape from the harsh realities of the cold war. Stone intuitively understood this. And yet, as will become more apparent, his version of Modernism, much of the time saturated with what is now understood as American glamour, was dangerously vulnerable to kitsch.

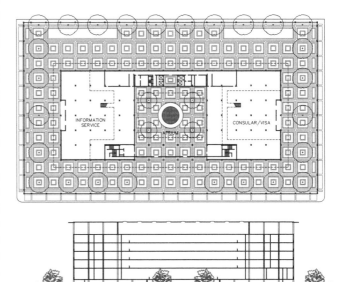

Fig. 5.12. American Embassy, London, first-floor plan and section.

6: FROM ARCHITECTURAL KITSCH TO POPULISM

I do not attempt to be universal, but I would say that my architecture allows great latitude for the individual to express himself.[1]

As Stone basked in the success of the New Delhi embassy and the Brussels pavilion, and their stylized offshoots, he embarked on two other conspicuous commissions—the Gallery of Modern Art at 2 Columbus Circle in New York City and the John F. Kennedy Center for the Performing Arts in Washington, D.C. Although dissimilar in many ways, both cultural institutions have provoked continual, widespread public responses and in critical reviews have generally been considered in relation to kitsch, often using the familiar but unreliable notion of kitsch as "bad taste."[2] And yet, significantly, they also helped bridge the gap between the cultured elite, who considered the art world its domain, and a new generation of mass consumers. Even so, while the Kennedy Center has maintained its position as an icon of popular culture, the Gallery of Modern Art ultimately could not endure the savaging of the critics.

Conceived in the midst of heated cold war threats, the Gallery of Modern Art was formulated by the vision of George Huntington Hartford II, an eccentric millionaire heir to the A&P supermarket chain, who was intent on conveying democratic values by challenging established notions of Modernism. He built his collection of some seventy, primarily figurative, nineteenth- and twentieth-century paintings in response to his belief that modern art, and especially Abstract Expressionism, was a form of Communist and revolutionary propaganda.[3] To express his antimodern position, he chose the architect who also built the Museum of Modern Art, which was his lifelong nemesis.[4]

In retrospect, it appears that Stone was a good fit for the job since he had already shown in his foreign work how adept he was at producing architecture that embodied American resistance to totalitarianism through the ideals of freedom and individualism. Though he clearly grasped Hartford's agenda, his design was not a repudiation of Modernism as some like to believe. Instead, the idiosyncrasy of the building—exemplifying the artistic freedom in which both architect and patron so fervently believed—illuminated the tension that persisted between steadfast adherents of Modernism and those open to reconciliation using contemporary currents.[5] Moreover, while Hartford may well have had politically and culturally inflammatory ideas, the occasion presented an opportunity for Stone to make Modernism more palatable to the larger public that the museum targeted.

The project was announced in the city newspapers in June 1956, even though Hartford had not yet picked an architect, nor finished building his collection.[6] He had done his homework, however, and knew he could erect a 150-foot-tall building (replacing a five-story office building) on the oddly shaped island on Columbus Circle he had purchased for about a million dollars (fig. 6.1).[7] He did not want extreme trends but rather a simple white, or off-white, building, to harmonize with the nearby white-brick Coliseum (1954–56; demolished), with

John F. Kennedy Center for
the Performing Arts (1958–71),
F Street N.W., Washington, D.C.

Gallery of Modern Art (1958–64;
redeveloped), 2 Columbus Circle,
New York. *Ezra Stoller*

Model of the Gallery of Modern Art, illustrated in *Architectural Record* 122 (July 1957): 168.

Stone with his wife Maria in front of the Doges Palace in Venice, 1958.

galleries, a theater, and a top-floor restaurant—a program just like the Museum of Modern Art's.[8]

Stone knew the small, awkward property, though centrally located, would present a challenge, but he wanted the commission. Following the public announcement, he immediately asked Hartford for an opportunity to discuss the "unique and marvelous architectural opportunity."[9] But the job did not come immediately. Hartford was also considering New York architects Perry M. Duncan and Alfred Easton Poor as well as Hanford Yang, a student of Pietro Belluschi who had already offered a plan Hartford liked a lot.[10] In fact, Hartford asked Stone to take on the young Yang, which made negotiations more delicate because Stone's staff thought Yang recalcitrant and his plan but a schoolboy solution.[11] Hartford was soon convinced, however, to collaborate only with Stone, whom he had come to appreciate for his old-world formality and lusty love of life.[12] He also shared Stone's view that all art forms should be enjoyed by the general public instead of by only a select few. Thus, the two reportedly got along well, working together for hours, readjusting models and experimenting with interior arrangements.[13]

Nonetheless, there were long lags in the design process, in part due to Hartford's uncertainty: while outwardly complimentary of Stone's work, he also sought other opinions—from his doorman and even the models in the agency he founded in 1948.[14] Further delays, including the eviction of an existing tenant, a lawsuit by the Museum of Modern Art over the new museum's name, a change in museum directors, and a strike by concrete truck drivers—as well as the unforeseen necessity of blasting through solid rock to bridge an underground stream and reduce subway vibrations—contributed to escalating costs (some $7.5 million instead of the initial $2.5 million estimate) and time (eight years instead of two).[15]

Though the building underwent extensive changes throughout the design process, its essence was founded on the unusual site: "I was, in effect, putting a watch together—and a miracle was needed to get an orderly, spacious gallery area," Stone later commented.[16] In July 1957, before he had officially received the commission, *Architectural Record* illustrated Stone's vision of a tall rectangular building to be encased with a veil of perforated terrazzo evocative of his grillwork. The proposed ground-floor colonnade, repeated at the top under a cantilevered roof to make a planted loggia, was historical in inspiration, but the persistence of the International Style was also visible, for example, in a design for interior sliding panels of plate glass and opaque screens that could be flexibly arranged in different combinations of walls and windows.[17] Stone was reportedly uneasy about the overall design, however. Its expression, at once historical, sentimental, and romantic, was here more pronounced than in his earlier work and thus contributed to the multiple studies he made in an effort to find a satisfactory solution.[18]

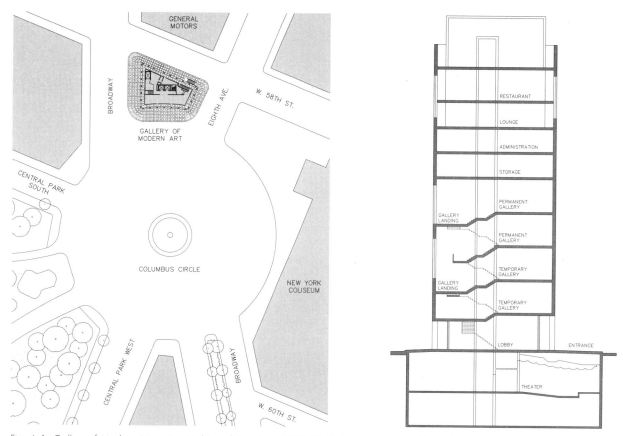

Fig. 6.1. Gallery of Modern Art section (right) and site plan of 1964 (left) showing its ground-floor plan.

In the end, he settled on a ten-story concrete structure covered with a veneer of 2-inch-thick square panels of gray-veined white Vermont Imperial Danby marble—to give the look of permanence he so admired in European examples. The circle theme was carried out in the bronze-plated windows, or "vision panels" (1,472 in all), consisting of four circles cut out of each marble square in the manner of plate tracery, which bordered all edges of the building.[19] Both the penthouse for the mechanical systems, sheathed in solid square marble panels, and the ground floor with plate-glass windows framed in bronze mullions on the front (and with Verde Antique marble on the other three sides) were equally set back from the principal façade, which echoes the 217-degree arc of Columbus Circle (see page 11).[20]

As an alternative to the stark glass-and-metal buildings that Stone disdained, one of the most distinctive features was the ground-floor arcade extending around the building—a feature prefiguring much of his later work. Although Stone knew it would take space away from the interior, he felt its unifying quality was essential because of the inconsistent façade dimensions.[21] Having experimented with various shapes for the supporting elements (from forked- to round-headed columns), Stone decided on stylized Venetian Gothic

columns inset with Swedish Red Rose granite ovals to lighten the appearance of the arches, designed not just for visual impact but also to subtly obviate the varying widths of the building sides.[22] He admitted to being under the spell of the architecture of Byzantium, the root of Venetian Gothic. In fact, as he told *Time*, the museum had a "probably unmistakable" resemblance to the Ca' d'Oro (1428–30; also known as the Palazzo Santa Sofia) and to the Doges Palace (1309–1424), both located in Venice, which Stone considered the "most marvelous place in the world," and which he had sketched as a Rotch scholar.[23]

The interior plan was cleverly organized around a central service core of elevators and public stairs, and the circulation pattern echoed that of Frank Lloyd Wright's nearby Solomon R. Guggenheim Museum, which had succeeded with the general public at its completion in 1959. Upon entering the ground-floor lobby, visitors took an elevator to the uppermost gallery on the fifth floor and descended to the other three gallery floors by way of double-height, half-level landings—a concept that probably evolved from the Yang plan that Hartford liked, though Stone did not admit as much (fig. 6.1).[24] Though originally conceived as places for smoking and reading, the landings were used as prominent exhibition spaces too. Since both Hartford and Stone

Gallery of Modern Art theater. *Ezra Stoller*

agreed the museum should imbue visitors with a desire to have works of art of their own, the interiors were presented more as an elegant, spacious home or private club than as a public setting.[25] Coordinated by the Stone office with Mildred Hull, Hartford's interior decorator, the choice of furnishings dramatically departed from those in International Style interiors and played to the contemporary narrative of American glamour that was now permeating Stone's work.[26] The below-ground, 154-seat theater—equipped for films, lectures, concerts, and slide presentations—was said to resemble a jewel box, with fabric-covered walls, wood grilles, red carpeting, and golden upholstery, as well as red curtains and bronze doors that employed the circle motif repeated throughout the building.[27] Its ceiling was covered with what by then was a Stone signature—gold-colored metal mesh of anodized aluminum discs. The ground-floor lobby had a coffered ceiling with bronze pin-spot fixtures; the terrazzo floor was embedded with marble roundels that had been cut from the exterior panels, the design for which continued outside to the curb line.

The four gallery floors, each containing a long main gallery with a convex wall running along the front and three smaller galleries around the service core, had alluring glimpses of Central Park through the small circular windows at the corners (so as not to detract from the art or take away hanging space).[28] The gallery floors were of oak parquet in the Versailles pattern and covered in places with thick red- and gold-colored rugs. The walls of the main galleries on the second and third floors were faced with cotton jacquard for changing exhibitions; the permanent galleries on the fourth and fifth floors had American white walnut veneer paneling.[29]

The sumptuous eighth-floor lounge, paneled in Macassar ebony, was given a South Seas theme in keeping with Hartford's collection of Oceanic art.[30] Correspondingly, the ninth-floor Polynesian restaurant, called the Gauguin Room, was richly decorated with a geometrically patterned grilled ceiling in walnut veneer with laminated fabric—the design reminiscent of the Starlight Roof at the Waldorf-Astoria and the library-study and guest room ceilings in Stone's duplex for Sam Spiegel (see pages 24 and 105). Banquettes cantilevered from large boxes of greenery (with silk matchstick dividers behind them), Chinese-red upholstered chairs, gold-colored carpeting, Rattan blinds, Japanese grass-cloth-covered walls, and a Chinese oven enhanced the exotic theme. In addition, there were tapestry copies of two paintings by Paul Gauguin: Over the buffet was *Tahitian Landscape* after the painting of 1891 (in the Minneapolis Institute of Arts); and on the west wall *Nave Nave Mahana* after the work of 1896 (in the Musée des Beaux-Arts de Lyon, France).[31] This complex mixture of eastern and western elements from both historical and contemporary contexts invited visitors to shed established beliefs in exchange for their own versions of paradise, where myths are perpetuated, and hierarchies of history, class, and race can be ignored. It was fantasy.

Though the museum's openings in March 1964 were said to eclipse all other social events that season in New York City, the message—that art could be appreciated by average people and not just the few privileged—was plainly heard.[32] During the first day the museum was open to the public, 3,358 visitors toured the building; 38,573 followed during the next two weeks.[33] Hartford's declaration that his museum represented the taste of the American people seemed accurate, at least during the first year, when attendance totaled about 330,000.[34] It fast became a tourist must, purportedly with ecstatic mobs packing the place like Macy's at Christmas.[35]

But after just five years, the museum went the way of Hartford's other ill-fated investments. Although constantly in the public eye, he had not been able to attract the contributions he needed to offset operating expenses; nor could he secure a comfortable niche in the New York City art world since the only consistent curatorial position was Hartford's denial of any form of abstraction. The situation was made worse by his inability to relinquish control to his expert staff.[36] Thus the

Gallery of Modern
Art permanent gallery.
Ezra Stoller

Gallery of Modern
Art Gauguin Room,
illustrated in *Interior
Design*, June 1964.

museum, along with its amateurish collection, became known as a statement of one man's taste.[37]

Hartford transferred ownership in 1969 to Fairleigh Dickinson University of New Jersey, which operated it as the New York Cultural Center until 1976, when it was purchased as a gift to the city by Gulf & Western Industries, by then headquartered on the other side of Columbus Circle (now the Trump International Hotel & Tower).[38] In 2002 the city agreed to sell the building to the Museum of Arts and Design (formerly the American Craft Museum), and in spite of a number of lawsuits and strong protests, a thorough redesign by Allied Works Architecture began in spring 2005 (see page 148).[39] This more recent history is relevant to Stone because it still generates ongoing commentary since for many the building is now considered the "Penn Station of Modernist Preservation."[40]

Since first introduced in the *Form Givers at Mid-Century* traveling exhibition in 1959, where its model was "the *most* discussed . . . a few liking it very much, most hating it," the unusual design of the museum has always been a magnet for controversy (see page 92).[41] During Hartford's occupancy, however, it was not the "ill-conceived museum that never caught on with the public or the press or the patrons" that Terence Riley proclaimed it to be in 2003 (as chief curator of the department of architecture and design at the Museum of Modern Art). Nor was it "a critical lightning rod from the very start" or unmercifully "savaged by critics," as has been claimed in revisionist evaluations in the *New York Times* and *Washington Post*.[42] Rather, the overall consensus in the initial reviews was that Stone had surmounted untold obstacles to make the building work.[43] Stuart Preston, art critic for *Apollo*, summed it up when he wrote, "There can be little criticism of the building itself."[44]

Even though not wrapped with the grillwork that had been his trademark, Stone considered the museum very much in the character of his other buildings.[45] Indeed, the polemics that had been provoked by the New Delhi embassy over decoration and its various associations are also present in the evaluations of this building. On the positive side, critics thought the interior was perfectly integrated with the exterior, its opulence setting a new standard in modern museum design.[46] The "Posh Place for Pictures," as a *New York Herald Tribune* headline read, was championed for its domestic scale and warm, humane atmosphere, in contrast to the severe utilitarian galleries prevalent in modern American museums.[47] But while there were those who believed its decorative beauty had no equivalent in the city, others associated it with bourgeois decadence or, more evocatively, the dangerous "other" perceived to be lurking just beneath the building's surface.[48] It led to charges of effeminacy, or worse, sexism: the windows were described as lacelike borders and long rows of eyelet, the columns as boudoir hand mirrors and dainty pillars, and the overall structure a ladylike apparition in immaculate fancy dress.[49] Olga Gueft's oft-repeated comment that "only a Bauhaus ogre with hardened arteries could fail to smile" at its details referenced—in an amusing and therefore not so threatening way—Modernism's forbiddance of feminine-gendered or even epicene design. Correspondingly, Huxtable's labeling of the building as "Stone's little seraglio," connoting shame, scandal, and exposure rather than wholesome beauty, points to a perception that Stone had transgressed modernist rationalism with sensual hedonism.[50]

Stone's proponents understood the building, from an urban-planning perspective, as a dazzling white palace set against a backdrop of drab, ordinary skyscrapers. They found it a welcome relief from the cluster of nondescript blocks and felt it brought a badly needed flair to the area, even making the adjacent buildings seem a little better.[51] On the contrary, there were those who thought its hemmed-in site made it look like an afterthought and that it stood defiantly unto itself in a swarm of traffic when compared to such neighbors as General Motor's nearby severe skyscraper of 1928.[52] Far more conspicuous was the building's overt reference to the past. Huxtable's often quoted and now famous statement that it was "a die-cut Venetian palazzo on lollypops" bears witness to the critical opinion that Stone again violated the great modernist taboo of decoration.[53] Interestingly, however, no one elucidated on its brazen classicism—in the tripartite organization of the façade and in the treatment of the wide staircase as the apex of the design.[54] Stone's own description of the building as "a grand staircase with the galleries serving as landings" cries out for comparison with the staircase in the foyer at Radio City Music Hall, and even more, the *grand escalier* in Charles Garnier's Beaux-Arts Opéra de Paris (1857–74), where public spectacle is an important function of the building—an essential feature in many Stone designs (see page 21).[55]

With each new phase of occupancy and as the building's destiny became more precarious, two polarized factions became increasingly outspoken about whether the building was a straightforward example of kitsch or a romantic variation of Modernism.[56] Their positions were not that mutually exclusive, however, if one takes into consideration the persuasive view that Romanticism—as a display of dramatic effect, pathos, and sentimentality—was the progenitor of the ethos of kitsch.[57]

Front façade of the Gallery of Modern Art. *Ezra Stoller*

According to the art critic Harold Rosenberg in his essay "Pop Culture: Kitsch Criticism" (1959), kitsch had become the daily art of the time. And yet, with the exception of the Washington, D.C., architecture critic Wolf Von Eckardt, who in 1957 referred to the building as "a big hunk of marble kitsch," it really was not until after Paul Goldberger's *New Yorker* Sky Line column titled "Landmark Kitsch," which appeared in 1997, that the building became commonly recognized as such.[58] "No one has yet made a persuasive case that the building is much more than kitsch," he wrote as he raised the issue of whether it should be preserved, and he likened it to the work of Claes Oldenburg, whose colossal art installations of quotidian objects were intended for the same popular culture as Stone's building.[59] Inevitably, Susan Sontag's influential essay "Notes on 'Camp'" (1964) has provided the most useful working construction for thinking about Stone's building in relation to kitsch. As an exemplar of the "outrageous aestheticism" about which she wrote, the Gallery of Modern Art perfectly exemplified "the proper mixture of the exaggerated, the fantastic, the passionate, and the naïve."[60] There seems no better description.

The criticism of the building is also imbued with the theory put forth by Clement Greenberg in his essay "Avant-Garde and Kitsch," first published in 1939 and, revealingly, republished in 1961.[61] According to Greenberg, kitsch exposes the volatile relationship between high art and mass culture, the latter of which he viewed as crude or retrograde because it was the product of an entrepreneurial economy.[62] Indeed, the words used by critics to describe the Stone building—lollypops and tennis rackets for the columns; punch cards, computer cards, and punched railroad tickets for the circular windows; and a marble egg, perfume bottle, superbly packaged chocolate box, and shoe emporium for the exterior—are all recognizable mass-produced objects of the very culture Greenberg wanted separated from the avant-garde.[63] Stone challenged this closed, limited system. He made the building a work of kitsch, albeit inadvertently, by bestowing on it a familiar and instantly identifiable vocabulary and saturating its atmosphere with hominess—all to evoke a passionate response from viewers.[64]

To attract a large audience and thus fulfill the expectations of the popular culture, Stone made a variety of historical and cultural references in the Gallery of Modern Art. Rather than taking an "either-or" stand, which at about this time Robert Venturi was associating with Modernism, Stone opted for a "both–and" approach, meaning that he created complexity and contradiction between heterogeneous elements, an aesthetic that eventually became part of Postmodernism.[65] Still, Stone fell short in his attempt to integrate his conscious sense of the past into a coherent whole, and he certainly lacked irony, wit, or humor, characteristic features of Postmodernism, which made the building all the more susceptible to criticism

Stone with President and Mrs. Dwight D. Eisenhower examining a model of the second scheme of the National Cultural Center (later the John F. Kennedy Center for the Performing Arts), 1962. *Ziegler*

in the years after completion. However, through the qualities of kitsch—embodied in the building's stylized historical memories, its challenge to the patently modern masculine disposition, and, what's more, its failed seriousness—Stone succeeded in engaging a general audience. Ironically, the building's kitschiness is remembered in its redesign, for the "lollypop" columns are symbolically enclosed by glass, ensuring for them in posterity a sense of the building's original sensationalism (see page 148).

Also enduring accusations of kitschiness, the Kennedy Center is, even more, the turning point for thinking about Stone's production as architectural populism: a "crowd pleaser . . . that all America can love," to quote Huxtable.[66] Initiated in the boom years of the late 1950s, which are characterized by social mobility, prosperity, and unparalleled consumerism, by the time the Kennedy Center was finished in 1971, the environment had radically changed into one of urban upheaval, generational conflict, social violence, and political resistance. The country's shattered self-confidence and precarious stability inevitably raised concerns not only about whether this deliberate spectacle was appropriate but also if it could break down established boundaries between high- and lowbrow cultures.[67]

In spite of the huge amount of controversy the project generated throughout its conception and implementation, over much of which Stone had no control, he understood from the get-go that the cultural center needed to gratify

First scheme for the waterfront entrance of the National Cultural Center, 1959.

vast numbers of people, and not just the privileged. He responded to their tastes—generally founded on popular forms of entertainment—by blending familiarity and comfort, fantasy and desire, and giving the whole work his own reassuring, unmistakable imprint.[68] As one observer aptly put it in the *Los Angeles Herald-Examiner*, "The cultural hounds don't seem to think much of it, but it appeals to my simple taste."[69]

Stone again had to work hard to obtain the commission. The building was to be located on an irregular, tongue-shaped site donated by the federal government on the east bank of the Potomac River known as Foggy Bottom, and, somewhat incredibly, he was able to hold on to it under three different presidential administrations. He was named architect of the project at the behest of Senator Fulbright, sponsor of the National Cultural Center Act, who shepherded it through many manifestations. With Fulbright's unyielding support, for about a year, beginning in 1958, Stone engaged the appropriate players, as he was so accomplished at doing—from the Fine Arts Commission and National Capital Planning Commission to the cultural center's Board of Trustees and its Advisory Committee on the Arts.[70] He was able to influence the selection process itself, advising against a competition, as the AIA had recommended, by offering his brand name, global recognition, and an established aesthetic—criteria deemed important. In June 1959, when he was named architect-adviser and charged only with the preliminary studies of the site, he was nonetheless confident he would be named the architect

for the entire project, informing Fulbright, "We will leave a monument to the Boys from the Ozarks."[71]

Stone offered two concepts differing considerably in land use and scope: one was for an arrangement of specialized buildings placed close together, as at Lincoln Center for the Performing Arts (then under construction); the other, which he favored "very strongly," was for a single monumental building. Though it would require the acquisition of additional parcels of land and the rerouting of the parkway system, Stone felt the single-building plan would produce a greater visual impact as well as be more efficient and economical—in land use, materials, utilities, maintenance, and personnel.[72] His soft sell restrained any potential criticism, and in an instant, at least as it seemed to Jarold A. Kieffer, the project's initial executive director, Stone convinced everyone to grant him the entire commission for what they envisioned as one of the world's greatest structures located on a magnificent park and river setting.[73]

Given that the country was gripped by cold war fear, Stone well knew that the building's message of cultural superiority was imperative.[74] Not only would the center be perceived as a proud symbol of American heritage and global leadership, but it would also be part of a great postwar trend that spawned a building boom of other cultural centers in more than seventy cities across the country.[75] In late October 1959 Stone presented his initial plan, described variously as equal in grandeur to the Lincoln and Jefferson memorials, in size to the courtyard of the Pentagon, and in character to the Louvre in Paris and the Houses of Parliament in London.[76] Wanting his design to harmonize with the monolithic classical white buildings scattered around the District, the first scheme consists of a circular white palatial building (referred to as a "cultural clam shell" in *Life*) containing a horseshoe-shaped opera house for 4,000, a symphony hall for 3,000, and a theater for 1,500, plus a smaller experimental theater and a recital hall.[77] Among the most imaginative details of the plan is a "ceremonial landing" on the western side extending 180 feet over the Potomac River, to be used for the reception of kings and queens and other dignitaries arriving by boat after passing between two spewing river fountains.[78] A stepped terrace would guide them into a glazed grand foyer surrounding a lower-level rotunda and topped by an illuminated gold-and-white dome. Determined to counter the "mechanistic functional appeaarance" of early Modernism, as he later explained, Stone looked to time-honored traditions of design, especially the theater, as he took his aesthetic to an extreme.[79] Grid-patterned white walls, crystal chandeliers, and red velvet carpets, all offset by gold-colored columns, wold embellish the sumptuous public spaces where audiences would be part of the drama. As only a romantic like Stone could imagine, the rotunda, he said, would be one of the world's most spectacular halls, on par with Louis XIV's baroque Grande Galerie at the Château de Versailles.[80] In spite of the many foreseeable roadblocks ahead, the sensationalism of his plan, certainly a symbol of national optimism, captivated the decision makers, and although estimated at $75 million, it was enthusiastically endorsed—even by President Eisenhower.[81] As Stone reported to Fulbright, it all was going "marvelously!"[82]

The project did not develop as smoothly as Stone anticipated, however, the biggest obstacle being the acquisition of funding from the private sector. After John F. Kennedy was inaugurated in January 1961, it began to look as if it would die a slow death in part due to the opinion of the president,

First scheme for the National Cultural Center grand foyer, 1959.

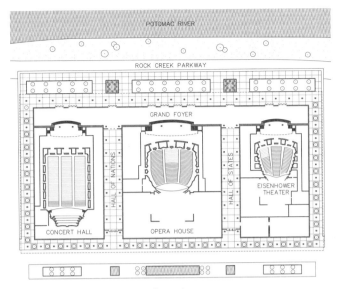

Fig. 6.2. Kennedy Center main-floor plan.

Kennedy Center opera house on opening night, September 8, 1971.

recognized for his moderation and independent judgment, that it was too expensive and grandiose.[83] Consequently, as the *Washington Post* reported, the design was quietly laid aside and Stone was forced to discuss alternatives, including a phased production of a single building or of three separate ones.[84] Though Stone stood firm on his concept of one unified building, and also its decorative scheme, his compromised second plan for a rectilinear structure was simpler but no less prominent. The model was previewed on September 11, 1962, by Jacqueline Kennedy, honorary cochair, at a publicity event at the Elms, in Newport, Rhode Island, and four days later by Mamie Eisenhower, the other chair, along with her husband at their farm in Gettysburg, Pennsylvania. The First Ladies' official backing of the cultural center, reduced to an estimated $30 million, gave it the much-needed reinvigoration and, eventually, the financial support (with the help of the federal government).

Although it endured further changes, as built, between 1967 and 1971, the cantilevered flat-roofed, marble-clad structure is supported on a delicate steel colonnade sheathed in bronze (see page 18). Entered from a spacious plaza embellished with fountains and plantings, the three main performance halls—a 1,100-seat theater, 2,700-seat concert hall, and 2,300-seat hall for opera, ballet, and musical comedy—are positioned side by side (fig. 6.2).[85] Two smaller common spaces, the Hall of Nations and the Hall of States, run between them and open onto an enormous grand foyer, 600 feet long, 60 feet high, and 40 feet wide (see page 149).[86] On the opposite side, the foyer opens onto a river terrace that protrudes dramatically over Rock Creek Parkway. On the roof there is a small pavilion (originally containing a 500-seat film theater, a multiuse facility, dining areas, and an atrium gallery) that was to have a retractable roof (as with Stone's Ideal Theater design; see page 105) but eliminated primarily because of anticipated jet noise.

The excitement that infused the groundbreaking ceremony in December 1964, attended by Rex Harrison and Audrey Hepburn (whose Academy Award–winning "My Fair Lady" opened that month), as well as Lauren Bacall, Mel Ferrer, and Jason Robards, to name but a few, foreshadowed the opening's two-week festival of music and dance in 1971. The debut gala was attended by 3,700 guests who walked the glittering grand foyer in what appeared as the Kennedys' Camelot brought back to life.[87] As a theatrical stage set, the cultural center offered an invitation for transformation—at least for a night—just as the Brussels pavilion had done through its shimmering fantasy. In short, Stone had united high art and entertainment to produce an American glamour on an unprecedented scale.[88] Subsequently, tourists and visitors, in "T-shirts and sneakers, hot pants and Bermudas, barefoot and barebellied," as Huxtable described them, poured into the magnificent people's palace.[89] Here,

Kennedy Center Hall of Nations.

the combination of democracy white, movie-house red, and imperial gold stirred aspirations of fame and fortune—the capitalistic mark of success—deepened by the poignant recollection of the slain president for whom the building was made a living memorial (see page 12).

Two years after its opening, critics had to concede that the well-attended and exceedingly functional center had unquestionably turned Washington, D.C., into a cultural capital.[90] Still, their criticisms of the building were unforgiving, and, as with Hartford's museum, were interjected with innumerable kitschy sobriquets, ranging from a glorified candy box and massive white marble Kleenex box to a great White Hoax and a white whale washed ashore.[91] The Kennedy Center is, they decided, kitsch for failing to reach a condition of greatness. It is a dramatic artifice for the masses with garish sentimentality, extreme nostalgia, and overwhelming presence.[92] More so, the architect's incandescence shows in the building itself—a sure sign of kitsch—leading one person to aptly comment about the building at the opening: "It's just Edward Stone, that's all!"[93]

Not long before Stone died he confessed, "It gives me great joy to see the throngs of people truly enjoy the facili-

ties provided."[94] He had good reason to feel satisfied, given that in its first ten years more than forty million visited the cultural center, making it the second most popular tourist attraction in the city after the Washington Monument.[95] But although Stone wanted to create an ageless building representing 2,500 years of western culture, rather than a contemporary cliché, or apotheosis of kitsch, his cultural center is very much a product of the moment—a showcase for, and now a monument to, the popular culture he helped to create and of which he was a part.[96]

What is especially enlightening about the Kennedy Center, and Hartford's museum, too, is how each illuminates the very fine line that Stone trod between modernist innovation and kitsch. As a "populist architect"—the title Fulbright rightfully accorded him at the completion of the Kennedy Center—Stone fearlessly integrated middle-class values and tastes into his hybrid aesthetic, even at the expense of critical approval.[97] It would not be until later in the 1970s, however, when the nervous but familiar certainties of the cold war gave way to détente that the professional critiques of Stone's work (intensified by the cultural revolution of the 1960s) would enter the mainstream.[98]

7: GOOD ARCHITECTURE
IS GOOD BUSINESS ...
FOR YEARS AND YEARS

I regard it as part of our obligation to Americans
unborn to plan well, permanently, and beautifully.[1]

In his final period of production, from the early 1960s to his retirement in 1974, Stone's distinct version of Modernism continued to attract a growing clientele because of its perceived predictability, efficiency, and prestige. He was riding the crest of a wave of global expansion—in education, science, commerce, and government. His ability to both grasp cultural issues and advance new trends is illustrated in his versatile output, from a Palm Beach luxury condominium built in 1962, when the concept of individually owned private space and joint ownership of public space was still relatively unknown, to Public School 199 in the Lincoln Square area, a gritty offshoot of New York City's most ambitious slum clearance and redevelopment program.[2] At the same time, his architecture increasingly appealed to the leaders of American industry, among them Levitt and Sons and Tupperware, prodigious contributors themselves to emerging patterns of American consumption in which Stone was also a participant.

In order to respond to the many opportunities coming his way, by 1966 Stone had expanded his staff by 25 percent, to a total of some two hundred employees, fifty of them architects, eight of whom were senior colleagues. But whenever he could, he collaborated with local architects, builders, and craftsmen to maximize cost-efficiency and to generate community support.[3] By 1968, when construction was the second-largest industry in the nation (with new structures accounting for about 10 percent of the gross national product, or $1 trillion),

his vast production contributed to the prevailing cultural current—not just in the United States but also overseas, particularly in the Middle East.

Even though Stone was by now less anxious about his publicity, he reportedly took his press clippings very seriously, an indication that he continued to cultivate the media, and announcements of his globe-girdling array of undertakings, propelled by his own press releases, were everywhere.[4] As a result, the world was familiar not just with his work but with the way it represented the architect himself, demonstrated by an Associated Press writer who perceptively observed that Stone's personality, a rich blend of the elegant and the earthy, was manifested in his lush style, which also respected function, honored simplicity, and bowed to tradition.[5]

At the beginning of the decade, Stone's architecture was generally well regarded for offering a restrained variation of his established aesthetic. It did not seem to matter that conceptually there was not much new—at least in the opinion of *Architectural Record*, which remarked approvingly on Stone's "gentle reinterpretations of his familiar, elegant, always relevant manner."[6] Importantly, in his heart was an ever-present predilection for classicism, with the prominent and unifying thin-stemmed colonnade standing on a grand podium now a defining element of his oeuvre. Other characteristics included white surfaces delicately incised with geometric pattern and slotted roof edges, as well as generous reflecting pools

400 South Ocean
Boulevard condominium
(ca. 1962), Palm
Beach, Florida.
Ezra Stoller

Atrium lobby of Levitt
and Sons (1963–65),
Lakeville Road, Lake
Success, New York.
Ezra Stoller

Public School 199 (1960–63), 270 West Seventieth Street, New York City. *Ezra Stoller*

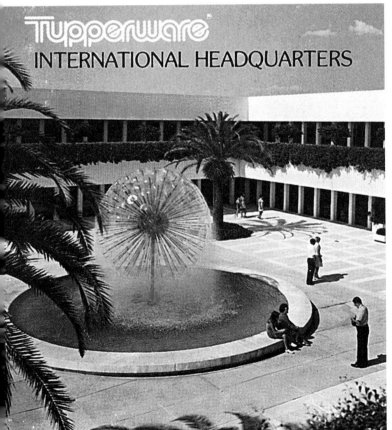

Tupperware International Headquarters (1969–71), on a postcard, South Orange Blossom Trail, Orlando, Florida.

with fountains, multiple skylights, and voluminous hanging planters (the latter so prevalent that they were the subject of another Alan Dunn cartoon for *Architectural Record*; see page 80).[7] Interior color schemes of red, white, and gold also abounded—their appeal to the mass consumer evident in Stone's new award-winning store for Hallmark on the south west corner of Fifth Avenue and Fifty-sixth Street in New York City. "The Red Carpet Is Out On Fifth Avenue," a 1964 advertisement pertinently proclaimed.[8] Even though Stone no longer used the New Delhi–patterned grille, its impact lingered: when in 1968 Bloomingdale's designer Barbara D'Arcy created an ultramodern room setting to represent Stone's personality, it was impossible not to feature it.[9]

Stone's exceptional ability at planning coherent spatial relationships was a dimension of his work often overlooked in reviews but especially relevant in this period. No matter how complex the program, his plans of Euclidian forms were straightforward, with explicit patterns of circulation.[10] Recapturing the grandeur of classical architecture, they were biased by his (corridor-avoiding) principle: that a building be centered by an "eventful" (as he called it), often multistoried, space contrasted with smaller rooms around the periphery. Three words—order, simplicity, and permanence—served as guideposts as he undertook increasingly complex commissions, often involving large-scale master planning—a logical progression for an architect of Stone's background and standing.

From a critical perspective, Stone was front and center in the clash between the technological determinism of Modernism and a formal artistic approach. In an exhibition review in 1964, Ada Louise Huxtable described the wide split between the two (and revealed her partiality for the former) when she declared that "the lines are drawn between the show-the-bones versus the cover-up or slipcover school, guts versus embroidery, steel versus lace."[11] This either/or perspective—containing the implicitly masculinist prejudice of Modernism—prevailed in evaluations of Stone's work, even though his architecture was already expressing the ambiguity that would characterize Postmodernism in the 1970s.[12] Still too early to be a part of that full-fledged movement, his 1960s designs epitomize this irresolute moment, largely because of his desire to expose the failures of Modernism. Stone's opinion that Modernism's glass-and-metal architecture of universalizing, straightjacketed environments was capable neither of producing a look of permanent beauty nor of responding to a desire for comfort and elegance contributed to his involvement with and advocacy of neighborhood renewal, urban public spaces, architectural preservation, green-space conservation, and downtown revitalization.[13] He was at the forefront.

His growing concern that the country's physical heritage was being despoiled by modern progress—unplanned and chaotic commercial development and its related "vulgar"

Proposed redevelopment
of Columbus Circle
(1964; unrealized),
New York City.

taste—was bolstered by Lyndon B. Johnson's Great Society, which Stone considered one of the administration's most significant policy statements. Deeply moved by Johnson's declaration in a speech at the University of Michigan in 1964 that "Our society will never be great until our cities are great," Stone wrote the president a letter of gratitude and expressed his long-held conviction that only with strong leadership (both political and private) could architects carry out their responsibility of replanning the nation. He became preoccupied with doing his part to create "an environment that will speak eloquently for the dignity of the people."[14]

Citing the noise and clutter of neon jungles, honky-tonks, filling stations, and billboards as well as the eye-searing blasts of commercial shopping centers with chain stores and large parking lots, his battle cry was: "We are a nation starved for beauty!" He attributed the blight of the American landscape to capitalistic compulsion for profitability over beauty; to haphazard, often speculative, development; and to changing cultural mores in favor of planned obsolescence, impermanency, standardization, and superficial novelty. He came to believe

there was not an urban building or space that had not been made obsolete by the automobile—an iconic symbol of Modernism that he came to view as "man's greatest curse."[15]

He pleaded with the public to "give a damn" by turning for inspiration to such exemplary antecedents as the ordered New England village greens and Ivy League quadrangles, the grand public spaces of the Seagram Building and Rockefeller Center, the cloistered hilltop towns of Italy and neat villages of France, the interior gardens of the Renaissance palaces of Spain, and the colonnades on the rue de Rivoli in Paris.[16] Attuned to the growing environmental and preservation movements around him and deploring "the mess" Americans had made of their country, Stone documented his forward-thinking ideas in "The American Landscape," a manuscript (left unpublished by E. P. Dutton), crafted intermittently between 1959 and 1961.[17]

Fully recognizing that it is not just words but actions that make a difference, early on Stone demonstrated his interest in architectural preservation. For the National Arboretum in Washington, D.C., he designed an open-air pavilion in 1963

Early plan for the International Trade Mart (1959; later World Trade Center), New Orleans, Louisiana, illustrated in *Progressive Architecture* 40 (May 1959): 97.

Busch Memorial Stadium (1962–66; demolished), St. Louis, Missouri.

reusing the early-nineteenth-century sandstone Corinthian columns that had been removed from the eastern façade of the United States Capitol. In spite of the support of a Kennedy Center trustee and Senator Hubert Humphrey, a lack of funding shelved the project (until 1990, when a new plan by Russell Page was used).[18] About a year later Stone similarly proposed to delineate Columbus Circle with a colonnade of twenty-four pink granite columns to be rescued from McKim, Mead and White's recently demolished Pennsylvania Station (1910). Envisioning an urban space as monumental as the Place Vendôme in Paris or even Saint Peter's Square in Rome, Stone planned to alter the roadway, enlarge the plaza with granite pavers, and plant flowering trees. But with an estimated cost of about $750,000, again there was not enough financial support to realize this "handsome episode" in an otherwise "asphalt jungle," as Stone explained.[19]

Although his attempts at preserving historical fragments were unsuccessful, Stone's architecture did express the postmodern interest in historical reference and reintroduction of ornament, suggestive of Robert Venturi's famous credo in *Complexity and Contradiction in Architecture* (1966): "I like elements which are hybrid rather than 'pure,' compromising rather than 'clean,' distorted rather than 'straightforward.' "[20] At first Stone was shameless in his derivations. His original plan for the International Trade Mart in New Orleans called for a circular arcaded piazza with an adjoining mall, all plainly modeled after the seventeenth-century Saint Peter's Square. In fact, a headline in *Progressive Architecture* proclaimed: "Stone Evokes Bernini in New Orleans," without, surprisingly, a negative implication.[21] Similarly, Stone's elliptical Busch Memorial Stadium in Saint Louis made an explicit reference to the ancient Roman amphitheater, specifically the Coliseum.[22]

It was the Taj Mahal, however, a monument Stone had come to revere as one of the most beautiful on earth, that most consistently provided him with inspiration—not specifically in form or even decoration but in the serene white classicism that prompted his primary work in the early part of this period. In *The Evolution of an Architect*, published at the same time, Stone was emphatic about his vision: "Now I debate a long time before departing from the classic purity of the all-white building."[23]

His extraordinarily diverse experiences, now coalesced as never before, enabled the mature architect to confidently give his modern designs a recognizable, highly sought-after gracefulness, exemplified by the Yardley of London finishing and distribution facility in Totowa, New Jersey (fig. 7.1). As in his other work environments, he achieved the popular country-club air by employing such characteristic features as shallow pools, hanging planters, and skylights.[24] More significantly, instead of enclosing the two exterior courtyards with his grillwork, as he had done at the similarly T-shaped Palo

Yardley of London finishing and distribution facility (1958–62; now P F Laboratories), Union Boulevard, Totowa, New Jersey. *Ezra Stoller*

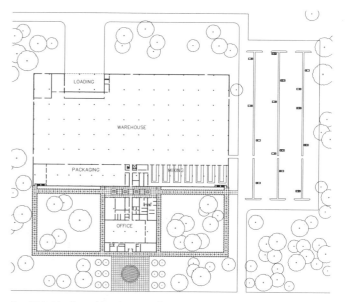

Fig. 7.1. Yardley of London site plan.

Alto Main Library (see page 100), Stone designed an elegant white brick classical colonnade that had the added advantage of uniting the building's two main functions.[25] His design for the Museo de Arte de Ponce in Puerto Rico, a two-story building Stone was "personally elated over," is even more dignified. Luxuriously clad with white marble aggregate, it won him the prestigious AIA Honor Award for its cool, white, tropical quality. Remembering both Mepkin Plantation and the Bruno and

Museo de Arte de Ponce (1961–65), Avenue Las Américas, Ponce, Puerto Rico. *John Betancourt*

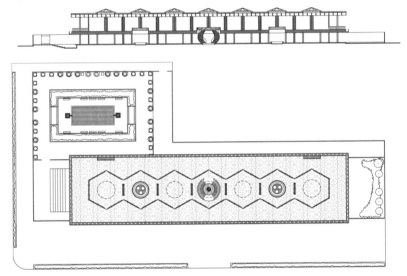

Fig. 7.2. Museo de Arte de Ponce section and site plan, showing second-floor galleries.

Museo de Arte de Ponce central staircase. *Ezra Stoller*

Josephine Graf house (see figs. 2.3 and 5.3), the ground-floor planar wall has a prominent role in the design not only as the façade but in defining the gardens (fig. 7.2). The second floor, defined by a thick protruding roof and floor slabs, holds an enfilade of seven hexagonal galleries surrounded by a capacious terrace. Distinguished by a graceful horseshoe stairway in the center, three of the galleries are open to floors with pools below and all have open metal wall grilles—originally for egress, ventilation, and light—as well as eighteen-sided skylights inserted into the hung ceiling of bold recessed triangles.[26] Yet another prominent example of this genre is the Community Hospital of the Monterey Peninsula in Carmel, California, a diagonally organized, low-lying structure that brought Stone an AIA Merit Award. As Stone had done with

Exterior of patient rooms at the Community Hospital of the Monterey Peninsula (1956–62), Holman Highway, Monterey, California, 1972. *Morley Baer*

Community Hospital garden court. *Ezra Stoller*

his International Style houses, the residentially scaled hospital stands conspicuously in its pine and cypress surroundings, but here the stark white surfaces are relieved with delicate patterns of radiating concrete squares (recalling Wright's concrete block houses).[27] Expanding on Stone's medical center at Stanford, the Monterey hospital has a gardenlike atmosphere, which was said to be responsible for reducing the average inpatient visit (fig. 7.3). Linking the two wings are a large central water court (a glass roof was added later by Stone) and two generous interior stairwells (located on the plan as "garden courts") topped with multiple ceiling bubbles for natural light.[28] Even more, each of the one hundred (uniquely private) patient rooms is arranged in clusters of four, opening to a small balcony or a patio.[29]

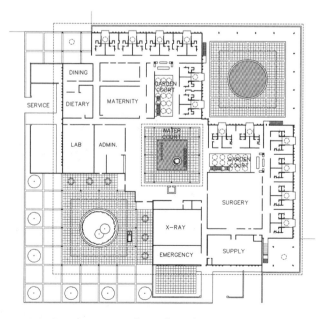

Fig. 7.3. Community Hospital main-floor plan.

Stuhr Museum of the Prairie Pioneer (1962–67), West Highway 34, Grand Island, Nebraska.

Aerial view of the Beckman Auditorium (1960–64) at the California Institute of Technology, South Michigan Avenue, Pasadena, California.

Now acclaimed for his curative, tranquil environments, Stone likewise designed the Eisenhower Medical Center (1967–71) in Rancho Mirage, California, but here positioned the severely classical structure in the center of a man-made lake.[30] He repeated the romantic gesture for the Stuhr Museum of the Prairie Pioneer in Grand Island, Nebraska. Brazenly situated on its island, everything about the square, white classical building is pure Stone—so much so that the museum's regional theme is missing from the architecture.

Similarly, at the Beckman Auditorium on the campus of the California Institute of Technology in Pasadena, the articulation of his personal aesthetic superseded all other considerations. Determined by soft, curvaceous lines, the visually arresting building is confidently positioned on a podium with four large, saucer-shaped pools with fountains. It is supported by diamond-shaped flared columns and topped with a prominent conical overhanging roof patterned with gold circles to complement the gold diamond pattern emblazoned on the exterior white walls. The lobby and 1,150-seat auditorium are equally opulent, not only using Stone's stately color scheme and refined patterned surfaces throughout but also his signature mesh ceiling, here festively swagged. The fantasy design, however, neither reflects the school's mission of advanced science and technology, nor harmonizes with other campus buildings, nor is sympathetic to the overall mood of a country engaged in social unrest and warfare, leading one critic

Beckman Auditorium exterior.
Ezra Stoller

Beckman Auditorium interior.
Ezra Stoller

Colonnades at Harvey Mudd College (1956–63) by Stone and Heitschmidt and Thompson, Architects (1955–65), Platt Boulevard, Claremont, California.

to candidly describe it as "so cute, so precious the over-all effect is to coat humans in an embossed environment of sweet unreality." [31]

When faced with complex planning programs with restricted budgets, Stone was more pragmatic, intent on creating unified formal compositions. When he designed the master plan for Harvey Mudd College in Claremont, California, in collaboration with Heitschmidt and Thompson, Architects, he insisted on an arcaded campus so that all the various elements would be united, recalling Thomas Jefferson's colonnaded "Academical Village" at the University of Virginia in

Charlottesville. [32] He utilized the same concept in the master plan for the International College, an American-sponsored preparatory school in Beirut, Lebanon. As envisioned (though not realized), sixteen concrete drum-shaped classrooms (each divided like pieces of a pie around a central atrium) were to be built as needed around the periphery of the elliptical plan—with a continuous colonnaded walk uneasily located in front of, but not connected to, each structure. [33]

Stone achieved a more successful integration of buildings at the University at Albany. [34] Under the governorship of Nelson Rockefeller, the university campus was the first of four in New York State to be constructed under a massive educational building program to meet the postwar demand for higher education. In contrast to the more typical American campus on which separate buildings are added over time on large open spaces, Stone was convinced that quadrangles of closely related colonnaded buildings (planned without automobiles, which he considered "fatal" to academic environments of "repose and meditation") would generate savings in construction, utilities, and maintenance costs. Other benefits, he said, included improved communication and circulation, protection against inclement weather, and the preservation of nature. He produced what is essentially a rigid (though expandable) megastructure consisting of semi-independent elements unified through proportion, materials, and repetition. Using a 20-foot-square structural grid, imposing three-story colonnades dominate the five quadrangles (see page 19). [35] While the four small dormitory quadrangles each enclose a twenty-two-story tower, the largest quadrangle, sometimes called the "academic podium," holds thirteen academic buildings (with little to distinguish them). In the center of the quadrangle is a sunken plaza containing a pool with fountains and a soaring white-and-gold-colored steel campanile with water storage. It is enclosed

Proposed master plan of the International College (1961–71), Beirut, Lebanon.

Master plan of the University at Albany (1961–70), State University of New York.

University at Albany academic podium.

University at Albany library. *Patrick Burns*

on the western side by the performing arts center and on the opposite side by the library—the latter with dramatically illuminated flared columns in the interior. Such showmanship, unusual for an institutional building, especially one with a tight budget and rapid construction schedule, reflects Stone's continued interest in appealing to a culture attracted to the theatrical icons of Disneyland, Miami Beach,

and Hollywood. In fact, the library, revealingly, served as a Saudi Arabian backdrop for the 1981 film "Rollover."[36] Even though his 1964 proposal for a similar quadrangle campus (this time with a domed circular building in the center) for the Nassau Community College in Mineola, New York, was never approved, Stone's preoccupation with systematic, ordered design persisted.[37]

Design for the Christian Science Pavilion (1962–64; demolished), New York World's Fair, 1964–65.

Billy Graham Pavilion (1963–64; demolished), New York World's Fair.

As a member of the design board of the New York World's Fair of 1964–65—along with Gordon Bunshaft, Henry Dreyfuss, Emil H. Praeger, and its chairman, Wallace K. Harrison—Stone was certain that Bunshaft's proposed donut-shaped, two-story building to contain all major industrial exhibits would be economically, functionally, and visually effective.[38] Estimated at $70 million, the mile-wide structure, to be surrounded by an island-strewn lake, would make more space available (as at the Brussels exposition) for the landscaped plazas Stone so relished. According to his former employee Ernest Jacks, Stone had a grand time dreamily sketching plans for imposing bold axes with avenues beautified by fountains, trees, lagoons, and canals—all in the best Beaux-Arts tradition.[39]

The president of the fair, Robert Moses, whom Stone considered "a great man and a militant leader," was impressed with the imaginative preliminary ideas.[40] But he told Harrison in July 1960 that the donut-shaped design, no matter how brilliant, intriguing, and significant, would not be appropriate since it did not conform to the existing layout and conditions of the 1939–40 World's Fair site in Flushing Meadow Park, Queens, which he wanted restored in the process.[41] A running dispute ensued, with Harrison and Stone holding out for the round design on a smaller scale.[42] But Moses sided with the industrial designer Walter Dorwin Teague (responsible for developing the fair's theme), who opined that one enormous building or even a dozen smaller ones by the same hand could be a dreadful bore.[43] Thus, as Moses made use of the extant formal Beaux-Arts site plan, he encouraged a range of con-

cepts by many architects. His decision, ultimately slammed by critics for inviting visual chaos, ran counter to Stone's inclination for thoughtful integrated environments.[44]

Even though Moses disbanded the stalemated design board, Stone managed to stay in his good graces and was asked to be on the visiting committee to Russia to promote the fair.[45] And although the official word from Moses was that he would not choose or recommend architects to exhibitors, he paved the way for Stone to be the architect of the Christian Science Pavilion (later relocated to Poway, California, and demolished with little fanfare in 2006).[46] Like the other three structures Stone designed for the fair, it was not particularly adventuresome or daring but presented an opportunity to broadcast his name and, even more, to indulge in the decorative fantasy he so adored. As one of the fair's five religious exhibits, the 35-foot-high pavilion (complemented by a smaller one with a reading room and offices) was shaped like a star, to symbolize the Christian Scientists' seven synonyms for God, and it was surrounded by a pool with fourteen illuminated fountains.[47] The protruding roof was pierced by a vivid seven-sided glazed dome surrounded by seven smaller domed pyramids also allowing for light to radiate into the interior.[48]

The octagonal pavilion Stone designed for the hugely popular evangelist Billy Graham, on the other hand, was intended to be unique in its simplicity. Nonetheless, it received extensive attention, attracting nearly 600,000 visitors in the first year alone and exposing Stone's brand to a new constituency. The "architectural jewel," as Graham referred to it, contained a chapel for 150, counseling rooms, and a 335-seat theater in

Stone's signature color scheme. Like Beckman Auditorium, the roof was patterned, here with gold bands, and crowned with a sunburst. An adjacent steel tower was covered by four thousand gold anodized discs, recalling his meshwork ceilings.[49] Set in an octagonal walled garden paved in multicolored marble, the evangelists felt their pavilion offered "a taste of heaven."[50]

For Julimar Farm, a commercial venture specializing in packaged garden units and out-of-the-ordinary food, Stone designed an airy glass pavilion, the smallest at the fair. It did not receive much publicity, however, because the exhibit was about its various gardens—designed by Stone's eldest son, Edward Durell Stone Jr., who in 1960 established a landscape architecture and urban design firm (now called EDSA) in Fort Lauderdale, Florida.

In contrast, *Look* magazine anticipated that Stone's three-bedroom demonstration house for a family of moderate income—one of three houses in the House of Good Taste exhibit—would be the most influential, thought-provoking modern home ever built.[51] Sponsored by the American Institute of Approval, composed only of socially prominent, non-professional women from across the nation, the house was presented as a giant do-it-yourself kit offering components that could be purchased in department stores.[52] With interiors decorated in a pedestrian manner by Sarah Hunter Kelly (with whom Stone had worked in the 1940s) and Esther Willcox, Stone's house was geared to average tastes.[53] Some critics thought the severely symmetrical plan—centered by an atrium with a circular pool and illuminated by a large faceted-

Model of Stone's House of Good Taste (1963–64; demolished), New York World's Fair. *Phillip Harrington*

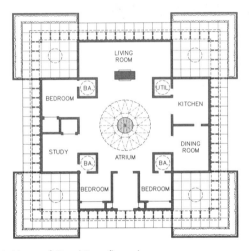

Fig. 7.4. House of Good Taste floor plan.

Model of Huntington Hartford's café (1960; unrealized) proposed for Central Park at Fifty-ninth Street and Fifth Avenue, New York City.

glass dome—audacious, but in truth it was merely a small variation on Stone's atrium house (fig. 7.4). Even so, it does contain the core of Stone's thinking at the time: concerned about the diminishment of the natural landscape, he advocated that such inward-facing houses be built side by side on small lots, with nature brought inside through walled courtyards, skylights, and pools.[54]

As part of his staunch commitment to beautify the urban environment, Stone engaged in a variety of other planning projects under the eye of Moses. For the Triborough Bridge and Tunnel Authority (of which Moses was chairman), he was one of three distinguished architects to advise on the Verrazano-Narrows Bridge (1959–69), which spanned the New York Bay between Brooklyn and Staten Island and was at the time the longest suspension bridge in the world.[55] When Stone designed the demountable open-air summer theater in Central Park in 1959, Moses, as chairman of the New York City Parks Department, thought it very fine (see page 105).[56] Later that year, in response to Huntington Hartford's plea for a promenade of outdoor cafés like those in Paris where the average person could while away leisure hours, Stone created a design for a sidewalk café to be built on Central Park South at Fifty-ninth Street, across from the Plaza Hotel (1907).[57] Mindful of Stone's inclination for enrichment, Moses wrote in a memorandum to his executive officer, "Please see Ed Stone before he goes very far with the design so that as to operations we shall have something practical; I don't doubt his imagination and talent."[58] Although Moses had wanted the Hartford Café to echo the touch of the masters who had given the park its character—Calvert Vaux and Frederick Law Olmsted—Stone's design, a rectangular concrete pavilion with sliding glass walls topped by a patterned cantilevered roof pierced with nine plastic domes and supported on thin columns, followed his established format.[59] Moses was satisfied with the design, but when its location at the edge of Central Park was made public, it was "about as popular as a baby on a doorstep," as the *New York Times* noted, initiating a six-year dispute that finally doomed the project's realization.[60] Stone lamented that New York City would continue to be "a living room without furniture."[61]

His unequivocal opinion that outdoor public spaces were "the scarcest commodity" of all may well have fueled his desire to situate his buildings on grand plazas or parks. The preeminent example is the PepsiCo World Headquarters relocated from Manhattan to a 168-acre polo field in Purchase, New York. Considered as lavish as a latter-day château, the three-story complex comprised seven square blocks, each gracefully rising into low inverted ziggurats of patterned concrete with recessed windows—originally with boxes of ivy outside them, in the Stone manner (fig. 7.5).[62] Linked by corner towers with elevators, stairs, and corridors, they are grouped around three slightly sunken outdoor planted quadrangles, each sur-

rounding the central circular pool. Landscaped by Stone Jr. with three thousand trees of thirty-eight varieties, one-third of them flowering, the site also features forty-five sculptures by well-known twentieth-century artists.[63] As described in *Architectural Record*, the composition is a skillful blending of architecture and nature, of the formal and informal, urban and rural.[64] It also had a strong sociological component, as Stone knew it would, resulting in higher morale and improved work habits as well as earning acceptance for the company in the bucolic, affluent community.[65]

As he became increasingly engaged in creating total environments for commercial enterprises, Stone focused on delivering his message against the pervasive glass-and-metal buildings, which in his opinion leaves the average person "unrequited."[66] Just as he had done with other typologies, he insisted on embellishing his high-rise buildings with aspects of naturalism, historicism, and other decorative variations. His effort was widely appreciated, as demonstrated by a journalist from Kansas who exclaimed to his readership, "This man from Arkansas has a way with boxes!"[67] A bold early attempt at creating a high-rise on a landscaped plaza is Perpetual Savings and Loan Association's eight-story building on Wilshire Boulevard in Beverly Hills, California. In the center of the plaza was a round pool with thirty-six fountain jets pointed toward *Sunburst*, a gold-plated, stainless-steel sculpture by Harry Bertoia (relocated in 1988 to the Milton R. Abrahams Branch of the Omaha Public Library in Nebraska).[68] A circular paving pattern of gray-and-white terrazzo and symmetri-

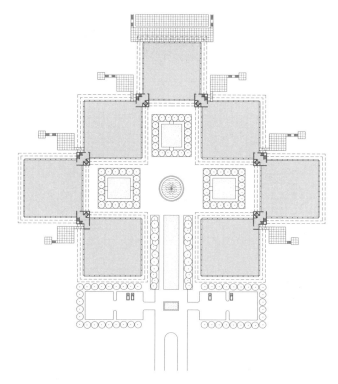

Fig. 7.5. PepsiCo first-floor plan.

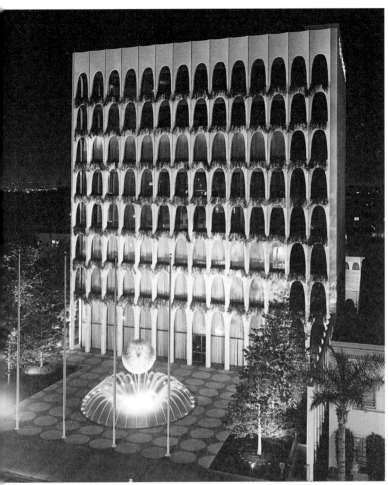

Perpetual Savings and Loan Association (1960–62),
Wilshire Boulevard, Beverly Hills, California. *Jack Laxer*

National Geographic Society (1960–64), 17th Street N.W.
at M Street, Washington, D.C. *Ezra Stoller*

cally placed flowering trees finished the plaza as an outdoor room. The building itself is wrapped with a shallow concrete tiered arcade, originally with boxes of ivy and bougainvillea (with a built-in watering system) draped over its concave parabolic arches to make a gigantic hanging garden.[69] Be it Romanesque, Expressionist, or biomorphic in inspiration, the fanciful arcaded façade was an extension of the grille concept, leading Esther McCoy to conclude sardonically in the *Los Angeles Times* that the anticurtain wall put the building in the realm of the pastry cook.[70] While playful exploitation of sensuous frivolity and exuberant naturalism is certainly entertaining, Stone's hesitancy to integrate such primary features into the structural form in a more fundamental way shows his susceptibility to kitsch.

On the other hand, the ten-story building for the National Geographic Society on M Street in Washington, D.C., is a forthright demonstration of Stone's reconciliation of Modernism with his decorated classical variation.[71] Set on a podium, its narrow vertical strips (or fins) of white Vermont marble rise from the canopied ground-floor colonnade to the overhanging slotted roof, sensitively contrasting and shading the predominating dark-gray glass windows. The black Swedish granite spandrels between floors harmonize with the glass as well as the bronze framing and are expressive of the horizontal structural elements (a modern feature Stone would omit in his later high-rise buildings). By inserting such traditional materials as marble, granite, and bronze into a building essentially of glass, Stone was able to achieve the look of permanency he was after.[72] *Washington Post* architecture critic Benjamin Forgey understood the effort by observing that by dressing up an ordinary curtain wall in white marble and by employing the classical colonnade, Stone successfully blended modern architecture with the city's image of itself.[73] Without succumbing to what Stone considered "mausoleum styling," the building communicates the monumental quality of governmental architecture, which had been forsaken by Modernism.[74]

Stone did the same for the North Carolina Legislative Building in Raleigh, leading *Architectural Forum* to conclude that he had originated a modern democratic, governmental style.[75] While its dash of pomp made an indelible impression when it opened, the genius of that building is its circulation, particularly in the separation of public and private space. Bypassing access to the first-floor joint committee rooms and offices as well as the second-floor House of Representatives and Senate chambers, upon entering the building, visitors immediately ascend a monumental red-carpeted staircase that leads directly to the third-floor mezzanine, where the public galleries flank the stately two-story, second-floor rotunda (fig. 7.6).[76]

No less prestigious but far more provocative is Stone's first skyscraper—the General Motors Building in the heart of

Staircase descending from the third-floor mezzanine in the North Carolina Legislative Building (1960–63), West Jones Street, Raleigh.
Ezra Stoller

General Motors Building (1963–68) during construction, 767 Fifth Avenue, New York City.

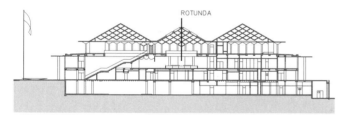

Fig. 7.6. North Carolina Legislative Building section.

New York City at Fifth Avenue and Fifty-ninth Street. Commissioned by the Savoy Fifth Corporation, a subsidiary of the vast British holding company, London Merchant Securities, General Motors was the building's largest tenant and a 50 percent owner. As the world's industrial leader, General Motors' goal was the showmanship for which Stone was branded. But for Savoy, represented by Cecilia Benattar (reputed to be the toughest woman in real estate), it was profitability. And so, Stone took advantage of the revised zoning code that offered height bonuses without setback restrictions (and thus more rentable space) when plazas or arcades were added.[77] The

fifty-story building, with a two-story wing extending to the sidewalk on each side, was thus situated on a 100-by-200-foot plaza with a sunken forecourt (since filled) with retail shops and restaurants—overtly echoing Rockefeller Center's plaza just down the avenue.

Although the associate architecture firm, Emery Roth and Sons (1938–96), was best known for its commercial high-rises throughout the city, Stone was anxious that his building not be perceived as one of their transitory-looking glass boxes.[78] So he alternated vertical rows of bronze-tinted glass bay windows with same-size concrete piers clad in white Georgian marble. Based on a 5-foot module, the bay windows (a concept taken from city row houses) provide panoramic views while limiting the amount of sunlight entering the building. They also help to distinguish individual interior spaces, unlike uniform glass walls. Even though Stone did not consider himself "the glassiest architect," the building does have 280,000 square feet of glass—although the casual viewer would never know it, since the white marble predominates visually.[79]

While all rentable space was spoken for well before the building was enclosed, it was controversial from day one—

Aerial view of the General Motors Building facing Grand Army Plaza (1913–16) and the Plaza Hotel (ca. 1907).

even provoking a stop-the-building rebellion led by socially prominent women.[80] First was the demolition of the existing buildings on the site, in particular McKim, Mead & White's thirty-seven-year-old Savoy Plaza Hotel facing Grand Army Plaza (1913–16) on Fifth Avenue.[81] While not one of the firm's most distinguished buildings, the Savoy's demise came on the heels of the fiercely contested demolition of Pennsylvania Station.[82] Equally disquieting was the perception that the structure would drastically modify the neighborhood's sedate gentility, epitomized by the stately Plaza Hotel on the other side of Grand Army Plaza (a building that even Stone considered the "last refuge and symbol of luxury and grace").[83]

Instead of the serene and classic formality that people had come to associate with Stone's work earlier in the decade, the General Motors building was disparaged by architecture critics for subscribing to sleek Cadillac styling, showing only glitz, vulgarity, and pretention, to use the descriptive words of Paul Goldberger in one of a number of vehement denunciations.[84] Equally contemptuous was its lack of urban sensitivity, especially the denial of the street line because of the building's setback and plaza: "Ever heard of a redundant plaza? This is it. Something like having two heads," Huxtable quipped in her article "How to Kill a City."[85] In short, it stood as an unforgiving symbol of the powerful consumer culture.

In spite of the criticism, the general public purportedly liked having an automobile showroom on Fifth Avenue and was mesmerized by the "outstandingly beautiful" building and its glamorous lobbies, also designed by Stone, of Greek Pentelic marble walls, tall ground-floor windows, and an enormous Orrefors sunburst chandelier.[86] Indeed, Stone's now-famous comment, "Every taxi driver in New York will tell you it's his favorite building," is indicative of its prevailing presence, and no doubt he would have been gratified had he known that in 2009 the building sold for $2.9 billion (a 101 percent increase over its sale price in 1998)—then the highest amount ever paid for an office building in the United States.[87]

Though the General Motors Building represents the clear dichotomy between popular appeal and critical disdain that increasingly defined Stone's architecture, he continued to be interested in masonry-clad high-rises, illustrated by his plans for the controversial fifty-story New York Civic Center (1963; unrealized), as well as for the Ahmanson Center on Wilshire Boulevard in Los Angeles, a complex that was to consist of a forty-story building (unrealized) positioned between two ten-story buildings curved around an elliptical plaza, which were built.[88] However, of the seven com-

General Motors Building lobby.

Model of the Ahmanson Center, parts of which were completed between 1965 and 1970, Wilshire Boulevard, Los Angeles. *Julius Shulman*

Standard Oil (Indiana) Building (1969–74; now Aon Building), East Randolph Street, Chicago.

Model of the Pakistan Institute of Nuclear Science and Technology (PINSTECH; 1961–74), Nilor, Pakistan.

missions Stone received as a direct result of the General Motors building, the dead ringer is the Standard Oil (Indiana) building in Chicago, built in association with the local firm of Perkins & Will.[89] At eighty stories high, the Standard Oil building advanced the structural technology of the taller John Hancock Center (completed nearby in 1970 by Skidmore, Owings & Merrill) but stood alone for its poised vertical piers of Carrara marble veneer (although in 1992 the 44,000 deteriorated marble panels had to be replaced with thicker Mount Airey granite).[90] Like its predecessor, the Standard Oil building has been censured for neighborhood incompatibility as well as for its inability to disclose structure and function—a fundamental requirement of Modernism. In spite of its arrogant, overwhelming height as the world's fourth-tallest building (inviting psychoanalytic readings of the narcissistic esteem of the ego, its decorative skin rekindled the earlier criticism of the feminine taint, exemplified by *Chicago Tribune* architecture critic Paul Gapp, who declared, "Standard Oil is a woman—an imperious, frigid pseudo-goddess." In agreement with Gapp, *Chicago Sun-Times* critic Rob Cuscaden named Stone "Worst Architect" of 1970.[91] What most concerned Standard Oil management, however, was the building's striking resemblance to Stone's other work. The vice president of public affairs complained to Stone in 1974 that the twelve-story Montgomery County Administration Building (1967–72) in Dayton, Ohio, was

too close in design for their liking, reminding Stone that he had been chosen (ironically) over Mies because the latter's buildings all looked too much alike.[92]

But it was this ubiquity that attracted the interest—at least initially—of foreign nations intent on emulating western success, especially fourteen-year-old Pakistan. The first and most consequential of Stone's Pakistani commissions was for the Institute of Nuclear Science and Technology (PINSTECH), which was built in two stages in Nilor, outside Islamabad.[93] Ishrat Hussain Usmani, chairman of the Pakistan Atomic Energy Commission, made it resolutely clear that he wanted to amplify the American image of science and technology and that Stone was the only architect of world fame who could also express the spirit of their culture by integrating regional traditions, climate, and topography into a modern design.[94]

A symbol of Pakistan's entry into the atomic age, PINSTECH is a self-contained grand quadrangle elevated on a podium. An encircling concrete colonnade with flared capitals, supporting a common roof pierced with translucent domes, unifies the diverse elements—an atomic reactor, laboratories, library, auditorium, and canteen. Decoration and function were combined throughout: in the reflecting pools (used for air-conditioning aeration) as well as in the 250-foot-high tower (used for the storage of water and the ventilation of gases).[95] Together with the nuclear reactor, inset with gold mosaic tiles, the tower provides a strong decorative accent to the axially organized plan. While touted as

Aerial view of the Presidential Palace (1966–ca. 1980) framed by other administrative buildings by Stone, Capitol Avenue, Islamabad, Pakistan.

Middle Eastern in flavor, the design of PINSTECH harks back to Stone's previous work—specifically, the Albany campus and, even earlier, the monastery Our Lady of Mepkin Abbey—the similarly colonnaded quadrangle Stone designed for the Cistercian monks in South Carolina (see pages 133 and 93). But here there is greater delicacy as well as enrichment and more reliance on classicism.

There is no question that Usmani's approbation helped to bring Stone fourteen other projects in Pakistan (not all of them realized)—residential (for Usmani himself and for Agha Hilaly, the Pakistani ambassador to the United States), commercial (for an airline sales office and a shipping company), and governmental (the National Water and Power Authority and the Secretariat in Lahore), among others. Most significant, however, was his work for the Capitol Development Authority (CDA), the agency in charge of implementing the master plan for Islamabad that had been completed in 1960 by the Greek architect Constantinos A. Doxiadis. With less than one architect for every million people in Pakistan and following such newly constructed capital cities as Le Corbusier's Chandigarh and Oscar Niemeyer's Brasília, the CDA turned to renowned foreign architects to design its administration buildings to be situated on the city's most imposing site—at the end of its main axis, Capitol Avenue.[96]

Stone was one of twenty-six architects sent a letter of inquiry in 1961 explaining that the program was to constitute a monumental design evocative of the great traditions of Muslim architecture. When asked if he was interested in being either one of the architects or the architect coordinator, Stone thought big and answered he would like to be the architect of the entire group of structures (using Pakistani architects and engineers for working drawings and construction) and also be the architect coordinator.[97] But it was not until 1966, after Usmani urged Stone to revive his offer, that Stone was awarded work.[98] (Though Doxiadas, Marcel Breuer, and Louis Kahn were also considered during the drawn-out decision process, buildings did go to Gio Ponti and Arne Jacobson; the coordinator job to Sir Robert Matthew.) While various forms of political agitation delayed construction and Stone did not live to see it all completed, he created a master plan for four administration buildings to be positioned and landscaped (by Stone Jr.) on the central square. He designed three of them himself—the president's estate (president's suite, guest house, office, secretariat, and other ancillary buildings), the foreign office, and the national assembly—and provided a schematic for the fourth, the supreme court (designed by Kenzo Tange between 1989 and 1993).[99]

The presidential estate, a white pyramidal building located on a summit at the end of the central square (with terraced gardens, foundations, and pools), is flanked by the two other administrative buildings by Stone.[100] Formal, symmetrical, and very much in keeping with his other colonnaded quad-

Model of the Presidential Palace.

Model of the University of Islamabad (1966–85; now Quaid-i-Azam University).

rangles on podiums, the front block of the estate building has public spaces, offices, and services on the lowest level and suites for state guests on the upper one; the presidential quarters, in a separate block behind, is set off by a colonnaded courtyard with a narrow pool spanning the main axis between the two buildings.

According to a press release generated by Stone, in addition to these government buildings, he was also committed to designing the Broadcasting House and Television Station (1965–77), also in Islamabad, as well as the University of Islamabad.[101] For the master plan for the postgraduate residential university, primarily determined by the steeply sloped 1,400-acre site at the foot of the Margalla Hills, Stone positioned a series of small, two-story quadrangles around an axial spine, centered by the library. The concrete buildings in each quadrangle had double roofs and walls with wide overhangs and louvers for climate control.[102] While some are connected to each other by bridges at the corners, most of the pedestrian circulation takes place outdoors.[103] Although criticized by government officials for looking like bunkers, Stone made an effort to comply with the building committee's insistence that there be as much differentiation as possible with varying surface textures, window patterns, and garden court.[104]

Stone's contribution to Islamabad, a city that arose within a single generation, has not been exempt from accusations of regimented sterility, nor from the prevailing tension that still exists there between Modernism and regional tradition.[105] Though criticized for the Islamization of modern architecture, the hybridization of eastern and western influences was, in fact, a requirement of the initial PINSTECH program. Moreover, while in the 1980s this architecture could be understood as a postmodern blending of stylistic references, Pakistanis considered it cultural imperialism, revealing that Stone's attempt to reprise a strategy that had been accepted as far back as the embassy in New Delhi in the 1950s was no longer welcomed.[106]

In the United States, too, the product Stone had developed and sold so successfully—and which earned him a reputation equal to Mies's, according to *Fortune* in 1967—was out of step with the high Sixties culture, distressed by political and social turmoil.[107] Top heavy with administrators—rather than enterprising talent—the financially troubled firm increasingly fell back on established format. When in 1971 a controversy arose about the height and style of Stone's design for the Florida State Capitol in Tallahassee, one of the alternatives simply offered a modified Kennedy Center topped with a traditional neoclassical dome.[108] The final design, featuring one of Stone's characteristic high-rises, which subjugates the much lower domed legislative wings as well as the original capitol (1845) in front, is compromised and lackluster. No longer responding to the particulars of the commission, Stone's trademark elements were simply being recycled, seemingly at random. His "new romanticism" is wanting.

Though the Florida State Capitol demonstrates the firm's inability to provide innovative, satisfying solutions towards the end of Stone's career, it must be remembered that when Stone was more vibrantly involved in the earlier part of the period, he was enormously productive because he could gauge current tastes and values. At the same time Stone was completing large public commissions, as an advocate of strategic urban planning and preservation, he also joined in the vocal critique of the 1960s. Unlike others who railed against the rampant disregard for the natural and historic built environments, Stone's position as someone both prominently located within his own discipline and deeply connected with the mass culture uniquely qualified him to identify current problems and to actively seek solutions. It brought him a level of appeal in many quarters of the globe on a scale that most architects never achieve.

Aerial view of the Florida State Capitol (1969–78), Apalachee Parkway, Tallahassee. *John Owen*

CONCLUSION

"DYMAXION RATING"
by Buckminster Fuller

Mepkin—
Conger Goodyear—
Museum of Modern Art
Edward Durell Stone

Off to a flying start
Martinis,
Scotch and sodas,
Palava—wartorn years
Edward Durell Stone
Locked in his lower gears
Panama Canal Zone
Brussells
Beirut Hotel
Edward Durell Stone
Doing very well

Rood-screened fenestration
New Delhi's
Sculptural Lace
Edward Durell Stone
Setting new era pace

Dignity
For Common Man
In Raleigh's white-green grace
Edward Durell Stone
In World Architects' First Place.[1]

Edward Durell Stone's ascent to populist architect is a compelling American story—that of an unlikely back-country boy who intuited unprecedented opportunities and climbed to international acclaim. As the title of his autobiography, *The Evolution of an Architect*, declares, Stone did not arrive on the scene with a fully formed aesthetic but developed it over the course of a long career. He absorbed ideas from assorted sources—from the buildings of antiquity to those of Frank Lloyd Wright—all of which were transformed by his creative vision of what modern architecture could mean for twentieth-century America.

Buckminster Fuller completely understood Stone's climb to greatness and chronicled it in a poem titled "Dymaxion Rating." But when Fuller penned it, in 1963, the final chapter in Stone's life had yet to be written. While the increasingly formal, classical elegance of his architecture appealed to the general public, architecture critics progressively considered his work routinized—a prepackaged aesthetic that had become ordinary and uninspired. What is more, their critical opinion of his work as stale began to overshadow his former success. The *New Yorker* noted in 1968, "Mr. Stone's pierced screens, delicate arches, and skylit interior courts, complete with jungle greenery and babbling pools, have lost much of their freshness for us through repetition."[2] Thus, though once considered among the few outstanding creative influences in architecture, Stone is often remembered today for simply giving his clients what they wanted.[3] The excitement of his early work—innovations that broke loose from the shackles of Modernism and prescient new approaches to city planning, historic preservation, and green environments—seems all but forgotten.

Stone in the third-floor library of his house at 130 East Sixty-fourth Street in New York City. *Pedro E. Guerrero*

At his peak in the late 1950s, Stone was perfectly in tune with the times, calculating that American culture, organized around a prospering mass media as never before, was in need of "richness, exuberance, and pure, unadulterated freshness," to use his own words.[4] Promoted by admirers as the most likely American architect to inherit the place of Wright, Stone must have expected that his immensely popular "new romanticism" would have enduring implications—so much so that he arranged for his own posterity by giving a large body of his papers to the University of Arkansas three years before his death.[5]

Looking back, though, Stone made a grave tactical error by not adhering to the basic rule of celebrity—namely, that to maintain his standing he had to be willing to constantly take risks and produce new and interesting material. He did not recognize that the permanence he was after is antithetical to the very notion of style, nor that in the realm of consumerism, in which Stone was indeed a player, architecture is just as vulnerable as any other commodity to rapid obsolescence.[6] And so, Stone's effort to create a postwar architecture for the media to circulate to great numbers of people eventually worked against a lasting appreciation of that very architecture.

It is fitting that Tom Wolfe, widely recognized for his flamboyant New Journalism style, was the first to resurrect Stone's public persona posthumously. In his book *From Bauhaus to Our House* (1981), Wolfe brought Stone back into the limelight, admiring

his effort to refute the accepted principles of Modernism and to challenge those who clung to them.[7] Though critics ranging from Robert Hughes to Michael Sorkin panned Wolfe's discourse, the popular response could not be ignored: In December 1981, *Progressive Architecture* noted that the short, little book had caused a stir in the architectural world, and by February 1982, *Architectural Record* claimed it had spawned more public attention than any other recently published book on architecture.[8]

From Bauhaus to Our House sensationally recaptures Stone's predilection for luxurious decoration, which, as Wolfe appreciated, "catered to the Hog-stomping Baroque exuberance of American civilization," even if many in Stone's own coterie considered it "poison."[9] Wolfe's implication—that an aesthetic not originated or cultivated by the avant-garde could not attain critical acclaim—echoes Clement Greenberg's argument that there can never be a positive exchange between mass culture and high art.[10] Critics and scholars have often taken this exclusionary stance in their evaluations of Stone's architecture. But what they have frequently missed is that the alternative Stone offered, integrating popular culture's ideas with modernist strategies, destabilized the barriers between the two extremes. Some have declared his architecture kitsch, using the inefficient understanding of kitsch as "bad taste."[11] But when considered in the context of Susan Sontag's "Notes on 'Camp'," Stone's variations on Modernism, some of which

were indeed kitschy, are precisely what allowed him to make modern architecture popular.

Early in this century, when Wolfe returned to the subject of Stone in three *New York Times* op-ed pieces about the proposed redesign of his former Gallery of Modern Art at 2 Columbus Circle, Wolfe brought home to his wide readership that (as only he could phrase it) "the greatest massing of cultural luminaries in a single cause since the antifascist crusades of the 1930s" had come to bear on an architect whose name at one time had represented nothing less than "imagination, daring, aloofness."[12] He rightly anticipated that the proposed reworking of the Columbus Circle building presented an opportunity to return to the burning deliberation about the meaning of Stone's architecture. Though its unstoppable redevelopment denied the opportunity to do what kitsch works are known to do best—to become even more fantastic with the passage of time—because the infamous "lollypop" columns are now enshrined inside the building, viewers can still enjoy the failure of Stone's attempt at ageless, permanent architecture, for this too is very much a part of kitsch.[13]

In retrospect, the controversy about 2 Columbus Circle overwhelmingly revealed that even though definitions of Modernism are now more inclusive, Stone has not been accommodated in the history of modern architecture. Conventional texts have not taken into consideration that he fully grasped the salient characteristics of the postwar culture and articulated them in an aesthetic expressive of the moment—in essence an architecture representative of a new consumer-driven society with

Museum of Arts and Design (2003–08; formerly Stone's Gallery of Modern Art), redesigned by Brad Cloepfil of Allied Works Architecture, 2 Columbus Circle, New York City. *Hélène Binet*

Detail of the Museum of Arts and Design. *Vicky Sambunaris*

a demand for variation, individual expression, and the convey-ance of American values. Nor have earlier histories taken into account the unprecedented tastemaking influence of the greatly enhanced systems of mass communication—particularly tele-vision and print—on Stone's professional life. For a time, the media was delighted by his aesthetic, and in particular his per-forated grille, even as he made it into a reproducible commodity, which demonstrated, in fact, a Pop Art sensibility, as famously characterized by Andy Warhol in his statement: "I like things to be exactly the same over and over again."

In anticipation of postmodern architecture, Stone's was a dis-tinct statement about the aspects of Modernism with which he was most dissatisfied. But his work was far from antimodern—as so many have contended. It was not an outward rejection of the International Style or any of the other expressions with which he experimented. Rather, Stone utilized all his experiences to develop a new set of relations in modern architecture. Facilitated by his Beaux-Arts training, he must be recognized for devising simple, straightforward solutions using geometric forms and then incorporating details absorbed from cultural, historical, regional, and natural surroundings to create a modern architecture that embodied the American ideals that high modernist dogma failed to sufficiently fulfill. In so doing, as the assessment of the criti-cism here reveals, Stone exposed the anxieties of modernists who feared their position was being overwhelmed by middle-class consumption. This inevitably contributed to his final undoing.

By the time Stone's story ended in 1978, his reputation had waned, as happens to populists when their interests no longer represent the people. And yet, as scholarly evaluations will

Demolition in 2005 of the Carlson Terrace dormitories, built in three phases between 1956 and 1964, University of Arkansas, Fayetteville.

undoubtedly continue to disclose, Stone's formidable presence places him firmly within the constellation of modern masters. If Modernism is to be fully documented and if restyling or, perhaps worse, out-and-out destruction of his buildings is to be avoided, it must be understood that Stone, even more than his contem-poraries who are already firmly ensconced in the ranks of the greats, created a wholly unique aesthetic, specifically American in spirit, a genuine expression of mid-twentieth-century popular culture. What is more, as Fuller aptly perceived, Stone singularly succeeded in giving dignity to the "Common Man."

Grand foyer, Kennedy Center for the Performing Arts (1958–71), Washington, D.C.

INTRODUCTION *pages 10–19*

1   Edward Durell Stone, quoted in John Peter, *The Oral History of Modern Architecture: Interviews with the Greatest Architects of the Twentieth Century* (New York: Harry N. Abrams, 1994), 68. The dates for the buildings throughout are from the time Stone received the commission to its completion.

2   J. William Fulbright, note on top of a *Congressional Record*, 117, no. 119 (July 28, 1971), Edward Durell Stone Papers, Ms St71/236, 1st accession (hereafter cited as acc.), box 30, Special Collections, University of Arkansas Libraries, Fayetteville (hereafter cited as Stone Papers).

3   See Alvin Toffler, *The Culture Consumers: Art and Affluence in America* (Baltimore: Penguin Books, 1965), 12–13; "Architect Stone in the Public Limelight: Limelight and Filigree," Architectural Forum 108 (April 1958): 77.

4   Nan Robertson, "Leading Architect Warns of Dangers in Progress," *New York Times*, April 3, 1959.

5   "Man with a Billion on the Drawing Board," Names and Faces, *Business Week*, October 8, 1966; "Spotlight on Business: The Architects Come Into Their Own," *Newsweek*, March 20, 1967.

6   Stone to Kenneth J. Conant, May 3, 1965, Stone Papers, MC340, 2nd acc., box 3.

7   Pietro Belluschi to Jury of Fellows, November 27, 1957, American Institute of Architects Archives, Washington, D.C. (hereafter cited as AIA Archives).

8   Wayne Andrews, "Three Who Made the Monuments of Our Time," *New York Herald Tribune*, November 25, 1962; Gordon Bunshaft to Jury of Fellows, December 5, 1957, AIA Archives; Philip Johnson to Stone, May 6, 1964, Stone Papers, 2nd acc., box 2; Max Abramovitz to Jury of Fellows, November 29, 1957, AIA Archives; George Rockwise, interview by Suzanne B. Riess, *Thomas D. Church, Landscape Architect*, vol. 1 (Berkeley: Regional Oral History Office, Bancroft Library, University of California, 1978), 348; Olgivanna Lloyd Wright, *The Shining Brow: Frank Lloyd Wright* (New York: Horizon Press, 1960), 242.

9   Octavio Méndez Guardia to the author, March 4, 2004.

10 Betty Beale, "Edward D. Stone Discusses His Views On National Cultural Center in Capital," Exclusively Yours, *Washington Star*, July 17, 1959; "More Than Modern," Art, Time, March 31, 1958; Jessica Dover, "Introduction of Edward Durell Stone at the Cosmopolitan Club," December 9, 1959, Stone Papers, 2nd acc., box 1; Clive Lawrance, "A 'Necessary Force' in Architecture: He Believes in Simplicity, Order, and Elegance," *Christian Science Monitor*, January 4, 1972.

11 George McCue, "The Evolution of an Architect: Edward Durell Stone's Homely Account of His Life and Designs," *St. Louis Sunday Post-Dispatch*, November 18, 1962.

12 Ernest E. Jacks, "The Elegant Bohemian: Tales of Architect Edward Durell Stone" (ca. 2000), 50, private collection.

13 Walter H. Kilham Jr., "Journeys in Two Worlds" (Cornwall, Conn.: privately printed, 1992); Reyner Banham, *Guide to Modern Architecture* (Princeton, N.J.: D. Van Nostrand, 1962), 18.

14 "More Than Modern"; George H. Favre, "Simplicity, Order, and Permanence," *Christian Science Monitor*, May 15, 1967.

15 Donald M. Kendall to Stone, June 15, 1971, Stone Papers, 2nd ac., box 37; Jarold A. Kieffer, *From National Cultural Center to John F. Kennedy Center for the Performing Arts: At the Front End of the Beginning* (Fairfax, Va: privately printed, 2004), 15–17. Much of the correspondence is in the John F. Kennedy Center for the Performing Arts Archives, Washington, D.C., as well as in Kieffer's private collection.

16 Stone to Fulbright, June 3, 1959, Stone Papers, 1st acc., box 70.

17 Kieffer, interview with the author, July 2004; Stone, The *Evolution of an Architect* (New York: Horizon Press, 1962), 95; John C. Hill to Stone, February 16, 1955, Stone Papers, 1st acc., box 62; Stone to Howard Eichenbaum, October 16, 1951, Stone Papers, 1st acc., box 23.

18 Francis Brennan, memorandum to Stone, November 23, 1964, Stone Papers, 2nd acc., box 71; Charles Strauss to Stone, September 20, 1946, Stone Papers, 1st acc., box 53; Edward L. R. Elson to Stone, October 23, 1959, Henry R. Luce Papers, box 45, Manuscript Division, Library of Congress, Washington, D.C. (hereafter cited as HRL Papers); Arthur Hanisch to Brennan, August 28, 1964, Stone Papers, 2nd acc., box 83.

19 John T. Caldwell to Marshall Scott Woodson, October 16, 1957, Stone Papers, 1st acc., box 63.

20 Leland King, telephone interview by Jane C. Loeffler, January 7, 1993, Jane C. Loeffler Collection (hereafter cited as Loeffler Collection).

21 Henry R. Shepley to Jury of Fellows, November 29, 1957, AIA Archives; Shepley, Nomination of Candidate, 1958, American Academy of Arts and Letters Archives, New York.

22 Jacks, "Elegant Bohemian," 186. See also "Howard Myers, 52, Housing Authority," *New York Times*, September 20, 1947.

23 Stone, *Evolution of an Architect*, 31.

24 Stone to Joseph C. Hazen, April 13, 1959, Stone Papers, 1st acc., box 70; Myers, office memorandum to Wesley Bailey, August 31, 1945, HRL Papers, box 98.

25 "Senator J. William Fulbright Remembers Edward Durell Stone," *Dimensions* [publication of the Arkansas Chapter of the AIA], vol. 5, no. 2 (1969): 9.

26 Fulbright, "American Architect Edward Durell Stone," *Congressional Record—Senate* 13311 (May 19, 1967).

27 Fulbright to Stone, March 21, 1949, J. William Fulbright Papers, LOC 869, box 21 Special Collections, University of Arkansas Libraries (hereafter cited as Fulbright Papers).

28 See Mary Anne Hunting, "Furniture Designed by Edward Durell Stone for Senator Fulbright," *The Magazine Antiques*, May 2004.

29 Bunshaft to Jury of Fellows.

30 Stone to A. L. Aydelott, March 29, 1955, Stone Papers, 1st acc., box 63.

31 Stone, "The Name of the Game Is Beauty," notes for a California Building Congress meeting, September 1967, private collection.

32 Lloyd Flood to Stone, March 12, 1958, Stone Papers, 1st acc., box 69.

33 Richard Atcheson, "Edward Durell Stone: Maker of Monuments," Show, March 1964.

34 Stone to Victorine DuPont Homsey, December 29, 1945, Stone Papers, 1st acc., box 82.

35 Emma Gene Hall, "Directions in Modern Architecture: A conversation with Edward D. Stone," *Gentlemen's Quarterly*, April 1959.

36 J. Seelye Bixler, citation, June 8, 1959, Time Inc. Archives, New York (hereafter cited as Time Archives).

37 "More than Modern"; Wolf Von Eckardt, *A Place to Live: The Crisis of the Cities* (New York: Dell, 1967), 216.

38 Jacques Barzun, "Romanticism: Definition of A Period," *Magazine of Art,* November 1949; Clement Greenberg, "Towards a Newer Laocoon," *Partisan Review* 7 (1940): 299.

39 Stone, "Modern Architecture on the Campus," *Stanford Review* (November 1960): 14; Hall, "Directions in Modern Architecture."

40 See "New Face For America Abroad," *Time,* July 11, 1960.

41 See, for example, Theo Wilson's articles in the New York Daily News, "Stones Smile and Roll Their Separate Ways," April 27, 1966 and "Stones Divorced: She Gets Million," May 10, 1966.

42 Wright, *The Shining Brow,* 242; Suzy Knickerbocker, Society, *New York Journal American,* November 10, 1964; Cranston Jones, *Architecture: Today and Tomorrow* (New York: McGraw-Hill, 1961), 14. See also the *Girl Talk* transcript, WABC-TV, July 30, 1965, Stone Papers, 2nd acc., box 71.

43 Kilham, "Journeys in Two Worlds."

44 Stone to Universe Krist, December 6, 1963, Stone Papers, 2nd acc., box 1.

45 Raymond Gomez, interview by the author, September 23, 2004.

46 Stone, quoted in "More Than Modern."

47 Von Eckardt, *A Place to Live,* 9.

48 Warren Wallace to Stone, June 8, 1959, Stone Papers, 1st acc., box 70; " 'Horizons' to Join WCBS Talk Shows," *New York Times,* September 28, 1964; recording of the Sam Yorty Show, August 20, 1967, Stone Papers, 2nd acc., box 139; transcript of the *Merv Griffin Show,* May 28, 1965, Stone Papers, 2nd acc., box 72. Stone appeared on T*oday* a number of times, including February 2, 1966. See also Beatriz Colomina, *Privacy and Publicity: Modern Architecture as Mass Media* (Cambridge, Mass.: MIT Press, 2000), 43.

49 Edward Durell Stone and Associates, marketing booklet, New York, October 1–2, 1971, Stone Papers, 2nd acc., box 4.

50 Henry Robbins to Stone, July 13, 1961, Stone Papers, 2nd acc., box 92; Robbins, memorandum to Alfred A. Knopf, n.d., Alfred A. Knopf Collection, Harry Ransom Humanities Research Center, University of Texas at Austin; M. Joseph Dooher to Stone, July 28, 1961, Stone Papers, 2nd acc., box 92.

51 Stone, "The American Landscape," Stone Papers, 2nd acc., box 92.

52 David K. Johnston, "Ben Raeburn, 86, Publisher of the Known and the Aspiring," *New York Times,* April 23, 1997.

53 Notes from a meeting between Martial and Co. and Ben Raeburn, October 31, 1962, Stone Papers, 1st. acc., box 78.

54 Stone, tape recording, July 11, 1964, Stone Papers, 2nd accession, box 81; "New Landmark for Wilshire Blvd.," *Concrete Facts* 9, n.d., and "How to Build A Landmark," *Southwest Builder and Contractor* (1962), Stone Papers, 2nd acc., box 51; Stone, "Modern Architecture on the Campus": 14; "End of the Glass Box?" Art, *Time,* May 25, 1962; Stone, draft for "The Case of the Tailfin Age," July 15, 1959, Stone Papers, 2nd acc., box 90; Stone, quoted in "Architecture Without Tears," People, *Architectural Forum,* 127 (November 1967): 91.

55 Stone, "Progress: Spare That Building!" *Harper's Bazaar,* May 1962.

56 Stone, draft, November 24, 1959, Stone Papers, 2nd acc., box 90.

57 Susan Sontag's "Notes On 'Camp,' " was originally published in Partisan Review 31 (Fall 1964): 515–30.

58 Sontag, "Notes on 'Camp'," in Sontag, *Against Interpretation and Other Essays* (New York: Farrar, Straus and Giroux, 1966): 277, 279; Matei Călinescu, "Kitsch," in *Five Faces of Modernity* (Durham, N.C.: Duke University Press, 1987), 223–62; Tomas Kulka, *Kitsch and Art* (University Park: Pennsylvania State University Press, 2002),100–13

59 Paul Gapp, "Ambiguous Statement Snarls Center Debate," Architecture, *Chicago Tribune,* June 30, 1974.

60 James T. Burns, "Edward Durell Stone? Who Ever Heard of a Book Called Edward Durell Stone?" *Progressive Architecture* 49 (April 1968): 222.

61 Allan Temko, "The Legacy of Edward Durell Stone," *San Francisco Chronicle,* August 21, 1978. See also Tom Cameron, "Building Designers Seek Place in Sun," Nailing It Down, *Los Angeles Times,* August 5, 1962; Gerald Nachman, "Dean of Architects," Close-up, *New York Post,* September 21, 1964; Blake Clark, "America's Unconventional Master Builder," *Readers Digest,* February 1965; Mary Burns to Barbara B. Freeman, January 24, 1963, Stone Papers, 1st acc., box 6.

1: AN ARTIST'S PATH: FROM PASTORAL OZARKIAN TO COSMOPOLITAN SAVANT *pages 20–25*

1 Edward Durell Stone, quoted in *The New Age of Architecture,* transcript of film produced by *Architectural Forum,* 1958, American Federation of Arts Records, Archives of American Art/Smithsonian, Washington, D.C. (hereafter cited as AFA Records).

2 Stone, *Recent and Future Architecture* (New York: Horizon Press, 1967), 8.

3 Blake Clark, "America's Unconventional Master Builder," *Reader's Digest,* February 1965.

4 "N.A.L. Co. Bird House Contest," *Fayetteville Democrat,* April 1, 1916; "Speech before the National Press Club," March 10, 1964, Stone Papers: 2nd acc., box 91.

5 Stone, "The Name of the Game Is Beauty," notes for a California Building Congress meeting, September 1967, private collection; Stone, *The Evolution of an Architect* (New York: Horizon Press, 1962), 16; "Urban Renewal Brings Back Memories," *Northwest Arkansas Times,* July 13, 1978.

6 William S. Campbell, *One Hundred Years of Fayetteville, 1828–1928* (1928; Fayetteville, Arkansas: Washington County Historical Society, 1977), 7–8.

7 Stone Record Sheet, College of Arts and Sciences, Office of the Registrar, University of Arkansas, Fayetteville, private collection.

8 Stone, *Evolution of an Architect,* 20.

9 "More Than Modern," Art, *Time,* March 31, 1958.

10 Barney Gruzen to Stone, March 28, 1958, Stone Papers, 1st acc., box 69; Kenneth J. Conant to Stone, January 1, 1964, Stone Papers, 2nd acc., box 2. For more on Hicks Stone see *Catalogues of the University of Arkansas, 1900–1906* (Fayetteville: University of Arkansas); *Boston City Directories; Harvard University Catalogues, 1912–1915* (Cambridge, Mass.: Harvard University).

11 *Stone, Evolution of an Architect,* 20–21.

12 Boston Architectural Center, "Dedication," 1966, Boston Architectural College Library.

13 Boston Architectural Center, "Dedication"; Stone Record Sheet.

14 Margaret Henderson Floyd, *Architectural Education and Boston: Centennial Publication of the Boston Architectural Center, 1889–1989* (Boston: Boston Architectural Center, 1989), 40–41; Rotch Committee, "Life Records and Envois," Rotch Travelling Scholarship Records, box 27, Institute Archives and Special Collections, MIT Libraries, Cambridge, Mass. (hereafter cited as Rotch Records).

15 Stone, *Evolution of an Architect,* 21.

16 Henry R. Shepley to George H. Edgell, April 25, 1925, private collection; Shepley to Jury of Fellows, November 29, 1957, AIA Archives.

17 Shepley Bulfinch Richardson and Abbott Archives, Boston.

18 Faculty of Architecture, *School of Architecture, 1927–28* (Cambridge, Mass.: Harvard University, 1927).

19 Edgell to M. A. Smith, January 3, 1930 and "Report on Standing," private collection; Walter H. Kilham Jr., "Journeys in Two Worlds" (Cornwall, Conn.: privately printed, 1992); Floyd, *Architectural Education and Boston,* 87.

20 Anthony Alofsin, *The Struggle for Modernism: Architecture, Landscape Architecture, and City Planning at Harvard* (New York: W. W. Norton, 2002), 55; Stone, *Evolution of an Architect,* 23.

21 Stone to Conant, July 6, 1964, Stone Papers, 2nd acc., box 2. Stone was referring to Sir Banister Fletcher's *History of Architecture for the Student, Craftsman, and Amateur, Being a Comparative View of the Historical Styles from the Earliest Period* (London: Batsford, 1896).

22 Alofsin, *Struggle for Modernism,* 54–55; 57.

23 Stone to Conant, May 3, 1965, Stone Papers, 2nd acc., box 2.

24 Alofsin, *Struggle for Modernism,* 19; "Official Register of the Department of Architecture" (Cambridge, Mass.: Harvard University, 1902), quoted in Alofsin, "Toward A History of Teaching Architectural History: An Introduction to Herbert Langford Warren," *Journal of Architectural Education* 37 (Fall 1983): 4.

25 Edward Durell Stone and Associates, marketing booklet, 1968, private collection.

26 "Report on Standing"; Alofsin, *Struggle for Modernism,* 32; John McAndrew, interview by Russell Lynes, Russell Lynes Papers, Archives of American Art/Smithsonian.

27 Kilham, "Journeys in Two Worlds," quoted in "More Than Modern."

28 Edgell to M. A. Smith, January 3, 1930, and to Stone, September 30, 1926, private collection.

29 Edgell to Board of Registration of Architecture, Department of Education, May 28, 1934; Edgell to Stone, July 3 and September 20, 1926; and Action of Council Report, 1925, private collection.

30 *Catalogue for 1926–1927* (Cambridge, Mass.: Massachusetts of Technology, 1926), 77–79; *Catalogue for 1927–1928* (Cambridge, Mass.: Massachusetts of Technology, 1927), 73–76, 245; Stone student file, Office of the Registrar, Massachusetts Institute of Technology, private collection; Edmund S. Campbell, "French Comrades in America: Jacques Carlu," *Pencil Points* 7 (May 1926): 283.

31 "Official Notification of Awards," *The Bulletin of the Beaux-Arts Institute of Design* 2 (June 1926): 4–5, and 3 (January 1927): 3, 11. See also Henry R. Sedgwick, "The Beaux-Arts Institute of Design," Year Book of the *Society of Beaux-Arts Architects* (1931): 61.

32 "Official Notification of Awards," *The Bulletin of the Beaux-Arts Institute of Design* 3 (May 1927): 5, 13.

33 "Tech Student Wins Rotch Scholarship," *Boston Harold,* May 4, 1927.

34 Clarence Henry Blackall, *A History of the Rotch Travelling Scholarship, 1883–1938* (Boston: privately printed, 1938); Rotch Records, box 1.

35 "Plan and Elevation of Prize Winning Design for 'An Architect's Office', by Edward D. Stone," *Pencil Points* 8 (July 1927): 440; Stone, *Evolution of an Architect,* 24.

36 Stone, *Evolution of an Architect,* 12–14, 23–29.

37 C. H. Blackall to Stone, October 25, 1927, and April 17, 1928, Rotch Records, box 3.

38 Rotch Committee Minutes, April 1928, Rotch Records, box 1; "Life Records and Envois"; Stone, *Evolution of an Architect,* 23.

39 Stone, *Evolution of an Architect,* 143.

40 Stone, quoted in Emma Gene Hall, "Directions in Modern Architecture: A conversation with Edward D. Stone," *Gentlemen's Quarterly,* April 1959.

41 Stone, *Evolution of an Architect,* 24–25.

42 See Marianne Lamonaca and Jonathan Mogul, eds., *Grand Hotels of the Jazz Age: The Architecture of Schultze and Weaver* (Miami Beach: Wolfsonian-Florida International University/New York: Princeton Architectural Press, 2005), 32–35, 229–43.

43 Stone to Orlean Vandiver, n.d., private collection.

44 Wallace K. Harrison to Jury of fellows, December 3, 1957, AIA Archives; Stone résumé, January 11, 1942, Stone Papers, 1st acc., box 2. See also Walter Rendell Storey, "Modern Decorations on a Grand Scale," *New York Times,* December 25, 1932; "New Movie Palace Gives City a Thrill," *New York Times,* December 30, 1932.

45 Kilham, *Journeys in Two Worlds;* Harrison to Jury of fellows, December 3, 1957, AIA Archives; Stone résumé; "The Reminiscences of Wallace Kirkman Harrison" (1978), 108, in the Columbia Center for Oral History Collection, Columbia University Libraries, New York.

46 "Preliminary Sketch for the Roxy Theatre at Rockefeller Center," *Pencil Points* 13 (September 9, 1932): 596; "Debut of a City," *Fortune,* January 1933.

47 Stone, *Evolution of an Architect,* 30; Daniel Okrent, *Great Fortune: The Epic of Rockefeller Center* (New York: Viking Press, 2003), 239; "Innovating Architect: Edward D. Stone," *New York Times,* April 18, 1958"; Stone to Clare Boothe Luce, September 26, 1961, and to Nat Hutchings, September 16, 1961, Stone Papers, 1st acc., box 78; "Life Calls on Vincent Astor at 'Ferry Reach' in Bermuda," *Life,* January 29, 1940; "Vincent Astor Buys Estate In Bermuda for Winter Home," *New York Times,* December 15, 1932; "Vincent Astor in Bermuda," *New York Times,* January 27, 1934.

48 Lewis Mumford, "Modernity and Commerce," The Sky Line, *The New Yorker,* October 2, 1936; Charles C. Savage, "Rockefeller Apartments," New York: Landmarks Preservation Commission, June 19, 1984, 8.

49 Harrison, quoted in Brendan Gill, "Wallace K. Harrison," in *A New York Life of Friends and Others* (New York: Poseidon Press, 1990), 157.

2: THE INTERNATIONAL STYLE: PIONEERING EXPERIMENTATION *pages 26–49*

1 Edward Durell Stone, quoted in "Recent Work by Edward D. Stone," *Architectural Forum* 75 (July 1941): 13.

2 Stone, *The Evolution of an Architect* (New York: Horizon Press, 1962), 31, 89. See also National Register of Historic Places, Richard H. Mandel house, Katonah, Westchester County, New York, NR #96000176.

3 Stone, *Evolution of an Architect,* 30–31; Gwendolyn Wright, *USA: Modern Architectures in History* (London: Reaktion Books, 2008), 114; Robert A. M. Stern, "International Style: Immediate Effects," The International Style at 50, *Progressive Architecture* 63 (February 1982): 105.

4. See Henry-Russell Hitchcock Jr. and Philip Johnson, *The International Style* (1966; first published in 1932 as International Style Architecture since 1922, New York: W. W. Norton, 1995), 29.

5 "Museum of Modern Art, New York City, Announces Exhibition of Modern Architecture," press release, n.d.; Museum of Modern Art, press release, January 24, 1932, Museum of Modern Art Library and Archives, New York (hereafter cited as MoMA Archives).

6 Hitchcock and Johnson, *International Style,* 15; Museum of Modern Art, press release, February 7, 1932, MoMA Archives.

7 Museum of Modern Art, *Modern Architecture: International Exhibition,* New York, February 10–March 23, 1932 (New York: Museum of Modern Art, 1932).

8 Alfred H. Barr Jr., " 'Tastemaking': Mr. Barr of the Museum of Modern Art Files a General Demurrer," *New York Times,* September 25, 1960; Ada Louise Huxtable, "Trend-Setting Departures and Pinnacles of Excellence in U.S.," Architecture, *New York Times,* May 18, 1965; Roxanne Kuter Williamson, *American Architects and the Mechanics of Fame* (University of Texas at Austin, 1991), 203; Beatriz Colomina, *Privacy and Publicity: Modern Architecture as Mass Media* (Cambridge, Mass.: MIT Press, 2000), 211–12. See also Aline B. Saarinen, "Our Cultural Pattern: 1929—and Today," *New York Times,* October 17, 1954; Hitchcock, interview by Russell Lynes, Lynes Papers.

9 Next Month, *House Beautiful,* November 1932.

10 Barr, foreword to *Modern Architecture: International Exhibition New York.* See also Talbot F. Hamlin, "The International Style Lacks the Essence of Great Architecture," *American Architect* 143 (January 1933): 12–16; "Architecture: The Turn it is Taking Under Modernistic Hands," *New York Herald Tribune,* February 14, 1932.

11 Stone, *Evolution of an Architect,* 32.

12 Transcript, Merv Griffin Show, WPTX-TV, Stone Papers, 2nd acc., box 72; Stone, *Evolution of an Architect,* 32.

13 Johnson to Ernestine M. Fantl, August 15, 1935, Curatorial Exhibition Files, Exh. #43, MoMA Archives.

14 Hitchcock, "International Style Twenty Years After," in Hitchcock and Johnson, *International Style,* 96.

15 "House of Richard H. Mandel," *Architectural Forum* 63 (August 1935): 79.

16 See "Automobiles," in Le Corbusier, *Towards A New Architecture* (1927; repr. New York: Dover)129–48.

17 See Stone's competition drawing, "A Summer School of Fine Arts," in The Bulletin of the Beaux-Arts Institute of Design 3 (May 1927): 13.

18 National Register of Historic Places, Wallace K. Harrison Estate, Huntington, Suffolk County, New York, NR #85002531; Victoria Newhouse, *Wallace K. Harrison, Architect* (New York: Rizzoli, 1989), 63–65; Kristina Wilson, Livable Modernism: Interior Decorating and Design During the Great Depression (New Haven, Conn.: Yale University Press/Yale University Art Gallery, 2004), 27–28, figs. 1.2–3.

19 "A $60,000 Dwelling Is Being Erected at Mount Kisco," *New York Times,* December 31, 1933.

20 Mary Fanton Roberts, *Inside 100 Homes* (New York: Robert M. McBride, 1936), 90.

21 Margaret B. W. Graham and Alec T. Shuldiner, *Corning and the Craft of Innovation* (New York: Oxford University Press, 2001), 145–46; A. E. Marshall to Armory Houghton, "Glass Construction Blocks," memo, March 14, 1931, box 33-5-3, Owens-Illinois Records, Glass Blocks folder, Corning Archives, Corning, New York.

22 Stone, Evolution of an Architect, 32; John Ely Burchard, "Glass in Modern Housing," *The Glass Industry* (December 1935): 379; Owens-Illinois Glass

Company, "Glass: 'Building the World of Tomorrow,'" (c. 1939), 21, Ward M. Canaday Center for Special Collections, University of Toledo. See also W. Fredwien, "Glass Block—New Building Maerial," *Scientific American* 149 (September 1933): 128.

23 "Washable Dinner Dresses," *Vogue*, May 15, 1935, and "Summer Cycle," June 15, 1935.

24 See Mary Anne Hunting, "The Richard H. Mandel House in Bedford Hills, New York," Living With Antiques, *The Magazine Antiques*, July 2001; David A. Hanks, "The Eric Brill Collection and The Richard H. Mandel House," *Sotheby's Important 20th Century Design*, December 9, 2005.

25 Sheldon Cheney and Martha Candler Cheney, *Art and the Machine: An Account of Industrial Design in 20th-Century America* (1936; New York: Acanthus Press, 1992), 164; "The Mandel House: A Home Resulting From Close Cooperation Between Architect, Decorator and Owner," *Interior Decorator* 95 (August 1935): 8.

26 Richard Guy Wilson, "Architecture in the Machine Age," in Wilson, Diane H. Pilgrim, and Dickran Dashjian, *The Machine Age in America, 1918–1941* (New York: Harry N. Abrams/Brooklyn Museum, 1986), 174.

27 Off the Record, *Fortune*, October 1935; Harry V. Anderson, "Modernity," Decorators Digest 5 (August 1935): 25.

28 Stone, *Evolution of an Architect*, 47.

29 Milton Mackaye, "Clare Boothe," *Scribners*, March 1939; Clare Luce, "The Victorious South," *Vogue*, June 1, 1937.

30 Quoted in W. A. Swanberg. *Luce and His Empire* (New York: Charles Scribner's Sons, 1972), 133.

31 Stephen Shadegg, *Clare Boothe Luce: A Biography* (New York: Simon and Schuster, 1970), 102; Stone, *Evolution of an Architect*, 33; "The New House of 194X," *Architectural Forum* 77 (September 1942): 65.

32 Illustrated in Le Corbusier and Pierre Jeanneret, *Oeuvre Complète de 1910–1929*, 4th ed. (Erlenbach-Zurich: W. Boesiger and O. Stonorov, 1946), 29.

33 See http://www.virginia.edu/academicalvillage/http://cti.itc.virginia.edu/~jjd5t/cww/1998/vi.03-uva-lawn-plan.jpg; accessed January 27, 2012.

34 Stone, *Evolution of an Architect*, 34.

35 Stone, *Evolution of an Architect*, 24.

36 Clare Luce to Allen Grover, January 4, 1941, Clare Boothe Luce Papers, box 85, Manuscript Division, Library of Congress (hereafter cited as CBL Papers).

37 Stone, *Evolution of an Architect*, 31; Howard Myers, office memorandum to Wesley Bailey, August 31, 1945, HRL Papers, box 98.

38 "Luce Plantation Slated To Become Monastery," *New York Times*, August 10, 1949; Stone, *Evolution of an Architect*, 34.

39 "Architects Award Prizes in 3 Fields," *New York Times*, April 22, 1937; "Homes of Varied Types Figure in Architect's Show," *New York Times*, May 2, 1937; "Modern in South Carolina," *House & Garden*, August 1937; "Mepkin Plantation, Moncks Corners, S.C.," *Architectural Forum* 66 (June 1937): 516.

40 "Frank Altschul: A Banker and Noted Philanthropist," *New York Times*, May 30, 1981; "Edward D. Stone Associates," *Interiors* 109 (July 1950): 89; "Recent Work by Edward D. Stone," *Architectural Forum* 175 (July 1941): 18.

41 Stone to Mrs. Henry Luce, February 15, 1940, CBL Papers, box 85; Stone, *Evolution of an Architect*, 38.

42 See the illustrations in Wilson, "Architecture in the Machine Age," 187–89, fig. 6:56; Daniel Okrent, *Great Fortune: The Epic of Rockefeller Center* (New York: Penguin Books, 2003), chapter 17.

43 Chuck Conconi, Personalities, *Washington Post*, May 18, 1990; "House for George P. Marshall," *Architectural Forum* 73 (July 1940): 20–21; John McAndrew, *Guide to Modern Architecture: Northeast States* (New York: Museum of Modern Art, 1940), 26.

44 See Le Corbusier et Jeanneret, *Oeuvre Complète de 1910–1929*, 98–99, 133, 176, 192.

45 "New York Men Win Architects' Award," *New York Times*, November 19, 1938.

46 See the biographical note in the *finding aid for the A. Conger Goodyear Papers, 1683–1964*, Buffalo and Erie County Historical Society, Buffalo, New York (http://libweb1.lib.buffalo.edu:8080/xtf/view?docId=ead/bechs/ bechs_c64_02.xml;query=;brand= ubdefault; accessed 2/27/11).

47 "Nelson Rockefeller … From a Center to a Citadel," *Time*, May 22, 1939; Cranston Jones, *Architecture: Today and Tomorrow* (New York: McGraw-Hill,

1961), 112; Alice T. Friedman, *American Glamour and the Evolution of Modern Architecture* (New Haven, Conn.: Yale University Press, 2010), 5.

48 Goodyear, *Sidelights* (1960).

49 Stone, *Evolution of an Architect*, 24; Elizabeth Mock, ed., *Built in USA since 1922* (New York: Museum of Modern Art, 1945), 42.

50 Stone, "Kitchens: Efficiency Is Not Enough," *Architectural Record* 91 (Mid-May, 1962): 5.

51 Stone, *Evolution of an Architect*, 89.

52 James Ford and Katherine Morrow Ford, *Design of Modern Interiors* (New York: Architectural Book, 1942), 59; The *Bulletin of the Beaux-Arts Institute of Design* 18 (January–March 1942).

53 Stone to Alexander Calder, December 30, 1946, Stone Papers, 1st acc., box 82.

54 "Recent Work by Edward D. Stone": 15; "Modern Gets a Break," *House & Garden*, October 1941; "Regional Design," *House & Garden*, November 1945.

55 "California in the East," *New York Times*, September 22, 1946.

56 Arthur Drexler, *Modern Architecture U.S.A.* (New York: Museum of Modern Art, 1965). See also Talbot Hamlin, *Forms and Functions of Twentieth-Century Architecture*, 4 vols. (New York: Columbia University Press, 1952), 2:258.

57 The "Futuramic" was introduced in *Life*, December 15, 1947; the Stone ad can be seen on page 14 of *Fortune*, April 1948.

58 John Fistere to Stone, November 11, 1947, Stone Papers, 1st acc., box 82. See also Colomina, *Privacy and Publicity*: 192.

59 Sarah Hershaw, "Saved Restored And Now for Sale," Big Deal, *New York Times*, July 3, 2011; National Register of Historic Places, A. Conger Goodyear house, Old Westbury, Nassau County, New York, NR # 03001246.

60 "Life Presents in Collaboration with the Architectural Forum Eight Houses for Modern Living Especially Designed by Famous American Architects for Four Representative Families Earning $2,000 to $10,000 a Year," *Life*, September 26, 1938.

61 Herbert Hoover, quoted in Kenneth T. Jackson, *Crabgrass Frontier: The Suburbanization of the United States* (New York: Oxford University Press, 1985), 187.

62 See United States Federal Housing Administration, *The FHA Story in Summary, 1934–1959* (Washington, D.C.: May 1, 1959), 1.

63 United States Federal Housing Administration, "Principles of Planning Small Houses," *Technical Bulletin* no. 4 (May 1, 1936; rev. April 1, 1937): 1–36. See also Delores Hayden, *Building Suburbia: Green Fields and Urban Growth, 1820–2000* (New York: Vintage Books, 2004), 4; Federal Housing Authority, *FHA Story in Summary*, 3; Joseph B. Mason, *History of Housing in the U.S., 1930–1980* (Houston: Gulf, 1980), 3, 10; Peter Blake, *No Place Like Utopia: Modern Architecture and the Company We Kept* (New York: Knopf, 1993), 139.

64 John T. Flynn, "A Good Place to Live," *Collier's*, March 28, 1936; George Creel, "Money To Build Your Home, *Collier's*, May 2, 1936; "Crowell's Have Largest Magazine Audience," *Springfield (Ohio) News-Sun*, November 1937.

65 The *Collier's* articles are: Flynn, "Good Place to Live"; Ruth Carson, "What's a Garden For?" April 11, 1936; Marie Beynon Ray, "Night Life at Home," April 25, 1936; Creel, "Money To Build Your Home"; Helen G. Thompson, "Home Is Like This," May 16, 1936; Betty Thornley Stuart, "The Cook Gets the Last Word," May 30, 1936. See also Next Week, *Collier's*, March 31, 1936.

66 "Co-Operative Exhibitions Attract Prospective Clients," *Architectural Record* 83 (June 1938): 84. For more about Theodore Conrad, see Carter B. Horsley, "Modelmakers' Work Gaining New Recognition," *New York Times*, July 28, 1974; David W. Dunlap, "Theodore Conrad, 84, Modeler And Architecture Preservationist," *New York Times*, August 20, 1994; "In Scale," The Talk of the Town, The *New Yorker*, July 7, 1956.

67 Meeting between Martial and Co. and Ben Raeburn, October 31, 1962, Stone Papers, 1st acc., box 5; Federal Housing Administration, "Principles of Planning Small Houses," 2.

68 Flynn, "A Good Place to Live."

69 National Register of Historic Places, Wallace-McGee house (part of the Columbia Multiple Resource Area submission), Columbia, Richland County, South Carolina, NR #79003379, and David Armstrong McNeill Sr. house, Thomson, Thomson-McDuffie County, Georgia, NR #92001637

70 "12th Annual Small House Competition," *House Beautiful*, March 1940.

71 "Charm in New Home: The Rooney House Is Modernistic in Design and Fit-

tings But It Possesses Comfort and Character—Furnishings in Many Tones of Green," *Hutchinson* (Kans.) *News*, May 10, 1937; "But People Do Live in Glass Houses," *Louisville Courier-Journal*, November 20, 1938; "Calls for Modern: Downey's Model Residence," *Downey (Calif.) Live Wire*, December 10, 1936. See also Gregory A. Luhan, Dennis Domer, and David Mohney, *Louisville Guide* (New York: Princeton Architectural Press, 2004), 286–87.

72 Stuart R. Carswell to Stone, January 15, 1948, Roy S. Johnson to Carswell, April 5, 1948, and Carswell to Stone, April 11, 1948, Stone Papers, 1st acc., box 82.

73 Thomas Crow, "Modernism and Mass Culture in the Visual Arts," in Francis Frascina, *Pollock and After: The Critical Debate* (New York: Harper and Row, 1985), 238, 256–58.

74 Aimee Larkin to Stone, February 19, 1936, box 87, Crowell-Collier Collection, Manuscripts and Archives Division, New York Public Library, New York; Ruth Carson, "Collier's Week-End House," *Collier's*, April 23, 1938.

75 Federal Housing Administration, "Principles of Planning Small Houses."

76 "For Week-Ends: Four Vacation Cottages Designed by Edward D. Stone," *House & Garden*, June 1938.

77 Fistere, "Space for Living" and Henrietta Murdock, "Living in Space," *Ladies' Home Journal*, April 1938.

78 "Miniature Home Shown," *New York Times*, March 13, 1938.

79 "Life Presents in Collaboration with the Architectural Forum Eight Houses"; "Life Houses: Houses for $2,000–$3,000 Income," *Architectural Forum* 69 (November 1938): 312–48. The houses are reprinted in *The 1940 Book of Small Houses by the Editors of Architectural Forum* (New York: Simon and Schuster, 1940).

80 "Life Houses," *Architectural Forum* 69 (October 1938): 2; Advertisement, *Architectural Forum* 69 (November 1938): 6; "Life Houses Open for Inspection," *Life*, December 12, 1938; "Life in Collaborating with the Architectural Forum Presents its Second Series of Eight Houses for Modern Living," *Architectural Forum* 73 (July 1940): 1.

81 For other Stone competitions see "Win $1,000 Prizes for Postoffices," *New York Times*, July 13, 1938; "The Curious Story of The Ventilating Tower," Forum of Events, *Architectural Forum* 75 (November 1941): 12.

82 James D. Kornwolf, "Introduction: The Competitions, the Thirties, and Architectural Issues Related to Them, Then and Now," in Kornwolf, ed., *Modernism in America 1937–1941: A Catalog and Exhibition of Four Architectural Competitions: Wheaton College, Goucher College, College of William and Mary, Smithsonian Institution* (Williamsburg, Va: Joseph and Margaret Muscarella Museum of Art, 1985), 3.

83 "Winners of National Theater Competition are Announced," *Architectural Record* 85 (April 1939): 61, 64; "Theatre Designs Put on Exhibition: Modern Museum Shows Prize Architectural Works for College in South," *New York Times*, March 1, 1939. See also Art, *Time*, March 13, 1939; Kornwolf, "College of William and Mary: Competition for a Festival Theatre and Fine Arts Center, November 1938–February 1939," in *Modernism in America*, 125–44.

84 "Modern Building Planned for Washington's 'Petrified Forest,'" press release, #40111-3, MoMA Archives; "Stone Is On Short List for Smithsonian Gallery of Art," *Architectural Forum* 70 (June 1939): 28.

85 "The Smithsonian Gallery of Art Competition," *Architectural Forum* 71 (July 1939): i–xvi; "Architects Named for Art Gallery," *New York Times*, May 12, 1939; "Father and Son Win Smithsonian Award," *New York Times*, June 29, 1939. See also Travis C. McDonald Jr., "Smithsonian Institution: Competition for a Gallery of Art, January 1939–June 1939," in *Modernism in America*, 177–95.

86 Leon Shimkin to Stone, July 15, 1964, Stone Papers, 2nd acc., box 2; *Current Biography* (1941), s.v. "Simon, Richard and Schuster, M. Lincoln." See also the film *Gentlemen's Agreement* (1947).

87 "Recent Work by Edward D. Stone": 24–25.

88 New York Museum of Science and Industry, *Science in Action* (New York, 1937), Nelson A. Rockefeller Personal Projects, box 168, Rockefeller Archive Center, Sleepy Hollow, New York (hereafter cited as NAR Personal Projects); Stone, *Evolution of an Architect*, 33; New York Museum of Science and Industry Pamphlet, NAR Personal Projects, box 127.

89 Mary Anne Staniszewski, *The Power of Display: A History of Exhibition Installations at the Museum of Modern Art* (Cambridge, Mass.: MIT Press, 2001), 10;

Cranston Jones, confidential report to James Linen and Harris K. Prior, AFA Records.

90 Conger Goodyear, *The Museum of Modern Art: The First Ten Years* (New York: Vrest Orton, 1943), 126.

91 For more about Philip Goodwin, see "James J. Goodwin Dead: Retired Financier, a Cousin of the Late J. P. Morgan, Expires at 79," *New York Times*, June 24, 1915; "Goodwin Left $30,000,000: Estate of Morgan's Cousin Divided Among Widow and Sons," *New York Times*, July 4, 1915; Goodwin to Rockefeller, April 10, 1939, NAR Personal Projects, box 130; Alfred H. Barr Jr., "The Philip L. Goodwin Collection," *The Bulletin of the Museum of Modern Art* 6 (Fall 1958); Goodwin to "Chick" Austin, October 25, 1935, October 28, 1941, and July 25, 1944, A[rthur] Everett Austin Jr. Papers, The Archives, Wadsworth Atheneum Museum of Art, Hartford, Conn. (hereafter cited as Austin Papers); "P. L. Goodwin Dies; Noted Architect," *New York Herald Tribune*, February 14, 1958; "Philip Goodwin, Architect, 72, Dies," *New York Times*, February 14, 1958; Lynes, *Good Old Modern: An Intimate Portrait of the Museum of Modern Art* (New York: Atheneum, 1973), 190; "'Brick House,' Woodside Circle, Hartford, Conn.: Philip L. Goodwin, Architect," *American Architect* 127 (May 20, 1925): pl. 126; "House of Ralph D. Cutler, West Hartford, Connecticut," *Architectural Record* 75 (February 1934): 158–60.

92 Goodwin, Suggested Outline for Competition for New Building for the Museum of Modern Art, February 21, 1936, NAR Personal Projects, box 126.

93 Goodwin to Rockefeller, March 10, 1936, NAR Personal Projects, box 126; Rockefeller to Goodwin, October 31, 1935, NAR Personal Projects, box 131; Goodwin to Austin, November 6, 1935, Austin Papers.

94 Goodwin, cable to Barr, July 17, 1936, NAR Personal Projects, box 126.

95 Goodwin, cable to Barr; Goodwin to Goodyear, June 8, 1936, NAR Personal Projects, box 126; Goodwin to Rockefeller, June 23, 1936, NAR Personal Projects, box 127.

96 Barr to Mrs. John D. Rockefeller, July 2, 1936, quoted in Rona Roob, "1936: The Museum Selects an Architect; Excerpts from the [Alfred Hamilton] Barr [Jr.] Papers of the Museum of Modern Art," *American Art Journal* 23 (1983): 24; John Canaday, "In the Gleaming: Twilight Seems to Be Settling Rapidly For Abstract Expressionism," *New York Times*, September 11, 1960.

97 John McAndrew, interview by Lynes, October 1971, Lynes Papers; Stone, *Evolution of an Architect*, 36; Rockefeller to Goodwin, August 2, 1937, NAR Personal Projects, box 126; Stone to Rockefeller, December 15, 1936, NAR Personal Projects, box 131.

98 Goodyear, *The Museum of Modern Art: The First Ten Years*, 127.

99 McAndrew, interview by Lynes.

100 Hitchcock to Barr, January 1, 1938, Curatorial Exhibition Files, Exh. #1518; Barr to Rockefeller, July 30, 1937, Barr Papers, MoMA Archives; Stone, *Evolution of an Architect*, 36.

101 Goodwin to Rockefeller, July 30, 1937, NAR Personal Projects, box 126.

102 Goodyear to Abby Rockefeller, July 30, 1937, Abby Aldrich Rockefeller Papers, box 8, Rockefeller Archive Center.

103 "Plans Filed for Art Building," *New York Times*, August 31, 1937; "New Art Museum to Flout Custom," *New York Times*, January 12, 1938; "New Building for Modern Art Museum," *Architectural Forum* 68 (February 1938): 7; Hitchcock to Barr, January 1, 1938, Curatorial Exhibition Files. Exh. #1518; Christine to Hitchcock, November 27, 1936, Early Museum History: Administration Records, 1.8, MoMA Archives.

104 Hitchcock to Barr, January 1, 1938.

105 Gordon Bunshaft, oral history taken by Betty J. Blum, April 4–7, 1989 (http://digital-libraries.saic.edu; accessed, February 1, 2010).

106 Stone to Rockefeller, February 4, 1938, and Rockefeller to Goodwin, February 9, 1938, NAR Personal Projects, box 127.

107 *Art in Our Time: An Exhibition to Celebrate the Tenth Anniversary of the Museum of Modern Art and the Opening of Its New Building* (New York: Museum of Modern Art, 1939); "Summary Report of the Department of Architecture," June 3, 1939, AHB [AAA:2166; 114], MoMA Archives. See also Hamlin, "Modern Display for Works of Art," *Pencil Points* 20 (September 1939): 615; "Record-Breaking Attendance at New Home of Museum of Modern Art," press release # 39606–24, n.d., MoMA Archives.

108 "Alfred H. Barr Jr. Director," *Magazine of Art* 32 (June 1939): 323. See also "New Art Museum to Flout Custom"; "Modern Museum," Art, *Time*, June 28, 1937.

109 "Modern Museum's New Plans," Field Notes, *Magazine of Art* 30 (August 1937): 496.

110 "Art Building Features: Glass Will Be Freely Used for 43rd St. Museum Building," *New York Times*, December 25, 1938.

111 Hitchcock, "1930 to the Mid-20th Century," in Americas: Art Since Columbus, *Encyclopedia of World Art*, vol. 1 (New York: McGraw-Hill, 1959), 272.

112 "The Museum of Modern Art," *Fortune*, December 1938; Ada Louise Huxtable, "A Dubious Survival Plan For the Modern," *New York Times*, August 7, 1977. See also Robert Hughes, "Revelation on 53rd Street," Art, *Time*, May 14, 1984.

113 "Museum of Modern Art Will Have Glass Walls," press release #381220–32, MoMA Archives; "Art Building Features: Glass Will Be Freely Used for 43rd St. Museum Building; "Rockefeller Site Given Museum," *New York American*, June 18,1937; "New Museum of Modern Art Opens May 10th: Tenth Anniversary Exhibit Will Inaugurate 5-Story, Glass-Walled Building," *New York Herald Tribune*, March 14, 1939; "The Glass-Temple Museum: Modern Art Display Takes Over Own Building In New York," Art, *Newsweek*, May 22, 1939.

114 Lewis Mumford, "Modernity and Commerce," The Sky Line, *The New Yorker*, October 3, 1936; Robert Wojtowicz, "Toward An Organic Architectural Criticism," in Elisabeth Blair MacDougall, "Lewis Mumford and American Modernism: European Theories for Architecture and Urban Planning," *Architectural Historian in America* 35 (1990): 246–47;

115 Marion Cook, "A Million Dollars Goes Modern," *Rockefeller Center Weekly*, July 16, 1937.

116 Edward Alden Jewell, "Museum of Modern Art Looks Ahead," *New York Times*, May 14, 1939; Royal Cortissoz, quoted in Lynes, *Gold Old Modern*, 210–11. See also "Modernistic Museum," *Lexington (Ky.) Leader*, June 29, 1937; Lynes, *Good Old Modern*, 194; "Modern Art Museum," *Washington Star*, June 20, 1937.

117 "Modern Art for the New Museum of Modern Art," *Architectural Record* 172 (October 1984): 164–65; Huxtable, "A Dubious Survival Plan for the Modern"; Huxtable, "The Modern Prepares for Expansion," *New York Times*, June 29, 1980.

118 Hilton Kramer, "MOMA Reopened: The Museum of Modern Art in the Postmodern Era," *New Criterion* (Summer 1984): 1, 44; Alan Wallach, "The Museum of Modern Art: The Past's Future," *Journal of Design History* 5 (1992): 210–11; Matilda McQuaid, draft for a text panel for A Modern Museum: The 1939 Goodwin/Stone Building, Curatorial Exhibition Files, Exh. # 1518, MoMA Archives.

119 Paul Goldberger, "A Wistful Ode to a Museum That Once Was," Architecture View, *New York Times*, June 11, 1989. See also Goldberger's *New York Times* articles, "The New MoMA," April 15, 1984, "The New MoMA: Mixing Art with Real Estate," November 4, 1979," "Architecture of Last 20 Years Surveyed at Modern," February 23, 1979, and "Museums That Build Glass Houses," January 26, 1978, as well as *his City Observed: New York, A Guide to the Architecture of Manhattan* (New York: Random House, 1979), 173; Dominic Ricciotti, "The 1939 Building of the Museum of Modern Art: The Goodwin-Stone Collaboration," *American Art Journal* 17 (Summer 1985): 70–73.

120 Nicolai Ouroussoff, "Art Fuses with Urbanity in an Aesthetically Pure Redesign of the Modern," Architecture Review, *New York Times*, November 15, 2004. See also Jed Perl, "Modern Immaturity," Jed Perl on Art, *New Republic* 231 (November 29, 2004): 33.

121 "Frank Lloyd Wright: Discussion between Frank Jennings and Stone," rough draft, May 7, 1959, Stone Papers, 2nd acc., box 90.

122 Mumford, "The American Tradition," The Sky Line, *The New Yorker*, March 11, 1939.

3: EMBRACING THE AMERICAN IMPULSE *pages 50–77*

1 Edward Durell Stone, quoted in "Meet Edward Stone," *House Beautiful*, September 1945.

2 Arthur Drexler to Henry-Russell Hitchcock Jr., July 9, 1952, Curatorial Exhibition Files, Exh. # 528, MoMA Archives.

3 Stone, *The Evolution of an Architect* (New York: Horizon Press, 1962), 90–92.

4 Elizabeth Mock, ed., *Built in USA Since 1932* (New York: Museum of Modern Art, 1945), 14.

5 "Modern Houses in America," *Architectural Forum* 71 (July 1939): 1–2.

6 Ann Natanson, "U.S. Pavilion in Brussels Inspired by Rome," *Daily American* (n.d.), Stone Papers, 2nd acc., box 97.

7 Emma Gene Hall, "Directions in Modern Architecture: A conversation with Edward D. Stone," *Gentlemen's Quarterly*, April 1959.

8 Roy McMullen, "A World of Your Own Choosing," *House Beautiful*, October 1953; "Here are 19 Ways to Create Interesting Interiors," *House Beautiful*, March 1957.

9 Ernest E. Jacks, "Elegant Bohemian: Tales of Architect Edward Durell Stone" (ca. 2000), private collection, 31.

10 Stone, "Hero Prophet Adventurer," *Saturday Review*, November 7, 1959.

11 See Ada Louise Huxtable, *Frank Lloyd Wright* (New York: Viking, 2004), xvi–xv, 55, 76, 87.

12 Stone, *Evolution of an Architect*, 90.

13 See Robert C. Twombly, "Usonia: Shelter in the Open, 1936–1947," in *Frank Lloyd Wright: His Life and His Architecture* (New York: John Wiley and Sons, 1979), 240–74.

14 David Weingarter, *Bay Area Style: Houses of the San Francisco Bay Region* (New York: Rizzoli, 2004), 12.

15 Elizabeth Kendall Thompson, "Backgrounds and Beginnings," in *Domestic Architecture of the San Francisco Bay Region* (San Francisco Museum of Art, 1949).

16 Stone to Henry Shepley, June 6, 1962, Stone Papers, 1st acc., box 79.

17 Stone, *Evolution of an Architect*, 92. See also "William Wilson Wurster," *Architectural Forum* 79 (July 1943): 45–65; "Meet Gardner Dailey," *House Beautiful*, October 1945; Marc Treib, ed., *An Everyday Modernism: The Houses of William Wurster* (San Francisco Museum of Modern Art, 1995); Sally Woodbridge, ed., *Bay Area Houses* (Salt Lake City: Peregrine Smith, 1988), 17, 147–58.

18 Robert N. Webb, "A House is Born," *Rockefeller Center Magazine*, June 1940.

19 "Home Exhibit Planned," *New York Times*, May 16, 1940; Henry H. Saylor, The Diary, *Architectural Forum* 73 (July 1940): 106; "Home Center Names Architect," *New York Times*, September 4, 1940.

20 Ruth Carson, "Collier's House of Ideas," *Collier's*, June 15, 1940; Webb, "A House is Born." The other *Collier's* articles, all by Carson, are "Living at Ease," July 20, 1940; "We Furnish the Home," August 10, 1940; and "Lights On!" September 14, 1940.

21 Stone, *Evolution of an Architect*, 93.

22 "Streamlined, It So Happens," *Rockefeller Center Magazine*, August 1940; Carson, "Collier's House of Ideas."

23 Carson, "Collier's House of Ideas."

24 "Miscellaneous Built-in Features," *Architectural Forum* 85 (July 1946): 139.

25 See "House Designed to Warm the Winter Scene," *Architectural Record* 115 (May 1954): 156; Marion Gough, "How to Harmonize a Fine House with Growing Children," *House Beautiful*, February 1950.

26 Thomas C. Linn, "Industrial Art Will Go On View," *New York Times*, April 21, 1940.

27 "Museum to Exhibit Art of Industries," *New York Times*, April 29, 1940; "Interior Decoration, 1940" *Pencil Points* 21 (July 1940): 433; Elizabeth B. Mock, *If You Want to Build A House* (New York: Museum of Modern Art, 1946), 73.

28 "Competition Announcements and Results," *Pencil Points* 22 (February 1941): 72.

29 "For Grand and Glorious Weekends," *Better Homes and Gardens*, April 1941.

30 See Kristin Szylvian Bailey, "Defense Housing in Greater Pittsburgh, 1945–1955," *Pittsburgh History* 73 (Spring 1990): 16–28.

31 "Low-Cost Housing," *Architectural Forum* 75 (October 1941): 212.

32 "Aluminum City Terrace Housing," *Architectural Forum* 81 (July 1944): 65–76. See also Zenia Kotval, "Opportunity Lost: A Clash Between Politics, Planning, and Design in Defense Housing for Pittsfield, Massachusetts," *Journal of Planning History* 2 (February 2003): 30.

33 See Talbot Wegg, "FLLW versus the USA," *AIA Journal* 53 (February 1970), 48–52; Clark Foreman to Frank Lloyd Wright, October 24, 1941, Frank Lloyd Wright Foundation, Taliesin West, Scottsdale, Ariz.

34 Paul R. Lusignan, "Public Housing in the United States, 1933–1949," *CRM*, no.1 (2002): 37; "Low-Cost Housing": 212; "Planning War Housing," *Architectural Forum* 76 (May 1942): 269.

35 "Planning War Housing": 268–69; "Today's House," *Architectural Forum* 85 (July 1946): 105.

36 "Victory on the Homes Front: A Report and a Blueprint, 1938–1944," (Pittsburgh: Allegheny County Housing Authority, ca. 1945); *Housing in Wartime Pittsburgh: Summary of Activities, 1943–1945* (Pittsburgh Housing Association, 1945), 9.

37 "Housing Sites Picked," *New York Times,* May 15, 1941; "Two Housing Projects Ready to Rent," *Pittsburgh Post-Gazette,* October 30, 1942.

38 "Planning War Housing": 270.

39 http://www.cherrypoint.usmc.mil/MCASCP/historycp.asp; accessed June 2009.

40 "Cherry Point Homes, North Carolina," *Architectural Forum* 79 (November 1943): 53.

41 Stone, *Evolution of an Architect,* 95.

42 "The New House of 194X," *Architectural Forum* 77 (September 1942): 65.

43 John Sargeant, *Frank Lloyd Wright's Usonian Houses* (New York: Whitney Library of Design, 1984), 22.

44 Andrew M. Shanken, *194X: Architecture, Planning and Consumer Culture on the American Home Front* (Minneapolis: University of Minnesota Press, 2009), 4; Various Stone résumés in the Stone Papers; Stone, presentation book, Foreign Office and Building (hereafter cited as FBO) Records, Bureau of Overseas Building Operations, United States Department of State, Washington, D.C.

45 Cranston Jones, *Architecture: Today and Tomorrow* (New York: McGraw-Hill, 1961), 112.

46 Col. G. M. Goodman, memorandum for Chief, Air Installation Division, August 17, 1945, Stone Papers, 1st acc., box 2; Stone to Henderson E. McGee, December 27, 1945, and to Richard Morse, January 29, 1947, Stone Papers, 1st acc., box 83; Stone, *Evolution of an Architect,* 95–96.

47 Edmond L. Leipold, *Famous American Architects* (Minneapolis: T. S. Denison, 1972), 45; Stone, *Evolution of an Architect,* 95.

48 Dolores Hayden, *Building Suburbia: Green Fields and Urban Growth, 1820–2000* (New York: Vintage Books, 2004), 131.

49 Hayden, *Building Suburbia,* 131; Paul Boyer, *Promises To Keep: The United States since World War II* (Boston: Houghton Mifflin, 1999), 12. See also "Life Presents Three Modern Houses," *Life,* April 28, 1947.

50 Announcements, *Architectural Forum* 84 (June 1946): 160. See also "Architect Buys House," *New York Times,* October 27, 1945.

51 Stone to Victorine DuPont Homsey, December 29, 1945, Stone Papers, 1st acc., box 82.

52 Charles B. Strauss to Stone, ca. 1946, Stone Papers, 1st acc., box 53; Stone to Mr. Parter, November 6, 1952, Stone Papers, 1st acc., box 73.

53 Stone to Colonel Musgrave Hyde, November 12, 1945, Stone Papers, 1st acc., box 82.

54 Verna Wear to Stone, December 10, 1947, Stone Papers, 1st acc., box 83; "The Arts Integrated," *New York Times,* November 9, 1947; Mary Roche, "Exhibit of Homes Will Open Today," *New York Times,* September 18, 1947.

55 "House That 'Lives,' " Theme of Exhibit," *New York Times,* September 20, 1948; "The Modern House Comes Alive," *Munson-Williams-Proctor Institute Bulletin* (February 1949); "The Modern House Comes Alive—1948–9," Munson-Williams-Proctor Arts Institute Library, Utica, N.Y.; Aline E. Louchheim, "Gallery, Decorator, and Work of Art," *New York Times,* September 26, 1948.

56 "Art for Interiors," Art, *Time,* October 5, 1953. See also Susan Sontag, "Notes on 'Camp,' " in Sontag, *Against Interpretation and Other Essays* (New York: Picador, 1966), 275–92.

57 Kiplinger Washington Letter, February 28, 1953, Stone Papers, 1st acc., box 64.

58 Richard Pratt, "Take Your Choice: Traditional and Modern," *Ladies' Home Journal,* March 1946; "House for Moderns," The Building Forum, *Good Housekeeping,* August 1946. See also Joseph B. Mason to Stone, February 7, 1949, Stone Papers, 1st acc., box 61.

59 Mason, *History of Housing in the U.S., 1930–1980* (Houston: Gulf Publishing, 1982), 53; Roche, "Modern Home Show Will Open Today," *New York Times,* May 4, 1946.

60 Pratt, "You Can Build Your Own Home for Half the Price," *Ladies' Home Journal,* April 1950; Stone, *Evolution of an Architect,* 110.

61 Donald R. Brann, "Here's a House You Can Build," *Los Angeles Times,* June 25, 1950.

62 Ingersoll Steel Division, "Presenting the Complete Ingersoll Utility Unit," Alden B. Dow Archives, Midland, Mich.; Roche, "Heart of the House," *New York Times,* September 8, 1946.

63 David A. Hanks with Jennifer Toher, *Donald Deskey: Decorative Designs and Interiors* (New York: E. P. Dutton, 1987), 126–30.

64 *MSA Weekly Bulletin* (October 1946), 4; Roche, "Heart of the House."

65 Lisa Germany, *Harwell Hamilton Harris* (University of Texas at Austin, 1991), 98.

66 "Eight Men on a Unit: A Group of Brilliant Young Architects Build Houses Round a Prefabricated Utility Package," *Interiors* 105 (May 1946): 92–93; "Presenting the Complete Ingersoll Utility Unit."

67 "Four Experimental Houses by Modern Designers Demonstrate the Application of a New and Versatile Building Material," *Architectural Forum* 91 (November 1949): 84–89; "New Homes for the Young Family: Hudson River Modern," *Today's Woman,* 1949, Stone Papers, 2nd acc., box 95; "The Hearth is the Heart, *Good Housekeeping,* June 1951.

68 Maron J. Simon, ed., *Your Solar House* (New York: Simon and Schuster, 1947), 7, 40–41; Roche, "New Ideas," *New York Times,* November 2, 1947.

69 "Residential Design," *Progressive Architecture* 32 (December 1951): 61–72.

70 Frank Seiberling, *Looking into Art* (New York: Holt, Rinehart and Winston, 1959), 120–22.

71 Karl Holzinger to Stone, July 17, 1941, Stone Papers, 1st acc., box 62.

72 Stone, *Evolution of an Architect,* 97; Notes, Stone Papers, 2nd acc., box 92.

73 Wallace W. Heath, "House Design for Mrs. Astor," *Woman's Home Companion,* November 1948.

74 "Life Houses: Houses for $3,000–$4,000 Income," *Architectural Forum* 69 (November 1938): 321–23; Treib, *An Everyday Modernism,* fig. 62; "House by William Wilson Wurster, AIA," *California Arts and Architecture* 60 (December 1943): 19–21.

75 Katherine Morrow Ford, "Indoor Patio," Designs for Living, *New York Herald Tribune* and *Los Angeles Times,* May 6, 1956.

76 "The Roman Touch," *Newark Sunday News Magazine,* August 22, 1954.

77 William A. Jenkins, "Dream House Combines Functionalism, Living Ease By Utilizing Natural Wood," *Bergen Evening Record,* January 20, 1951; Jenkins, "Novel Twists Add Beauty, Economy," *Bergen Evening Record,* January 27, 1951.

78 Jenkins, "Dream House Combines Functionalism."

79 Carol Richter, "Home and Personality Are Blended," *Sunday Sun,* March 11, 1956.

80 See John Sergeant, Frank Lloyd Wright's Usonian Houses (New York: Whitney Library of Design, 1984), 52–53; Riley, ed., with Peter Reed, *Frank Lloyd Wright: Architect* (New York: Museum of Modern Art, 1994), 230, 240, 242.

81 Andrew Thurnauer to the author, May 15, 2009.

82 Thurnauer to the author; Virginia Lambert, "Living With—And In—A Landmark," *Sunday Record,* May 30, 1971.

83 Stone, quoted in Paul Heyer, *Architects on Architecture: New Directions in America* (New York: Walker, 1966), 175; Stone, *Evolution of an Architect,* 97.

84 "Architect Urges Community Plans," *New York Times,* May 18, 1950.

85 Stone to C. A. Wyman, May 29, 1946. Stone Papers, 1st acc., box 83; Peter Blake to Douglas Haskell, September 29 and October 5, 1950, Douglas Putnam Haskell Papers, Drawings and Archives, Avery Architectural and Fine Arts Library, Columbia University, New York.

86 Ford and Thomas H. Creighton, *The American House Today* (New York: Reinhold, 1951), 32.

87 Stone to R. M. Kearns, May 16, 1949, and to Mr. and Mrs. W. T. Grant, December 7 and 30, 1948, and January 7, May 6, and May 9, 1949, Stone Papers, 1st acc., box 61.

88 John A. Bradley, "Many Structural Feats Are Accomplished In Remodeling of the Victoria Theatre," *New York Times,* October 31, 1948; "Theater: New York, N.Y." *Progressive Architecture* 31 (May 1950): 59–62.

89 "Edward Durell Stone: Rotch Scholarship Sketch Books, 1927–1929," private collection.

90 See "Theater: New York, N.Y.," 62; United States Patent Office, "Flexible fabric for use as a ceiling wall drape, divider or the like," filed February 20, 1958,des. 187,464, issued March 22, 1960; "Building 'Skin,' " *New York Times,* March 26, 1960.

91 "15 New Bathroom Plans," *House & Garden,* February 1957.

92 Floor plan, June 15, 1949, Stone Papers, 2nd acc., M-13.

93 Stone to Fred Jones, April 28, 1953, Stone Papers, 1st acc., box 50; Thomas D. Church to Stone, May 7, 1953, Stone Papers, 1st acc., box 1; Stone to

Henry Mudd, August 31, 1960, and Church to Earl Heitschmidt, September 6, 1960, Stone Papers, 1st acc., box 64; Landscape plans of the Ludwig Lauerhass house and Stuart Pharmaceutical Company, Ludwig Lauerhass Papers, Huntington Library, San Marino, Calif. (hereafter cited as Lauerhass Papers); Treib, *Thomas Church, Landscape Architect: Designing A Modern California Landscape* (San Francisco: William Stout, 2003); Elizabeth Barlow Rogers, *Landscape Design: A Cultural and Architectural History* (New York: Harry N. Abrams, 2001), 449–50.

94   See Mary Anne Hunting, "From craft to industry: Furniture designed by Edward Durell Stone for Senator Fulbright," *The Magazine Antiques*, May 2004.

95   F. P. Rose, "The Springfield Wagon Company," *Arkansas Historical Quarterly*, vol. 10, no. 1 (Spring 1951): 97; Randall Bennett Woods, *Fulbright: A Biography* (New York: Cambridge University Press, 1995), 9; Monthly Stock Letter, J. H. Phipps Lumber Company, Fayetteville, Arkansas, May 1, 1928, Fulbright Papers (unless noted otherwise the records in the Fulbright Papers are in BCN 105, folders 2–6).

96   "Senator J. William Fulbright Remembers Edward Durell Stone," *Dimensions* vol. 5, no. 2 (1969): 9; "Leaders in the Industry," *Furniture Manufacturer* 72 (May 1951): 46.

97   Frank G. Lee to Fulbright, March 1, 1950, Fulbright to Mrs. Edward D. Stone, May 5, 1950, and Fulbright to Alfred Auerbach, April 10 and 19, 1950, Fulbright Papers.

98   Stone to Hal Douglas, June 15, 1950, Stone Papers (unless noted otherwise the Fulbright Industries furniture records in the Stone Papers are in the 1st acc., boxes 48 and 61); Fulbright to Auerbach, November 25, 1950, Fulbright Papers.

99   "Acquisition of Arkansas Baskets for University Museum," memorandum from James A. Scholtz to Dean R. C. Anderson, June 29, 1977, University Museum, University of Arkansas.

100 See "Organic Design in Home Furnishings," *Pencil Points* 22 (October 1941): 634.

101 *Modern by Edward Stone* (Fayetteville: Fulbright Industries, 1951), private collection.

102 Roche, "There's Increasing Evidence of America's Own Style," *House Beautiful*, June 1951. See also "Out of Plow Shares and Wagon Wheels," *Interiors* 110 (May 1951): 16; Betty Pepis, "Oak Strips used in New Furniture," *New York Times*, March 21, 1951; Sheila Hibben, "About the House," *The New Yorker*, May 19, 1951.

103 Lee to Fulbright, May 14, 1951, Fulbright Papers.

104 Auerbach to Lee, July 13, 1951, and Fenner F. Stice to Fulbright, July 28, 1951, Fulbright Papers; Stice to Stone, January 16, 1952, Stone Papers.

105 Fulbright to Auerbach, August 18, 1951, and Auerbach to Fulbright, August 8, 1951, Fulbright Papers.

106 Stone to Fulbright, April 24, 1951, Fulbright Papers; Stone to Lloyd Flood, May 17, 1951, Stone Papers, 1st acc., box 69.

107 Interoffice memo to Fulbright, February 27, 1950, and Auerbach to Fulbright, July 11, 1950, Fulbright Papers; "The Year's Work: 12th Annual Collection," *Interiors* 112 (August 1952): 87; "Architectural Interiors," *Architectural Record* 113 (January 1953): 147, 152; Lee to Stone, Mary 7, 1952, Stone Papers.

108 Lee to Fulbright, December 17, 1956, and Fulbright to Lee, December 20, 1956, Fulbright Papers; Fulbright to Lee, December 20, 1956, Fulbright Papers; Stone, *Evolution of an Architect*, 99.

109 Hall, "Directions in Modern Architecture"; Stone, manuscript for *Evolution of an Architect*, Stone Papers, 2nd acc., box 92.

110 "Sixth Avenue's Tomorrow," *Rockefeller Center Magazine*, July 1938.

111 "Blueprint for an Avenue," Art, *Time*, June 23, 1941; Millard Henlein, "The Sixth Avenue Association Brags a Bit," *Boulevard* (Spring 1939): 10; *From Humble Beginnings to Architectural and Commercial Greatness: The Saga of the Avenue of the Americas* (New York: Avenue of the Americas Association, 1974), and "25th Annual Report," 1950, Avenue of the Americas Association Archives, New York (hereafter cited as AAA Archives); Lewis Mumford, "Cloud Over Sixth Avenue—Home on the Park," The Sky Line, *The New Yorker*, December 21, 1940.

112 "Blueprint for an Avenue"; Directories of the Faculties, 1937–42 (New York: New York University).

113 "Study for an Avenue of the Americas by Edward D. Stone for the United States Gypsum Company," *Architectural Forum* 75 (August 1941): 1–5. See also "Sixth Ave. To Help Hemisphere Trade," *New York Times*, June 12, 1941.

114 "Plan 'Avenue of the Americas,' *New York Sun*, June 12, 1941; "Trees for Sixth Avenue," *New York Times*, June 16, 1939.

115 "Student's Exhibit," The Record Reports, *Architectural Record* 102 (December 1947): 132; "Out of Schools: Training for Architects," For your information, *Interiors* 107 (December 1947): 10; Stone, quoted in Maria M. and Louis di Valentin, *The Everyday Pleasure of Sculpture* (New York: James H. Heineman, 1966), 108.

116 Stone, "Study for the Avenue of the Americas," 2; "Avenue of Americas Plans Master Plan," *New York Herald Tribune*, January 25, 1950.

117 Stone, "American Landscape," April 26 and June 1, 1960, Stone Papers, 2nd acc., box 67.

118 Harvie Branscomb to Dr. H. Kaplan, January 26, 1953, University Records, box 300, Special Collections and University Archives, Vanderbilt University, Nashville, Tenn. (hereafter cited as Vanderbilt Archives).

119 John T. Caldwell to Branscomb, April 16, 1957; Branscomb to Caldwell, April 26, 1957, box 300, Vanderbilt Archives.

120 "Report of the Study of Suggested Recommendations for the Fine Arts Building to be Built on the Campus of the University of Arkansas," Norman Bel Geddes Theater and Industrial Design Papers, Job no. 582, Harry Ransom Center, University of Texas at Austin.

121 Minutes of Special Meeting of the Board of Trustees, University of Arkansas, Little Rock, April 5 and November 2, 1945, University Records, Special Collections, University of Arkansas Libraries. See also Lewis Webster Jones to Stone, November 21, 1952, Stone Papers, 1st acc., box 74.

122 Stone to Haralson and Mott, Architects, March 23, 1948, Stone Papers (unless noted otherwise, the Fine Arts Center records in the Stone Papers are in the 1st acc., boxes 22 and 23); Minutes of Special Meeting of the Board of Trustees, January 6 and February 19, 1948, University Records.

123 Norman deMarco, "A University Art Center," *Library Journal* 78 (July 1953): 1217; "Dr. Edward Stone, Architect of International Prominence, Firm Believer in University of Arkansas Program," *Northwest Arkansas Times*, January 15, 1958; "Modern Architecture on the Campus," *Stanford Review* (November 1960), 12–14.

124 Fulbright to Stone, March 21, 1949, Stone Papers, 1st acc., box 21; Haskell to Robert M. McCambridge, October 29, 1952, Haskell Papers; "University Art Center," Architectural Forum 95 (September 1951): 165; Louchheim, "Architecture Unites Art Center," *New York Times*, November 1, 1953.

125 "Schools and Galleries," *Interiors* 109 (February 1950): 14.

126 "A Program Prepared by Norman Bel Geddes for Edward Stone and Associates," April 1948, Bel Geddes Papers; Stone to Reginald Allen, July 18, 1958, Stone Papers, 1st acc., box 63.

127 "University Art Center": 168; "Estimate for Furniture for Fine Arts Building," August 22, 1949, Stone Papers.

128 Paul Goldberger, "Toward Different Ends," in Barbaralee Diamonstein, ed., *Collaboration: Artists and Architects in Celebration of the Centennial of the Architectural League* (New York: Whitney Library of Design, 1981), 56-57.

129 Press release, March 10, 1950, Architectural League of New York Records, Archives of American Art/Smithsonian (hereafter cited as Architectural League Records); Alexander Calder to Stone, January 3 and July 9, 1951 and June 3, 1955, Calder Foundation, New York. See also Diamonstein, ed., *Collaboration: Artists and Architects*; Joan Ockman, comp., *Architecture Culture 1943–1968: A Documentary Anthology* (New York: Columbia Books of Architecture/Rizzoli, 2003): 64–65, 100–102; Sarah Williams Goldhagen and Réjean Legault, "Introduction: Critical Themes of Postwar Modernism" in *Anxious Modernisms: Experimentation in Postwar Architectural Culture* (Montreal: Canadian Centre for Architecture, 2000), 16.

130 George Rockwise, interview by Suzanne B. Riess, *Thomas D. Church, Landscape Architect*, vol. 1 (Berkeley, Calif.: Regional Oral History Office, Bancroft Library, University of California), 348.

131 Octavo Méndez Guardia to Giuseppe Gigante, January 21, 1954, Stone Papers, 1st acc., box 63.

132 "Statement by Edward Durell Stone for Concrete Products magazine," Stone Papers, 2nd acc., box 65; "Hotel Made for the Tropics," *Architectural Forum* 94 (April 1951): 142.

133 See "Freiderica Hotel," *Architectural Forum* 76 (June 1942): 378–82; "For

Arkansas Travellers," *Interiors* 101 (March 1942): 22–29; H. Ray Burks to Stone, March 2, 1942, Stone Papers, 1st acc., box 64.

134 Stone, *Evolution of an Architect*, 39; Leilani Hotel drawings, Stone Papers, 2nd acc., K24–26.

135 "Hotel Made for the Tropics": 141.

136 Lee to Florence Bates Hayward, April 1, 1950, and to Auerbach, August 1, 1950, Stone Papers, 1st acc., box 61. See also Hunting, "From craft to industry."

137 Back of photograph dated January 6, 1956, in the *New York Times* Photograph Archives, New York.

138 Louchheim, "New Design Proves Worth in Hotels," *New York Times*, June 11, 1950. See also "The Year's Work," *Interiors* 111 (August 1951): 95.

139 "Beehive in the Tropics," *Life*, January 27, 1952; Octavio Méndez Guardia to Stone, February 29, 1952, Stone Papers, 1st acc., box 65.

140 Méndez Guardia to the author, January 19, 2004.

141 Lieutenant General H. R. Harmon to Brigadier General Colby M. Myers, August 28, 1951, and Myers, memorandum to Harmon, September 13, 1951, Special Collections, Academy Libraries, United States Air Force Academy, Colorado Springs.

142 See " 'If I Were Doing It Over Again,' " *Architectural Forum* 98 (January 1953): 106–11.

143 Emily Genauer, "Architect, in Project for New Hotel, Employs Artists' Work Extensively," *New York Herald Tribune*, January 4, 1953.

144 Charles B. Strauss to Stone, c. 1946, Stone Papers, 1st acc, box 53; "Is This the Year to Build Your House?" *House & Garden*, February 1947.

4: A PROVOCATIVE NEW AESTHETIC: NEW ROMANTICISM
pages 78–89

1 Rough draft of "Frank Lloyd Wright Discussion between Frank Jennings and Edward Durell Stone," May 7, 1959, Stone Papers, 2nd acc., box 90.

2 John Kenneth Galbraith, "For Public and Potent Building," *New York Times Magazine*, October 9, 1960.

3 Stone, "Words to Live By: 'Break the Rules!' " *New York Herald Tribune This Week Magazine*, May 8, 1960.

4 J. William Fulbright, "Fayetteville's Ed Stone: A Giant on America's Cultural Stage," *Northwest Arkansas Times*, November 12, 1962.

5 The cartoon, *Meetings and Miscellany*, is in *Architectural Record* 44 (March 1959): 25; Bureau of Overseas Building Operations, United States Department of State, *The Secretary of State's Register of Culturally Significant Property*, Publication 11192 (June 2005), Property no. X1001 (http://www.state.gov/documents/organization/66242.pdf; accessed September 4, 2010).

6 "More than Modern," Art, *Time*, March 31, 1958; Stone, *Evolution of an Architect* (New York: Horizon Press, 1962), 138.

7 Leland King to Stone, July 17, 1953, Loeffler Collection; King, "Notes for the period 1937–1954 on the Office of Foreign Buildings: A History, April 24, 1987," private collection.

8 King, "Abstract of correspondence," November 20, 1950, private collection.

9 Loy Wesley Henderson, interview by Jane C. Loeffler, Loeffler Collection.

10 Loeffler, *The Architecture of Diplomacy: Building America's Embassies* (New York: Princeton Architectural Press, 1998), 58.

11 King to Andree Lynn Abecassis, March 22, 1960, Loeffler Collection. See also Jane de Hart Mathews, "Art and Politics in Cold War America," *American Historical Review* 81 (October 1976): 778, 787; Alfred H. Barr Jr., "Is Modern Art Communistic?" *New York Times*, December 14, 1952; Eva Cockcroft, "Abstract Expressionism, Weapon of the Cold War," in Francis Frascina, ed., *Pollock and After: The Critical Debate* (New York: Harper and Row), 125–34.

12 Mary Anne Staniszewksis, *The Power of Display: A History of Exhibition Installations at the Museum of Modern Art* (Cambridge, Mass.: MIT Press, 2001), 224.

13 G. E. Kidder-Smith to Philip Johnson, October 2, 1953, Curatorial Exhibition Files, Exh. # 543, MoMA Archives. See also "Architect Leland King Dies at 96: Commissioned Bold Embassies," *New York Times*, May 7, 2004.

14 Aline B. Louchheim, "State Department Opens Show Today," *New York Times*, October 7, 1953; Nickie King to Stone, March 26, 1957, private collection.

15 Allan Temko, "Lifting the Federal Façade," *Horizon: A Magazine of Art*, Janu-

ary 1960; "U.S.A. Abroad," *Architectural Forum* 107 (December 1957): 115; King, telephone interview by Loeffler, January 7, 1993, Loeffler Collection.

16 "Statement of Department of State's Architectural Policy and Specific Functions of the Architectural Board for Foreign Buildings," 1954, Shepley Papers.

17 Pietro Belluschi, memorandum to Nelson A. Kenworthy, January 27, 1954, Loeffler Collection.

18 William J. R. Curtis, *Modern Architecture Since 1900* (1982; London: Phaidon Press, 1996), 428.

19 Colin Rowe, Introduction to *Five Architects: Eisenman, Graves, Gwathmey, Hejduk, Meier* (New York: Oxford University Press, 1975), 3–7; Belluschi, "The Meaning of Regionalism in Architecture," *Architectural Record* 118 (December 1955): 131–39.

20 FBO, "Architectural Policy Issued July 7, 1954," Loeffler Collection (unless noted otherwise the FBO Records are in the Loeffler Collection).

21 Stone to Henry Shepley, April 12, 1954, Shepley Papers.

22 Stone to Fulbright, April 13, 1959, Stone Papers, 1st acc., box 70.

23 FBO, Architectural Advisory Meeting Minutes (hereafter cited as AAC Minutes), January 21, August 19, and September 17, 1954, Loeffler Collection.

24 AAC Minutes, March 29, 1955 and July 30, 1956; William P. Hughes to Ellsworth Bunker, March 26, 1957, Stone Papers, 1st acc., box 15.

25 AAC Minutes, March 29, 1955 and Ralph Walker, memorandum to Shepley, Belluschi, and Harry A. McBride, August 15, 1955; Shepley, notes on India, April 26–May 15, 1955, Shepley Papers.

26 "U.S. Embassy for New Delhi," *Architectural Forum* 102 (June 1955): 114.

27 Stone, description of the United States Pavilion at the Brussels Exposition and the American Embassy in New Delhi, India, c. 1959, Stone Papers, 2nd acc., box 51.

28 "U.S. Embassy Building," *Marg* 10 (December 1956): 68.

29 AAC Minutes, October 20, 1954; Stone, telegram to Isamu Noguchi, November 15, 1957, Stone to William P. Hughes, October 3, 1957, Isamu Noguchi Papers, Noguchi Museum Archives, Long Island City, N.Y.; Noguchi to Stone, February 11, 1957 and March 6, 1955, Stone Papers, 1st acc., box 75.

30 AAC Minutes, September 17, 1954; telex, June 8, 1965, on back of the image on p. 82 (bottom).

31 United States Patent Office, "Wall Block," des. 184,463, filed September 18, 1957, issued February 17, 1959.

32 Neil Levine, *Architecture of Frank Lloyd Wright* (New York: Princeton University Press, 1996), 152.

33 Winthrop Sargeant, "From Sassafras Branches: Edward Durell Stone," Profiles, The New Yorker, January 3, 1959.

34 Anne-Marie Sankovitch, "Structure/Ornament and the Modern Figuration of Architecture," *Art Bulletin* 80 (December 1998): 686–717.

35 Stone, description.

36 John Ruskin, *The Stones of Venice*, rev. ed. by J. G. Links (1960; New York: Da Capo Press, 1985), 46.

37 Stone to Kenneth John Conant, May 3, 1965, and Conant to Stone, January 1, 1965, Stone Papers, 1st acc., box 2; Conant, *Carolingian and Romanesque Architecture, 800 to 1200* (Baltimore: Penguin Books, 1959), xxv.

38 "India: American Taj," *Time*, January 12, 1959"; Loeffler, *Architecture of Diplomacy*, 193.

39 "A New Public Architecture," *Architectural Forum* 110 (January 1959): 84. See also Temko, "Lifting the Federal Façade"; Robert A. M. Stern with Raymond W. Gastil, *Modern Classicism* (New York: Rizzoli, 1988), 53.

40 Eero Saarinen to Stone, June 6, 1955, Stone Papers, 2nd acc., box 74.

41 Maria Stone to Douglas Haskell, August 1, 1955, and Haskell to Maria Stone, August 9, 1955, Haskell Papers.

42 "Its News When Wright Lauds an Architect," *Palo Alto Times*, August 3, 1955.

43 Arthur Drexler, "American Architecture: The New Patrons (Tentative Title)," 1957, Curatorial Exhibition Files, Exh. #615, MoMA Archives; Drexler, "Buildings for Business and Government in America," *Zodiac* 1 (1957): 137. See also "A Design Tour de Force Destroys Walls to Turn Illusion into Reality," *Interiors* 116 (May 1957): 132–35.

44 "An Architecture of Space and Grace," *Architectural Forum* 122 (July 1957): 154; Joseph Hudnut, "A New Eloquence for Architecture," *Architectural Record* 122 (July 1957): 179.

45 "India's Great Builder," *Architectural Forum* 110 (February 1959): 55; "More Than Modern."

46 Bunker to Stone, April 8, 1959, Stone Papers, 2nd acc., box 1.

47 "India: American Taj"; Bunker to Henderson, Hughes, and George Allen, November 18, 1958, Office of Foreign Building Operations Records, record group 59, box 689, National Archives and Records Administration, College Park, Md.

48 "An American Builds His Taj," *Statesman*, November 26, 1958. See also Norma Evenson, *The Indian Metropolis: A View Toward the West* (New Haven, Conn.: Yale University Press, 1989), 229; "Diplomatic Temple: America's Embassy Wins India's Praise," *Life*, January 26, 1959.

49 "First Honor Award: United States Embassy," *AIA Journal* 35 (April 1961): 70; Wolf Von Eckardt, *Mid-Century Architecture in America: Honor Awards of the American Institute of Architects, 1949–1961* (Baltimore: John Hopkins Press, 1961), 26. See also Committee on Foreign Relations, "Amendments to the Foreign Service Buildings Act of 1926," August 21, 1962, Loeffler Collection; Fulbright, HR 5207, 88th Cong., *Congressional Record* 109 (May 7, 1963).

50 Paul Goldberger, "Edward Durell Stone Services Will Be Held Tomorrow," *New York Times*, August 8, 1978.

51 Ada Louise Huxtable, "Buildings That Are Symbols, Too," *New York Times*, April 5, 1959, and "Sharp Debate: What Should an Embassy Be?," *New York Times*, September 18, 1960.

52 Goldberger, "Landmark Kitsch: A New Generation of Architects Tries to Save the City's Ugly Ducklings," *The Sky Line*, *The New Yorker*, August 18, 1997; Robin Boyd, "Decoration Rides Again," *Architectural Record* 122 (September 1957): 183. See also Serge Chermayeff, "The Shell Game," *Architectural Forum* 109 (July 1958): 54, 56; William H. Jordy, "The Formal Image: USA," *Architectural Review* 127 (March 1960): 163.

53 Huxtable, "The Patronage of Progress," *Arts*, April 1957; Jordy, "The Formal Image": 163.

54 Stone, quoted in Richard Atcheson, "Edward Durell Stone: Maker of Monuments," *Show*, March 1964; Adolf Loos, "Ornament and Crime," in Ludwig Münz and Gustav Künstler, *Adolf Loos: Pioneer of Modern Architecture*, trans. Harold Meek (New York: Frederick A. Praeger, 1966), 226. See also Reyner Banham, "Ornament and Crime: The Decisive Contribution of Adolf Loos," *Architectural Review* 121 (February 1957): 86.

55 Jordy, "The Formal Image": 159. See also "Le Néo-Classicisme Américain," *L'architecture d'aujourd'hui* 29 (April 1958): 46.

56 Colin Rowe, "Neo-'Classicism' and Modern Architecture I," in *The Mathematics of the Ideal Villa and Other Essays* (Cambridge, Mass.: MIT Press, 1987), 122. See also Von Eckardt, "Las Vegas Is Not Almost All Right," in *Back to the Drawing Board!: Planning Livable Cities* (Washington, D.C.: New Republic Books, 1978), 87; William J. R. Curtis, "Modern Architecture, Monumentality and the Meaning of Institutions: Reflections on Authenticity," *Harvard Architecture Review* 4 (Spring 1984): 67.

57 Spiro Kostof, *History of Architecture: Settings and Rituals* (New York: Oxford University Press, 1985), 729.

58 Mary McLeod, "Undressing Architecture: Fashion, Gender, and Modernity," in Paulette Singley, ed., *Architecture: In Fashion* (New York: Princeton Architectural Press, 1994), 43; Lilian S. Robinson and Lise Vogel, "Modernism and History," *New Literary History* 3 (Autumn 1971): 185. See also Valerie Jaudon and Joyce Kozloff, " 'Art Hysterical Notions' of Progress and Culture," *Heresies: A Feminist Publication on Art and Politics* 4 (Winter 1978): 38–42; Norma Broude, "The Pattern and Decoration Movement," in Broude and Mary D. Garrard, *The Power of Feminist Art* (New York: Harry N. Abrams, 1994), 208; Griselda Pollock, "Modernity and the Spaces of Femininity," in Broude and Garrard, *The Expanding Discourse: Feminism and Art History*, (New York: IconEditions, 1992), 264–65.

59 Le Corbusier and Amédée Ozenfant, quoted in Broude and Garrard, *Feminism and Art History: Questioning the Litany* (New York: Harper and Row, 1982), 15.

60 Herbert Muschamp, "The Secret History," *New York Times*, January 8, 2006.

61 John Burchard and Albert Bush-Brown, *The Architecture of America: A Social and Cultural History* (Boston: Little, Brown and Company, 1966), 489–90; Henry-Russell Hitchcock, *Architecture: Nineteenth and Twentieth Centuries*, 3rd ed. (Harmondsworth, England: Penguin Books, 1963), 430. See also Herbert Muschamp, *File Under Architecture* (Cambridge, Mass.: MIT Press, 1974), 40.

62 Joseph Hudnut, "The Baroque Revival and Its Clients," *ARTnews* 56 (March 1957): 31; Stone, notes, 2nd acc., box 92.

63 Belluschi, "The Meaning of Regionalism in Architecture," 138.

64 John M. Jacobus, *Twentieth-Century Architecture: The Middle Years, 1940–65* (New York: Frederick A. Frederick A. Praeger, 1966), 150–52.

65 Evenson, *Indian Metropolis*, 229.

66 José Luis Sert, Fernand Léger, and Sigfried Giedion, "Nine Points on Monumentality," in Joan Ockman, comp., *Architecture Culture, 1943–1963: A Documentary Anthology* (New York: Rizzoli, 1993), 27. See also Sigfried Giedion, "The Need for a New Monumentality," in Ann Eden Gibson, *Abstract Expressionism: Other Politics* (New Haven, Conn.: Yale University Press, 1997), 54; Louis Kahn, "Monumentality," in Ockman, comp. *Architecture Culture*, 48–54.

67 "More Than Modern."

68 "A New Public Architecture": 84.

69 Public Affairs Office of the U. S. Commissioner General to the Brussels World's Fair–1958, "Status of Construction: U.S. Pavilion," press release no. 42, n.d., International Conferences, Commissions, and Expositions, record group 43, box 22, National Archives and Records Administration (hereafter cited as Exposition Records); Harry Gilroy, "Million Gay Visitors Close Brussels Fair," *New York Times*, October 20, 1958.

70 Dillard Stokes, "Bureaucrats and the Brussels Fair: Why America Is Slated for a 'Humiliation,' " *Human Events* 15 (April 14, 1958): 15.

71 The baron Moens de Fernig to Frederick M. Alger, December 13, 1955, Exposition Records, box 1.

72 Paul Child, dispatch to Joseph B. Phillips, May 9, 1955, Exposition Records, box 16.

73 The baron Moens de Fernig to Alger.

74 Landreth M. Harrison, "Brussels Fair—AIA—Purvis—Building," memorandum for the files, February 27, 1956, and "Brussels Fair-1958-Building Plans—AIA," memorandum for the files, March 2, 1958, Exposition Records, box 8. See also Dianne Ludman Frank, *Hugh Stubbins and His Associates: The First Fifty Years* (Cambridge, Mass.: Stubbins, 1986), 26–27, 132; Barbara Miller Lane, "The Berlin Congress Hall, 1955–1957," *Perspectives in American History* 1 (1984): 131–85; "Dedication of Berlin Congress Hall," *Memo: A Newsletter*, no. 171 (September 9, 1957), AIA Archives.

75 Edmund R. Purves to Harrison, March 14, 1956, Exposition Records, box 8; AIA advisory committee, "The Report of the Activities on the Brussels International Exposition Building for the Department of State," October 4, 1956, Stone Papers, 1st acc., box 18; Harrison, "Brussels Exhibition 1958—State—AIA Meeting on Architectural Matters," memorandum for the files, March 19, 1956, Exposition Records, box 8; AIA advisory committee, "Report of the Activities," and Earl Heitschmidt to Jury of Fellows, December 10, 1957, AIA Archives.

76 Heitschmidt to Jury of Fellows.

77 "Special International Report: World's Fair—Brussels '58," *Newsweek*, April 1, 1957; Harrison, "Brussels Exhibition 1958—Architectural Meeting," memorandum for the files, October 3, 1956, Exposition Records, box 8; AIA advisory committee, "Report of the Activities"; Stone, description; Ken Frizzell to Harrison, October 23, 1956, Exposition Records, box 11.

78 Haskell, memorandum to staff, August 7, 1958, Haskell Papers; Joe Reddy, "Circarama Showing American Spectacle at Brussels Fair," press release #9945, Walt Disney Archives, Burbank, Calif.

79 "5 U.S. Sculptors for Fair Chosen," *New York Times*, October 27, 1957; Ogden Tanner, "The Best of Brussels," *Architectural Forum* 108 (June 1958): 80; Jean-Louis Lhoest, "This Is America! This Candy-Box in White and Gold Lace Is a Fantastic Surprise-Box," *Le Peuple*, April 23, 1958.

80 Forrest Wilson, *Emerging Form in Architecture: Conversations with Lev Zetlin* (Boston: Cahners Books, 1975), 83–84; Henry J. Cowan, *Science and Building: Structural and Environmental Design in the Nineteenth and Twentntational eth Centuries* (New York: John Wiley and Sons, 1978), 180. See also Hitchcock, *Modern Architecture: Romanticism and Reintegration* (New York: Payson and Clark, 1929), 207.

81 Cowan, *Science and Building*, 180; Stone, *Evolution of an Architect*, 146. See also Brigitte Schroeder-Gudehus, "Popularizing Science and Technology During the Cold War," 157–80; "The Brussels Exhibition," *Architects' Journal* 127 (May 29, 1958): 790–845.

82 Quoted in Robert W. Rydell, *World of Fairs: The Century-of-Progress Expositions* (Chicago: University of Chicago Press, 1993), 202.

83 Sargeant, "From Sassafras Branches."

84 "Memorandum on the Design of the United States Pavilion Brussels Exposition," Stone Papers, 1st acc., box 18. See also "A Final Look at Brussels," *Architectural Forum* 109 (October 1958): 104–9.

85 "An Architecture of Space and Grace": 156; Stone to James Plout, March 11, 1958, Stone Papers, 1st acc., box 21.

86 Stone, "Address Given to the NAEA Conference, Kansas City [Mo.]," 1963, Stone Papers, 1st. acc., box 2.

87 See Sir Banister Fletcher, *A History of Architecture on the Comparative Method*, rev. by R. A. Cordingley, 17th ed. (London: Athlone Press/University of London, 1961), 210–13.

88 Eddy Gilmore, "Russia Expected to Outshine U.S. World's Fair," *Roanoke Times*, March 27, 1958.

89 Christopher Rand, "Letter from Brussels," *The New Yorker*, March 29, 1958. See also Gaston Coblentz, "Reds at Brussels Outdo Low-Budget U.S. Show," *New York Herald Tribune*, February 5, 1958; United States Information Agency, European Press Reaction: Comments on U.S. Pavilion and Others, 1958, Exposition Records, box 13; "More Than Modern"; "Brussels ... A Special Report: Where East Meets West, The U.S. at the Fair," *Newsweek*, April 14, 1958.

90 Malcolm Stevenson Forbes, Fact and Comment, *Forbes*, July 1, 1958. See also "U.S. Faces Task at Brussels Fair: Lack of Funds May Bring Loss of World Supremacy in Showmanship to Russia," *Los Angeles Times*, March 23, 1958; Jerry Hulse, "Miniature World Unfolds at Fair," *Los Angeles Times*, April 23, 1958.

91 Howard Taubman, "Brussels: American Mistakes and Lessons: A 'Hotchpotch' Approach, Says a Visitor, Has Marred America's Portrait at the Fair," *New York Times Magazine*, June 1, 1958. See also Keith N. Morgan and Richard Cheek, "History in the Service of Design: American Architect-Historians, 1870–1940," *Architectural Historian in America* 35 (1990): 72; Maura Reynolds, "Bernard Rudofsky, 82, Architect and 'Outspoken' Social Analyst," *New York Times*, March 13, 1988; Heitschmidt to Harrison, April 24, 1956, and Stone to Harrison, April 27, 1956, Stone Papers, 1st acc., box 18; Harrison to Heitschmidt, June 14, 1956, Exposition Records, box 8. See also Harrison, memorandum to staff, September 19, 1956, Exposition Records, box 16; Harrison to Purves, September 27, 1956, Exposition Records, box 8; United States Department of State, "Howard Cullman Sworn in as the United States Commissioner General," press release, October 3, 1956, Exposition Records, box 16.

92 John D. Morris, "Brussels Exhibit Irks Eisenhower," *New York Times*, June 18, 1958; George V. Allen, Statement about the Brussels Pavilion, June 39, 1958, Exposition Records, box 11.

93 Statements of Adlai Stevenson and of Herbert Hoover, July 5, 1958, Exposition Records, box 11; "An Architect Goes East," *Newsweek*, November 17, 1958. See also P.G. Nicholson to Stone, July 7, 1958, Stone Papers, 1st acc., box 69.

94 The letters are in the Exposition Records, box 11.

95 "Brussels '58: The United States Speaks to the World": 158; Rydell, *World of Fairs*, 11. See also Sarah Williams Goldhagen and Réjean Legault, "Introduction: Critical Themes of Postwar Modernism," in *Anxious Modernisms: Experimentation in Postwar Architectural Culture* (Montreal: Canadian Centre for Architecture, 2000), 17.

96 See Deborah Desilets, *Morris Lapidus* (New York: Assouline, 2004), 14.

97 Haskell, "Architecture and Popular Taste," *Architectural Forum* 109 (August 1958): 106.

98 Haskell, memorandum to staff, August 7, 1958, Haskell Papers.

99 "A Final Look at Brussels": 105.

100 Cullman, "Opening of the United States Pavilion at the Brussels Universal and International Exhibition," *News from the Office of the US Commissioner General*, April 17, 1958, Exposition Records, box 22.

5: ARCHITECTURE AS COMMODITY pages 90–109

1 Edward Durell Stone, "This Is Our Own, Our Native Land," Stone Papers, 2nd acc., box 92.

2 "More than Modern," Art, *Time*, March 31, 1958.

3 See Mary McLeod, "Architecture and Politics in the Reagan Era: From Postmodernism to Deconstructivism," *Assemblage* 8 (February 1989): 23–59.

4 "Most talked-about house in New York City," Vogue's Fashions in Living, *Vogue*, February 1, 1958.

5 Stone, "The Case Against the Tailfin Age," *New York Times*, October 18, 1959. See also "One Man's Revolt Against the Tailfin Age," *Reader's Digest*, February 1960.

6 See, for example, "Innovating Architect: Edward D. Stone," *New York Times*, April 18, 1958; John M. Jacobus, *Twentieth-Century Architecture: The Middle Years, 1940–65* (New York: Frederick A. Frederick A. Praeger, 1966), 152–53.

7 "Forecast 1959," *House & Garden*, January 1959.

8 "A New Public Architecture," *Architectural Forum* 110 (January 1959): 84.

9 Thomas H. Creighton, "The New Sensualism," *Progressive Architecture* 40 (September 1959): 145.

10 Ada Louise Huxtable, "The Lollipop Building: The Best Way to Preserve 2 Columbus Circle? A Makeover," *Wall Street Journal*, January 7, 2004.

11 Huxtable, "Pop Architecture Here to Stay: Mass Taste Creates a Mass Art that Reveals Face of America in the Sixties," *New York Times*, October 4, 1964.

12 Stuart Ewen, *All Consuming Images: The Politics of Style in Contemporary Culture* (New York: Basic Books, 1988), 231; Joseph Bensman and Bernard Rosenberg, *Mass, Class, and Bureaucracy: The Evolution of Contemporary Society* (Englewood Cliffs, N.J.: Prentice-Hall, 1963), 345; John W. Cook and Klotz Heinrich, *Conversations with Architects* (New York: Frederick A. Praeger, 1973), 198.

13 *Ed Sullivan Show*, SOFA Entertainment, February 2, 1958.

14 "Most talked-about house"; Stone, interview by Gary Moore, *Person to Person*, CBS, February 14, 1958.

15 *What's My Line?* Mark Goodson Bill Todman Production, August 10, 1958.

16 "Most talked-about house"; Stone to Allison Bisgood, February 12, 1958, Stone Papers, 1st acc., box 75; "More than Modern." See also Ludwig Lauerhass to Edward R. Murrow, October 26, 1956 Lauerhass Papers.

17 Stone to Harris K. Prior, August 12, 1958, AFA Records. See also *Form Givers At Mid-Century* (New York: Time Inc./American Federation of Arts, 1959).

18 A copy of the script is in the Time Archives.

19 "More than Modern"; "Honor for Architects: Four Here are Among Twenty Elected to Institute," *New York Times*, April 27, 1958; "First Honor Award: The Stuart Company," *AIA Journal* 30 (July 1958): 32; "Architects' Institute Selects Best Building Design of Year," *New York Times*, May 26, 1958; "Honor Awards," *Memo: A Newsletter*, no. 186 (May 26, 1958): 2, AIA Archives; Lauerhass to Stone, May 5, 1958, Stone Papers, 1st acc., box 69.

20 Douglas Haskell, memorandum to staff, September 13, 1957, Haskell Papers.

21 See Harry Anderson, "Edward Durell Stone: Architect," *Interior Design* 30 (May 1959): 126A.

22 "Dr. Edward Stone, Architect of International Prominence," *Northwest Arkansas Times*, January 15, 1958.

23 Lauerhass to Stone, May 15, 1958, Stone Papers, 1st acc. box 69.

24 "U.S. Pavilion Architect to Build 'Trade Temple,' " *New York Times*, August 17, 1958.

25 Stone to Clare Boothe Luce, May 26 and September 5, 1958, CBL Papers.

26 Luce to Stone, August 21, 1958, CBL Papers. See also "Luce Plantation Slated To Become Monastery," *New York Times*, August 10, 1949; Father M. Benedict Gemignani, *An Account of the Foundation of Our Lady of Mepkin of the Cistercian Order of the Strict Observance in South Carolina and Its Subsequent History, 1949–1964* (Moncks Corner, S.C.: Our Lady of Mepkin, 1964), CBL Papers.

27 Stone to Luce, September 5, 1958, CBL Papers.

28 "New Work in the Office of Ed Stone," *Architectural Forum* 115 (October 1961): 127. See also "Stone Designs a Sylvan Retreat for Monks," *New York Times*, April 11, 1965.

29 Stone to Peter Pfisterer, October 30, 1951, Stone Papers, 1st acc., box 38; "600 Bed Hospital in Arkansas Changes the Health Map," *Architectural Forum* 93 (July 1950): 90–95.

30 Stone to Señor Doctor Don Armando Montes de Peralta, February 18, 1955, Stone Papers, 1st acc., box 63.

31 Stone to Pfisterer.

32 "Peru Hospital Sets New Standards," *Progressive Architecture* 36 (October 1955): 81; "Two Approaches to Hospital Design," *Architectural Record* 122 (October 1957): 231. See also "Big Double Hospital," *Architectural Forum* 96 (June 1952): 138–44.

33 John Long Wilson, chapter XXXVII, "Stanford University School of Medicine

and the Predecessor Schools: An Historical Perspective," 1998 (http://elane.stanford.edu/wilson/html/toc.html; accessed March 23, 2010).

34 Stone to Haskell, July 28, 1950, Stone Papers, 1st acc., box 23; "600 Bed Hospital in Arkansas": 90–95; Stone to Shepley, August 11, 1955, Stone Papers, 1st acc., box 73; John Carl Warnecke to Stone, May 11, 1955, Stone Papers, 1st acc., box 14; Stone, *Evolution of an Architect* (New York: Horizon Press, 1962), 40; Harvie Branscomb to Dr. H. Kaplan, January 28, 1953, box 300, Vanderbilt Archives.

35 "Consultants for P.A., Stanford Hospitals are Called Pioneers in Design by Magazine," *Palo Alto Times*, November 16, 1955; "The Flattened-Out Hospital," *Architectural Forum* 103 (November 1955): 166–69; Lewis Mumford, Memorandum on Planning, 1947, Planning Office, box 2, Special Collections and University Archives, Stanford University Libraries, Stanford, Calif.

36 Ernest E. Jacks, "The Elegant Bohemian: Tales of Architect Edward Durell Stone" (ca. 2000), 58–59, private collection.

37 Stone to Shepley, August 11, 1955; George J. Young (for John C. Hill) to Mary Jane Lightbown, October 31, 1959, Stone Papers, 1st acc., box 51.

38 "Garden Hospital Design Approved by University," *Palo Alto Times*, January 25, 1956; "Medicine's New 'Taj Mahal,'" *Architectural Forum* 111 (December 1959): 98.

39 "Garden Hospital Design Approved"; "Dedication to Begin New Medical Era," *Daily Palo Alto Times*, September 15, 1959.

40 Young to Lightbown.

41 Laura Jones, "A Little Versailles for the Sick," *Sandstone and Tile* [publication of the Stanford Historical Society] 32 (Fall 2008): 3.

42 Medicine's New 'Taj Mahal' ": 98. See also "Stone's 'Garden Hospital' Approaches Completion," p/a news report, *Progressive Architecture* 40 (April 1959): 81; "New $21 Million Medical School," *Life*, November 2, 1959.

43 Alice T. Friedman, *American Glamour and the Evolution of Modern Architecture* (New Haven, Conn.: Yale University Press, 2010), 5; Joseph Rosa with others, eds., *Glamour: Fashion + Industrial Design + Architecture* (San Francisco Museum of Modern Art/Yale University Press, New Haven and London, 2004).

44 Matei Călinescu, *Five Faces of Modernity* (Durham, N.C.: Duke University Press, 1987), 241.

45 Stone to Stanley Torkelsen and Dick Snibbe, August 9, 1955, Stone Papers, 1st acc., box 75.

46 Stone to Torkelson and Snibble; Person to Person, CBS, New York, February 14, 1958.

47 "Award Citations with Commendation," *Progressive Architecture* 37 (January 1956): 82. See also Paige Phelps, "Dallas Couple Wins National Award for Restoring Historic Home," *Dallas Morning News*, October 24, 2008; "Updating A Classic," *Architectural Digest*, October 2008.

48 "Tile Council Bathroom—Guiding Principles," August 3, 1954, Stone Papers, 1st acc., box 48.

49 Stone to William H. Patterson, October 4, 1956, University Records, South Caroliniana Library, University of South Carolina, Columbia (hereafter cited as USC Records).

50 Haskell to staff, August 28, 1957, Haskell Papers; Stone to Patterson; "Poetic Space—A Private Retreat," *Town & Country*, August 1958. See also Curtis Besinger, "The Traditional Graces Give Elegance to this New Environment," *House Beautiful*, November 1959; "Contrast in Texas," *Architectural Forum* 109 (July 1958): 82–87; "The Super-American State: IV—You and Non-You," Profiles, *The New Yorker*, April 8, 1961.

51 "Poetic Space—A Private Retreat"; "Architecture of Ideas," *House & Home* 21 (March 1962): 121.

52 AAC Minutes, July 26, 1957; Stone to William P. Hughes, June 11, 1959, and Harry Turko to L. V. Del Fabero, November 19, 1959, Stone Papers, 1st acc., box 16; Stone to R. Stanley, February 15, 1960, Stone Papers, 1st acc., box 76.

53 John Kenneth Galbraith, *Ambassador's Journal: A Personal Account of the Kennedy Years* (Boston: Houghton Mifflin, 1969), 42. See also Stone to R. Stanley Sweeley, January 15 and February 15, 1960, Stone Papers, 1st acc., box 76.

54 "Open Diplomacy," Design, *Time*, April 12, 1963; Richard Critchfield, "Our Fancy Embassy in India: A White Elephant is Put to Work," *San Francisco Chronicle*, May 20, 1964.

55 Critchfield, "Our Fancy Embassy." See also Charlotte Curtis, "Décor Ideas are Chosen by Women," *New York Times*, July 20, 1962; "Costly 16-Bed Hotel: U.S. Envoy Spurns New Delhi Mansion," *Los Angeles Times*, September 27, 1963;

Galbraith to Anne D. Nissen, December 7, 1981, Loeffler Collection; Thomas F. Brady, "U.S. Embassy in New Delhi Offers a Challenge," *New York Times*, March 20, 1963."

56 Huxtable, "Idlewild: Distressing Monument to Air Age," *New York Times*, November 25, 1962; Norval Whitle and Elliot Willensky, *AIA Guide to New York City*, rev. ed. (New York: Macmillan Publishing, 1978), 528; Jacks, "Elegant Bohemian," 298; "Port Authority Re-Elects Heads," *New York Times*, April 12, 1957.

57 "The World's Most Beautiful Service Station," *Orange Disc* (May–June 1960), Collection of Policy, Government and Public Affairs, Chevron Corporation, San Ramon, Calif.

58 "Palo Alto to Dedicate New Main Library Saturday," *Palo Alto Times*, July 17, 1958. See also "Educational Work of Edward D. Stone," *Architectural Record* 123 (February 1958): 192–95; "The Work of Edward Durell Stone," *Architectural Record* 125 (March 1959): 164–69; Dale R. Wirsing, "Palo Alto Builds Main and Branch," *Library Journal* 84 (December 1, 1959): 3677–79; Frederick Mulholland, "A New Building with a Difference," *California Librarian* 20 (January 1959): 48–71.

59 "Palace for Pills," Art, *Time*, January 20, 1958; "The Stuart Company, Owner, Pasadena California," promotional material, June 1958, Stone Papers, 2nd acc., box 51. See also National Register of Historic Places, Stuart Company Plant and Office Building, Pasadena, Los Angeles County, Calif., NR #94001326.

60 Stone to Torkelson and Snibbe, August 2, 1955, Stone Papers, 1st acc. Box 11; Thomas Dolliver Church, *Gardens are for People: How to Plan for Outdoor Living* (New York: Reinhold, 1955), 38, 43, 216.

61 Robert C. Agee, article draft, May 7, 1958, Lauerhaus Papers.

62 Jacks, "Elegant Bohemian," 78; Arthur Hanisch to Stone, October 16, 1958, Stone Papers, 1st acc., box 70; Hanisch to Francis Brennan, August 28, 1964, Stone Papers, 2nd acc., box 83; Joyce C. Hall to Lauerhass, September 22, 1958, Stone Papers, 1st acc., box 69; Hanisch to Stone, May 28, 1959, Stone Papers, 1st acc., box 70; Stone to Hanisch, July 15 and August 18, 1960, Stone Papers, 1st acc., box 77. See also Huxtable, "Some New Faces on Fifth Avenue," *New York Times*, November 8, 1964; "The Red Carpet Is Out on Fifth Avenue," *Los Angeles Times*, June 21, 1964; "Plans for Pasadena Cultural Center Drawn," *Los Angeles Times*, November 27, 1960; Henry J. Seldis, "Plans for Pasadena's Culture Center Shown," *Los Angeles Times*, January 26, 1962.

63 "A Delicately Screened Factory," *Architectural Forum* 108 (April 1958): 9. See also "Splendor in the Factory," *Architectural Record* 123 (April 1958): 161–68; "Selected Factories at Home and Abroad," *Architectural Design* 29 (August 1959): 320–22.

64 "New Work, Serene and Classic":142.

65 Lauerhass to Elizabeth Gordon, May 2, 1958, Lauerhaus Papers.

66 "Architects Institute Selects Best Building Designs of Year," *New York Times*, May 25, 1958; "'Ten Top Plants of 1959' Get Factory Awards," The Record Reports, *Architectural Record* 126 (November 1959): 48; "City's Architecture Reflects History," *(Pasadena) Star-News*, April 22, 1963.

67 "Palace for Pills"; "Plush Headquarters: $3 Million Business Plant Holds Opening," *Star-News*, January 8, 1958.

68 Haskell, "Ornament Rides Again," editorial, *Architectural Forum* 108 (April 1958): 85.

69 Stone, *Evolution of an Architect*, 196.

70 Jacks, "Elegant Bohemian," 38.

71 Harmon to Stone, August 13, 1956, USC Records.

72 Stone to Patterson, July 18, 1956, USC Records; Harmon to Stone, November 2, 1956, Stone Papers, 1st acc., box 65.

73 Edward Waugh and Elizabeth Waugh, *The South Builds: New Architecture in the Old South* (Chapel Hill: University of North Carolina Press, 1960), 67; Allan Temko, "The Dawn of 'High Modern,'" *Horizon: A Magazine of the Arts*, September 1959.

74 Museum of Modern Art, *Modern Architecture U.S.A.* (New York: Museum of Modern Art, 1965), figs. 40, 41.

75 "Educational Work of Edward Durell Stone": 184; "An Embassy Too Beautiful to Enlarge," *Atlanta Journal*, June 10, 1965.

76 Jacks, "Elegant Bohemian," 73–74.

77 "More than Modern"; "'Character' Keynoted in City Houses," *New York Herald Tribune*, June 14, 1959.

78 "Most talked-about house," 171; Huxtable, *Four Walking Tours of Modern*

Architecture in the City of New York (New York: Museum of Modern Art/Municipal Art Society, 1964): 63.

79 Robert Venturi, Denise Scott Brown, and Steven Izenour, *Learning from Las Vegas: The Forgotten Symbolism of Architectural Form* (1977; Cambridge, Mass: MIT Press, 2001), 74.

80 Cynthia Kellogg, "Filigree Arrives," *New York Times Magazine*, December 1, 1957.

81 Winzola McLendon, "Jet-Age Architect Stone: Cupid's Arrow Outflew His Plane," *Washington Post*, November 29, 1959.

82 McLendon, "Jet-Age Architect"; Eleanor Early, "Consulting Architect for National Cultural Center is Man of Monumental Achievement," *Diplomat*, August 1959; Stone, *Evolution of an Architect*, 142.

83 Haskell to Lightbown, May 23, 1957, and to Hazen, November 13, 1957, Haskell Papers; "Profile of an Architect," *Christian Science Monitor*, September 26, 1962.

84 "Most talked-about house"; "More than Modern"; Person to Person; Early, "Consulting Architect for National Cultural Center"; "Innovating Architect."

85 Timothy M. Rohan, "Rendering the Surface: Paul Rudolph's Art and Architecture Building at Yale," *Gray Room* 1 (Fall 2000), 209–10.

86 Maria Stone to Bisgood, May 19, 1960, Stone Papers, 1st acc., box 77; "Fantasia," *Modern Living*, *Time*, April 13, 1962. See also "Duplex on Park," *Interior Design* 31 (August 1960): 82–87; John Anderson, "Park Avenue Penthouse," *Interiors* 120 (August 1960): 60–65. See also Natasha Fraser-Cavassoni, *Sam Spiegel: The Biography of a Hollywood Legend* (London: Time Warner Paperbacks, 2004), 227.

87 "Arena-Style Theater-in-Park Ready July 15," *New York Herald Tribune*, June 3, 1959; Jo-ann Price, "Central Park Theater Over the Skating Rink," *New York Herald Tribune*, July 6, 1959; Walter Terry, "Opening Night of the Central Park Theater," *New York Herald Tribune*, July 17, 1959.

88 Ken Cole, telex, November 24, 1959, Time Archives; Stone to Lloyd Flood, September 8, 1958, Stone Papers, 2nd acc., box 69; "The Work of Edward Durell Stone":170–72.

89 Eldon Elder and Stone, "Two thousand seat open-air theater," and Elder to Stone, January 26, 1962, Stone Papers, 1st acc., box 61; "Ideal Theater: Daring Theatrical Exhibit Displayed," *Los Angeles Times*, January 30, 1962; Margaret Cogswell, ed., *Designs for Eight New Theaters* (New York: American Federation of Arts, 1962); Ideal Theatre folder, AFA Records.

90 Early, "Consulting Architect for National Cultural Center."

91 A selection of articles about the house include: "The Celanese Family of Fibers," *American Fabrics* 51 (Fall 1960–Winter 1960): 75–82; "The Celanese House," *Interiors* 119 (September 1959): 132–39; "Edward Stone Puts Fanciful Ideas to Practical Use," *House & Home*, September 1959; "The House with the Built-In Sky," *House & Garden*, October 1959. See also Jay Fielden, "From Glass House to Your House," *Departures*, May/June 2011.

92 Modern Homes Surveys, New Canaan, Conn. (http://www.preservationnation.org/travel-and-sites/sites/northeast-region/new-canaan-ct/sites/celanese-house.html; accessed April 10, 2010).

93 Ralph Blumenthal, "Cattle Display Draws Many in the Field," *New York Times*, September 12, 1966; "New Work, Serene and Classic": 138–41.

94 "Bold New Plan for Best Land Use," *Life*, September 22, 1958. See also "Famed Architect Ed Stone Designed This House," *Architectural Forum* 14 (November 1958): 128–31; "Demonstration Home by Edw. Stone Shown," *Los Angeles Times*, January 18, 1959; Jeffrey Head, "Unearthing Stone," January 2, 2008 (http://www.metropolismag.com/story/20080102/unearthing-stoneag.com; accessed September 22, 2009).

95 "Bold New Plan for Best Land Use."

96 Stone, "The American Landscape," April 18, 1960, Stone Papers, 2nd acc., box 92.

97 ". . . Architect Edward D. Stone Has A Remedy," *Oakville* (Ontario Canada) *Record-Star*, November 20, 1958.

98 "Florida Should Consider New Concept in House," *Tampa Tribune*, October 5, 1958.

99 Stone, quoted in Emma Grace Hall, "Directions in Modern Architecture: A conversation with Edward D. Stone, *Gentleman's Quarterly*, April 1959"; Stone, "Hero Prophet Adventurer," *Saturday Review*, November 7, 1959.

100 Stone, "The Name of the Game is Beauty," notes for a California Building Congress meeting, September 1967, private collection.

101 Kenneth J. Conant to Stone, January 1, 1965, Stone Papers, 2nd acc., box 2; Jacks, "Elegant Bohemian," 223–25.

102 William S. Culbertson to Stone, June 23, 1959, HRL Papers, box 45; Jacks, "Elegant Bohemian," 223.

103 Stone, *Evolution of an Architect*, 152, 224–25; National Presbyterian Church fact sheet, Stone Papers, 1st acc., box 64.

104 Brennan to Henry R. Luce, December 16, 1959, Francis Edwin Brennan Papers, box 18, Manuscript Division, Library of Congress (hereafter cited as Brennan Papers).

105 Emmie Nollen to Luce, April 6, 1960, Brennan Papers, box 18; Brennan to Luce, March 30, 1960, HRL Papers, box 18.

106 Architectural League of New York, "Exhibition of Competition Drawings for the London Embassy," press release, June 1956, Architectural League Records; "Candidates Named for U.S. London Embassy Design Contest," People, *Architectural Forum* 103 (December 1955): 29.

107 "New US Embassy for London," *Architectural Forum* 108 (April 1958): 140; "Winning Design for American Embassy in London," *Architect's Journal* 122 (April 12, 1956): 346–48.

108 Reginald Allen, memorandums, July 17 and 18, 1958, Lincoln Center for the Performing Arts Archives, New York.

109 Antonio Román, *Eero Saarinen: An Architecture of Multiplicity* (New York; Princeton Architectural Press, 2003), 2–23.

110 Walter McQuade, "The Architects: A Chance for Greatness," *Fortune*, January 1966.

6: FROM ARCHITECTURAL KITSCH TO POPULISM
pages 110–121

1 Edward Durell Stone, quoted in Richard Atcheson, "Edward Durell Stone: Maker of Monuments," *Show*, March 1964.

2 See Gillo Dorfles, *Kitsch: The World of Bad Taste* (New York: Bell, 1968); Tomas Kulka, *Kitsch and Art* (University Park: Pennsylvania State University Press, 2002), 16.

3 Huntington Hartford, "Pushovers," in *Art or Anarchy? How the Extremists and Exploiters Have Reduced the Fine Arts to Chaos and Commercialism* (Garden City, N.Y.: Doubleday and Company, 1964), 63. See also Serge Guilbaut, "The New Adventures of the Avant-Garde in America," in Francis Frascina, ed., *Pollock and After: The Critical Debate* (New York: Harper and Row, 1985), 153–66; Guilbaut, *How New York Stole the Idea of Modern Art: Abstract Expressionsim, Freedom, and the Cold War* (Chicago: University of Chicago Press, 1983).

4 "Here is the Gallery of Modern Art, *New York Village Voice*, June 13, 1956; "The House That Hartford Built," Emily Genauer on Art, *New York Herald Tribune*, September 1, 1963.

5 See "One Man's Taste," Art, *Time*, March 27, 1964; Katharine Kuh, "The Ironies of Art," The Fine Arts, *Saturday Review*, September 25, 1965, and "New York's Modern Merry-Go-Round," The Fine Arts, *Saturday Review*, March 21, 1964; Stuart Preston, "More Space for Modern Art," Letter From New York, *Apollo* (March 1964): 244–45; John Canaday, "Those Pre-Raphaelites," *New York Times*, April 26, 1964; Carl J. Weinhardt Jr., "Why Manhattan Needs Another Museum," *Show*, March 1964; Olga Gueft, "Non-Conformity on Columbus Circle," *Interiors* 123 (June 1964): 92; "A Gallery of Modern Art," *Regina (Canada) Leader-Post*, May 15, 1964; "Hartford Has Nearly Everything," *West Palm Beach Post-Times*, February 9, 1964.

6 Sanka Knox, "Art Museum at Columbus Circle Planned by Huntington Hartford," *New York Times*, June 11, 1956; "Here is the Gallery of Modern Art."

7 Adrian H. Phillips to Hartford, August 16, 1957, New York Cultural Center Collection, Fairleigh Dickinson University Library, Florham-Madison Campus, Madison, N.J. (hereafter cited as NYCC Collection).

8 Knox, "Art Museum at Columbus Circle."

9 Stanley [Torkelsen], memorandum to Stone, June 12, 1956, Stone Papers, 2nd acc., box 62; Stone, memorandum [to Torkelsen], June 14, 1956, Stone Papers, 1st acc., box 81.

10 Charles Nagel to Winslow Ames, September 26, 1957, Pietro Belluschi to Hartford, April 29, 1957, and Hartford to Belluschi, May 13, 1957, NYCC Collection; "Architect Picked for Art Museum," *New York Times*, May 19, 1958; Harry Turko to Stone, April 29 1958, Stone Papers, 1st acc., box 69; "Ed

Stone to Design Manhattan Art Gallery," *Architectural Forum* 109 (July 1958): 11; Douglas Haskell to Stone, July 3, 1958, and Mar Lib Young, memorandum to Haskell, July 3, 1958, Haskell Papers.

11 Turko to Stone.

12 Hartford, interview by Paul Cummings, May 19, 1970, Archives of America Art/Smithsonian (http://www.aaa.si.edu/collections/oralhistories/transcripts/hartfo70.htm; accessed May 18, 2010); Hartford, *You Are What You Write* (New York: Macmillan, 1973), 292–93.

13 Hartford, interview by Cummings; Stone, "What Architecture Should Be," *Show*, March 1964; Stone, *The Evolution of an Architect* (New York: Horizon Press, 1962), 150.

14 Turko to David Sher, September 20, 1960, Stone Papers, 1st acc., box 77; Ernest E. Jacks, "The Elegant Bohemian: Tales of Architect Edward Durell Stone" (ca. 2000), 133, private collection; Lisa Rebecca Gubernick, *Squandered Fortune: The Life and Times of Huntington Hartford* (New York: G. P. Putnam's Sons, 1991), 73–75; 125–26; Suzanna Andrews, "Hostage to Fortune," *Vanity Fair*, December 2004

15 Stone to Bill Bierach, January 22, 1959, and to Sher, December 2, 1960, Stone Papers, 1st acc., box 78; David Lyle, "Art Gallery Wins, Shoe Store to Go," *New York Herald Tribune*, February 29, 1960; Aline B. Saarinen, "Museums Go to Law for Right To A Name," *New York Times*, February 1, 1959"; Canaday, "Hartford Names His Gallery Head," *New York Times*, August 28, 1963; Grace Glueck, "Director Leaves Modern Gallery," *New York Times*, October 19, 1965; Hartford, interview by Cummings.

16 Stone, "What Architecture Should Be."

17 "An Architecture of Space and Grace," *Architectural Record* 122 (July 1957): 167–68.

18 Jacks, "Elegant Bohemian," 132.

19 Stone, *Evolution of an Architect*, 204.

20 "Here is the Gallery of Modern Art"; "Huntington Hartford to Build Art Gallery," *New York Herald Tribune*, June 11, 1956.

21 Laurence Vail Coleman to Hartford, August 7, 1958, and Ames to Hartford, August 11 and 19, and September 3, 1958; NYCC Collection; Stone to Hartford, August 30, 1961, Stone Papers, 1st acc., box 78.

22 Ames to Hartford, June 18, 1959, NYCC Collection; Stone, "What Architecture Should Be;" Emma Grace Hall, "Directions in Modern Architecture: A conversation with Edward D. Stone, *Gentleman's Quarterly*, April 1959."

23 "The New Architecture," *Time*, April 27, 1959; Atcheson, "Stone: Maker of Monuments"; Stone, manuscript for *Evolution of an Architect*, Stone Papers, 2nd acc., box 92.

24 Hartford, interview by Cummings; Jean Lincoln to Ames, September 4, 1958, NYCC Collection; Jerome Zukosky, "A Posh Place For Pictures," *New York Herald Tribune*, September 9, 1962.

25 "Art Gallery," *Architectural International* 1 (1965): 82; William Wolf, "World's Tallest Museum: Hartford Art Gallery Opens Friday," March 1964, NYCC Collection; Stone, "What Architecture Should Be."

26 Ames to Samuel Baum, December 19, 1960, NYCC Collection; Mildred Hull obituary, *Palm Beach Daily News*, December 11, 1993.

27 "House That Hartford Built."

28 Peter Blake, "The Museum Explosion," *Art in America*, no. 2 (1964): 103.

29 Hartford, interview by Cummings; Ames to Stone, November 24, 1959, NYCC Collection.

30 Hartford, cablegram to Ames, July 1, 1959, NYCC Collection.

31 William Rollins, "Is UN Nitery a Museum Piece?" *New York Standard*, February 6, 1963.

32 Preston, "Conservative Realism Resurgent: Other Shows Eclipsed by Hartford Opening," *Art*, *New York Times*, March 21, 1964; Andrew A. Bradick, letter to the editor, *Time*, April 10, 1964.

33 Thomas Buckley, "Huntington Hartford's White Marble Tower Is Open," *New York Times*, March 22, 1964; "4,719 at Modern Gallery Set Attendance Record," *New York Times*, April 2, 1964.

34 Richard F. Shepard, "Hartford Talks of Varied Plans," *New York Times*, December 11, 1964; Genauer, "The First Year on Columbus Circle," *New York Herald Tribune*, March 8, 1965.

35 Genauer, "The First Year"; Blake, "Museum Explosion": 102; Brian Doherty, "A Millionaire Art Buff Takes on the Bad Guys," Review, *Life*, November 27, 1964.

36 Grace Glueck, "Hartford to Shut His Artist Colony," *New York Times*, April 2, 1965; Gubernick, *Squandered Fortune*, 23; Doherty, "Millionaire Art Buff"; Thomas B. Morgan, "George Huntington Hartford, II: Peripatetic Patron," *Esquire*, March 1961. See also Gueft, "Non-Conformity on Columbus Circle": 92; Ames to Hartford, July 31, 1961, and Julius S. Held to Hartford, December 27, 1962, NYCC Collection.

37 Canaday, "Hartford Collection," *Art*, *New York Times,* March 17, 1964; L. A. W. to Hartford, February 7, 1962, NYCC Collection.

38 "Cultural Center Appoints Director," *New York Times*, January 2, 1970; Glueck, "Gulf and Western Gives New York A Cultural Center," *New York Times*, December 9, 1976. See also C. Gerald Fraser, "Columbus Circle Museum Gets a New Cultural Life," *New York Times*, November 7, 1980; David W. Dunlap, "Acquiring a Taste for Marble Lollypops: 2 Columbus Circle, Much Despised, is Now Somewhat Admired," Metropolitan Desk, *New York Times*, December 11, 1998.

39 See Dunlap, "Museum Wins a Court Battle on Columbus Circle Renovation," *New York Times*, February 25, 2005; Leonard M. Kliwinski and Alan Hess, "Two Columbus Circle," National Register of Historic Places Registration Form, January 31, 1994, sec. 8, p. 7, private collection.

40 Roberta Brandes Gratz, "When Is a Landmark A Landmark?" August 21, 2011 (http://www.huffingtonpost.com; accessed March 12. 2012).

41 Cranston Jones to Virginia Field, December 4, 1959, AFA Records.

42 See Celestine Bohlen, "Oregon Firm to Design for Museum," *New York Times*, November 5, 2002; Terence Riley, "What a Building Says About Us," letter to the editor, *New York Times*, October 15, 2003; Julie V. Iovine, "On Columbus Circle: Fighting a Face-Lift," *New York Times*, January 22, 2004; Linda Hales, "At Columbus Circle, Going Round and Round Over a Building's Fate," *Washington Post*, May 29, 2004.

43 Ada Louise Huxtable, "Huntington Hartford's Palatial Midtown Museum," *Architecture*, *New York Times*, February 25, 1964; Blake, "Museum Explosion": 102; Gueft, "Non-Conformity on Columbus Circle": 95; " 'Healthy New Force,' " *Art*, *Newsweek*, September 9, 1963; "A Gallery of Modern Art."

44 "More Space for Modern Art": 244.

45 Sanche De Gramont, "Huntington Hartford Files Plans for 10-Story Museum," *New York Herald Tribune*, April 28, 1959.

46 Inez Robb, "An Elegant Showcase," *New York World-Telegram and the Sun*, December 11, 1963.

47 Zukosky, "A Posh Place For Pictures"; Thomas Buckley, "Huntington Hartford's White Tower to Open," *New York Times*, March 22, 1964.

48 Alfred Frankfurter, "Caviare?—New York's Newest Museum," *ARTnews* 63 (March 1964): 60; Blake, "Museum Explosion," 102.

49 Ann Eden Gibson, *Abstract Expressionism: Other Politics* (New Haven, Conn.: Yale University Press, 1997), 45–54; Herbert Muschamp, "The Secret History," *New York Times*, January 8, 2006, and "The Short, Scorned Life of an Esthetic Heresy"; *New York Times*, July 31, 1996; Sally Hammond, "Huntington Hartford And His Museum," *New York Post*, March 15, 1964; Martin Filler, "Goodbye Columbus," *New Republic* 223 (August. 28, 2000): 30; "Hartford Has Nearly Everything"; Burt Wasserman, "News and Notes," October 1964, NYCC Collection; Gueft, "Non Conformity on Columbus Circle": 92.

50 Gueft, "Non-Conformity on Columbus Circle": 95; Huxtable, "Architecture Stumbles On," *New York Times*, April 14, 1963.

51 "A Gallery of Modern Art"; Zukosky, "A Posh Place For Pictures"; "House That Hartford Built."

52 Gueft, "Non-Conformity on Columbus Circle": 92; Brian O'Doherty, "Hartford Gallery: Old Wine, A New Bottle," *New York Times*, January 12, 1964; "Home for 'Wholesome' Art," *Life*, April 3, 1964; Huxtable, *Will They Ever Finish Bruckner Boulevard?* (New York: Collier Books, 1970), 159.

53 Huxtable, "Huntington Hartford's Palatial Midtown Museum"; "Eye on the Environment," *Press*, *Newsweek*, August 23, 1965; Muschamp, "The Short, Scorned Life of an Esthetic Heresy."

54 See Kliwinski and Hess, "Two Columbus Circle," section 8, p. 1.

55 "New York's Newest Museum," *Architectural Record* 135 (April 1964): 13.

56 Dunlap, "Museum Wins a Court Battle."

57 Kulka, *Kitsch and Art*, 15l; Hermann Broch, "Notes on the Problem of Kitsch," reprinted in Dorfles, *Kitsch: The World of Bad Taste*, 49–67.

58 Harold Rosenberg, "Pop Culture: Kitsch Criticism," in *The Tradition of the*

New (New York: Horizon Press, 1959), 265; Wolf Von Eckardt, *A Place to Live: The Crisis of the Cities* (New York: Dell, 1967), 215.

59 Paul Goldberger, "Landmark Kitsch: A New Generation of Architects Tries to Save the City's Ugly Ducklings," The Sky Line, *The New Yorker,* August 1997.

60 Susan Sontag, "Notes on 'Camp,' " in Sontag, *Against Interpretation and Other Essays* (New York: Picador, 1966), 283. See also Mary Anne Hunting, "Edward Durell Stone: Perception and Criticism." (Ph.D. diss., City University of New York, 2007), 259–68.

61 See Clement Greenberg, "Avant-Garde and Kitsch," in *Art and Culture: Critical Essays* (Boston: Beacon Press, 1961), 21–33.

62 See Robert Storr, "No Joy in Mudville: Greenberg's Modernism Then and Now," in *Modern Art and Popular Culture: Readings in High and Low*, eds. Kirk Varnedoe and Adam Gopnik (New York: Museum of Modern Art, 1990), 179.

63 Huxtable, "Huntington Hartford's Palatial Midtown Museum"; Huxtable, "The Lollypop Building: The Best Way to Preserve 2 Columbus Circle? A Make-over,," *Wall Street Journal*, January 7, 2004; Daniel J. Wakin, "An Effort To Preserve A Monolith: Derived Building Has Big-Name Help," *New York Times*, April 15, 2000; Joseph L. Eldredge, "Today's Architecture: Master Milliner's Touch," *Boston Globe*, July 1966; "House That Hartford Built"; " 'Healthy New Force' "; Muschamp, "The Short, Scorned Life"; Robin Boyd, "The Counter-Revolution in Architecture," *Harper's Magazine*, September 1959; Frankfurter, "Caviare?—New York's Newest Museum."

64 Andreas Huyssen, *After the Great Divide: Modernism, Mass Culture, Postmodernism* (Bloomington, Indiana: University of Indiana, 1986), ix.

65 Robert Venturi, Complexity and Contradiction in Architecture (1966; repr. New York: Museum of Modern Art, 2002), 13.

66 Huxtable, "Architecture: A Look At the Kennedy Center, *New York Times*, September 7, 1971.

67 Benjamin Forgery, "John F. Kennedy Dream Is Reality At Center," *Washington Star*, September 5, 1971.

68 Huxtable, "Some Sour Notes Sound at Kennedy Center," *New York Times*, September 19, 1971; "A Noble Edifice To Glorify Creative Arts," *Life*, September 28, 1962.

69 Lee Belser, "Kennedy Arts Center Gets Congressional Approval," *Los Angeles Herald-Examiner*, September 8, 1971; "Buildings of the Future—As a Noted Architect Sees Them: Interview with Edward Durell Stone," *U.S. News & World Report*, August 15, 1977.

70 The correspondence is in the Stone Papers, 1st acc., boxes 69 and 70.

71 Edmund R. Purves to Charles Montooth, October 22, 1958, Stone to Robert W. Dowling, April 16, 1969, and to William Fulbright, May 6, 1959, Stone Papers, 1st acc., box 70.

72 Dowling to Arthur S. Fleming, July 8, 1959, Fulbright Papers, series 93, sub-series 2, box 4; Jarold A. Kieffer, memorandum for the record, August 19, 1961, Jarold Kieffer Personal Papers, John F. Kennedy Presidential Library, Boston, Mass. (hereafter cited as Kieffer Papers); Gene Gleason, "Stone Outlines Designs: Entrance for State Visits Planned In Cultural Center on the Potomac," *Washington Post*, October 7, 1959.

73 Kieffer, *From: National Cultural Center To: John F. Kennedy Center for the Performing Arts: At the Front End of the Beginning* (Fairfax, Va.: privately printed, 2004), 27; Kieffer, diary, March 29, 1960, Kiefer Papers.

74 Sophy Burnham, "Kennedy Center—Culture With a Capital K," *Los Angeles Times*, July 2, 1967.

75 Elizabeth Ford and Maxine Cheshire, "Dinner is Centered on the Arts," *Washington Post*, May 26, 1960; Kieffer, *From: National Cultural Center*, 21; Huxtable, "From a Candy Box: A Tardy and Unpleasant Surprise," *New York Times*, August 22, 1965; Stone, Speech at National Cultural Center Dinner, Washington, D.C., May 25, 1960, Stone Papers, 1st acc., box 2.

76 Grace Bassett, "D.C. Cultural Center Details Are Revealed," (Washington, D.C.) *Sunday Star*, November 22, 1959.

77 Russell Baker, "The Kennedy Center Was Talking," (Washington, D.C.) *Evening Star*, January 7, 1971; Jerry Landauer, "Architects 'Vision' of Cultural Center Approved," *Washington Post*, July 21, 1959; Fine Arts Commission Minutes, October 14, 1959, and David E. Finley, Fine Arts Commission News Release, October 14, 1959, Fine Arts Commission Records, Washington, D.C.; "Stone Pares Down His Cultural Clam Shell," *Life*, February 7, 1964.

78 "National Cultural Center Plans Now Approved," Buildings in the News,

Architectural Forum 127 (January 1960): 10; "Cultural Center Design Shown," *Progressive Architecture* 41 (January 1960): 48.

79 Becker, *Miracle on the Potomac*, 55; "Statement by Edward Durell Stone, Architect for the Kennedy Center," October 31, 1969, Stone Papers, 1st acc., box 80.

80 "New National Cultural Center Plan Unveiled," *Los Angeles Times*, November 22, 1959.

81 "Culture on the Potomac," *Washington Daily News*, November 24, 1959; Kieffer, notes, September 30 and November 16, 1959, Kiefer Papers.

82 Stone to Fulbright, October 12, 1959, Fulbright Papers, BCN 123 folder 38.

83 Kieffer, notes, March 1 and 7, April 21, September 20, 1961, Kiefer Papers; Tony Judt, *Reflections on the Forgotten Twentieth Century* (New York: Penguin Books, 2008), 337–38.

84 Paul Hume, "Shape of Cultural Center is Changing," *Washington Post*, January 7, 1962; Kieffer, notes, November 9, 1961; Ralph E. Becker, *Miracle on the Potomac: The Kennedy Center from the Beginning* (Silver Spring, Md.: Bartleby Press, 1990), 41; Arthur Gelb, "Cultural Center Sets Lower Goal," *New York Times*, February 4, 1962.

85 Stone, "Address Given at the NAEA Conference, Kansas City [Mo.]," 1963, Stone Papers, 1st acc., box 2.

86 Burnham, "Kennedy Center—Culture With a Capital K."

87 Betty Beale, "Glamour Galore on the Potomac River," Washington Letter, *Washington Star*, December 13, 1964; "It's a Dream Come True," *San Gabriel Valley Tribune*, May 29, 1966; Donald Sanders, "Preview of Kennedy Center of Performing Arts," *Baltimore Sun*, May 23, 1971; Robertson, "Scores of Notables Attend Preview of Kennedy Center," *New York Times*, May 28, 1971; "Fireworks and Champagne: The John F. Kennedy Center for the Performing Arts Has a Gala Debut in Washington With 3,700 Guests," *Life*, June 11, 1971.

88 Alice T. Friedman, *American Glamour and the Evolution of Modern Architecture* (New Haven: Yale University Press, 2010), 7.

89 Huxtable, "A Look At the Kennedy Center." See also Von Eckardt, "Kennedy Center is More than Art Shelter," Cityscape, *Washington Post*, March 22, 1964; "A Noble Edifice to Glorify Creative Arts"; "Stone Revises Design for Cultural Palace," *Progressive Architecture* 43 (October 1962): 75; Nan Robertson, "Board Approves Kennedy Center," *New York Times*, May 18, 1965.

90 Von Eckardt, "If Only It Looked as Good As It Works," *Washington Post*, September 8, 1973; Walter McQuade, "Architecture," *Nation*, September 3, 1960. See also McQuade, "A Deadly Décor for the Lively Arts," *Life*, November 20, 1970.

91 Stone to Leslie Cheek Jr., January 15, 1963, Stone Papers, 2nd acc., box 1; Von Eckardt, "A Critical Look at the John F. Kennedy Center," *Washington Post*, July 28, 1973; Von Eckardt, "Kennedy Center: The Monument That Isn't," *Washington Post*, December 26, 1970.

92 Charles Jencks, *Modern Movements in Architecture* (Garden City, NY: Anchor Press, 1973), 192; Susan Sontag, "Notes on 'Camp,' " 275–92.

93 "Kennedy Center Opens With a Party," *Evening Sun*, May 28, 1971; Sontag, "Notes on 'Camp,' " in Sontag, Against Interpretation, 286.

94 "Buildings of the Future—As a Noted Architect Sees Them."

95 Andrea O. Dean, "Cultural Colossi: Kennedy Center at 10," *AIA Journal* 70 (August 1981): 29.

96 Beale, "Edward D. Stone Discusses his Views on National Cultural Center in Capital," *Washington Star*, July 17, 1959; Gene Gleason, "Stone Outlines Designs: Entrance for State Visits Planned in Cultural Center on the Potomac," *Washington Post*, October 7, 1959.

97 Fulbright, note written on top of a copy of *Congressional Record*, 117, no. 119 (July 28, 1971), Stone Papers, 1st acc. box 30.

98 Judt, *Reflections*, 341–42.

7: GOOD ARCHITECTURE IS GOOD BUSINESS . . . FOR YEARS AND YEARS *pages 122–145*

1 Edward Durell Stone, quoted in Ernest E. Jacks, "The Elegant Bohemian: Tales of Architect Edward Durell Stone," (ca. 2000), 130, private collection.

2 "Condominium Comes of Age," *House & Home* 31 (March 1967): 86; Robert A. M. Stern, Thomas Mellins, and David Fishman, *New York 1960: Architecture*

and Urbanism Between the Second World War and the Bicentennial, 2nd ed. (New York: Monacelli Press, 1997), 677, 680, 717.

3   Stone, quoted in "We Hitch our Wagons to a Star: Guest Editors Interview Five Celebrities," *Mademoiselle*, August 1961.

4   Stone, press release, ca. 1964, Stone Papers, 2nd acc., box 95: Stone to All Principals and Associates, February 13, 1970, Stone Papers, 2nd acc., box 40; "That anti-Chicago obelisk," Rob Cuscaden/Architecture, *Chicago Sun-Times*, October 11, 1970.

5   Jules Loh, "Edward Durell Stone: At 71, He Has the Vigor of an Idealist Beginner," *Arkansas Gazette*, October 28, 1973.

6   "New Work Serene and Classic, by Edward Durell Stone," *Architectural Record* 132 (October 1962): 129.

7   Alan Dunn, "Now This Is Where Ed Stone and Me Go Our Separate Ways!" *Architectural Record* 136 (October 1964): 23.

8   "The Red Carpet Is Out On Fifth Avenue," *Los Angeles Times*, June 21, 1964. See also Glenn Fowler, "Park Ave. Tower Wins Recognition: 'Lighthouse' on 59th Street and 2 Stores Also Honored," *New York Times*, May 8, 1966; Ada Louise Huxtable, "Some New Faces on Fifth Avenue," *New York Times*, November 8, 1964.

9   Lisa Hammel, "Furniture Settings With Personality," *New York Times*, September 26, 1968.

10   Jacks, "Elegant Bohemian," 336.

11   Ada Louise Huxtable, "Dams, Domes and the Battle of Styles," *New York Times*, July 5, 1964.

12   See Mary McLeod, "Architecture and Politics in the Reagan Era: From Postmodernism to Deconstructivism," *Assemblage* 8 (February 1989): 23–59.

13   See "Urban Renewal—Art in Architecture," *New York Herald Tribune*, May 6, 1962.

14   Stone, "The American Landscape," April 18, 1960, Stone Papers, 2nd acc., box 92; Stone, *Recent and Future Architecture* (New York: Horizon Press, 1967), 7; "Are Most Cities Too Ugly to Save?" *U.S. News & World Report*, November 30, 1964; Stone, Speech Before National Press Club, March 10, 1964, Stone Papers, 2nd acc., box 91; Stone to Lyndon B. Johnson, January 12, 1965, WHCF, WE 9, box 25, Lyndon B. Johnson Presidential Library, Austin, Tex.

15   "We Hitch our Wagons to a Star"; Stone, "American Landscape," July 13, 1960.

16   See Stone, *Recent and Future Architecture*, 9.

17   The manuscript is in the Stone Papers, 2nd acc., box 92. See also "Edward Durell Stone Deplores 'Mess We've Made of Country,' " *New York Times*, August 27, 1964.

18   "Columns From Capitol Urged for Arboretum Pavilion," *New York Times*, December 22, 1963; National Arboretum fact sheet, July 3, 1963, Stone Papers, 2nd acc., box 36; Barbara Gamarekian, "History for Sale, $41,000 per Stick," *New York Times*, February 11, 1986; "The Temple of Flora," in *A Different Stripe: Notes on NYBR Classics*, (http://nyrb.typepad.com/classics/2007/04/index.html; accessed October 29, 2010); "Use of Capitol Columns at National Arboretum," *Congressional Record—Senate* (December 4, 1963): 23194–95.

19   Stone to Cranston Jones, February 18, 1964, Time Archives; "Redevelopment of Columbus Circle: Report on Current Status of Job," 1964, and Francis Brennan to Mary Lasker, July 20, 1964, and to Barbara Platoff, October 14, 1964, Stone Papers, 2nd acc., box 78; "Beautifying Where It Counts," *New York Times*, February 12, 1964; William Borders, "Fountain (No City Water Used) Is Dedicated in Columbus Circle," *New York Times*, October 12, 1965.

20   Robert Venturi, *Complexity and Contradiction in Architecture* (1966; repr., New York: Museum of Modern Art, 2002), 16.

21   "Stone Evokes Bernini in New Orleans," p/a news report, *Progressive Architecture* 40 (May 1959): 97.

22   Busch Memorial Stadium fact sheet, Stone Papers, 2nd acc., box 50.

23   Stone, *The Evolution of an Architect* (New York: Horizon Press, 1962), 143.

24   Stone, quoted in "New Work Serene and Classic": 130.

25   Stone, *Evolution of an Architect*, 143.

26   Museo de Arte de Ponce fact sheet, Stone Papers, 2nd acc., box 51; Stone to Julius Held, March 28, 1962, Julius S. Held Papers, box 49, folder 5, Getty Research Institute Library, J. Paul Getty Trust, Los Angeles. See also Walter McQuade, "Puerto Rico's Newest Art Museum," Structure and Design, *For-*

tune, April 1966; "New Art Museum Attracts Tourists to Ponce," *New York Times*, January 23, 1966; "Three Museums," *Architectural Record* 139 (April 1966): 196–99.

27   "Award of Merit: Edward Durell Stone," *AIA Journal* 39 (May 1963): 44.

28   "An Elegant Exception in Hospital Design," *Architectural Forum* 117 (October 1962): 109

29   "An Elegant Exception in Hospital Design": 108; Sam Lubell, "Two: Community Hospital Monterey, California," *Architectural Record* 196 (August 2008): 120; " 'A Room of One's Own'—Patients Love It," *Modern Hospital*, 1963; "To Improve Patient Care," *Medical World News*, March 19, 1965.

30   "Medical Center Architect Chosen," *San Francisco Chronicle*, May 1, 1967; "Two California Hospitals by Edward Durell Stone Set a Challenging Pace in Design and Economics," *Architectural Record* 152 (September 9, 1972): 142.

31   Art Seidenbaum, "Caltech Art Beachhead Is Cause for Celebration," Spectator, 1966, *Los Angeles Times*, May 5, 1966; "Classic Temple in California Olive Grove," *Progressive Architecture* 46 (May 1965): 59.

32   Stone to Earl Heitschmidt, September 6, 1960, Stone Papers, 1st acc., box 64. See also http://www.virginia.edu/academicalvillage/http://cti.itc.virginia.edu/~jjd5t/cww/1998/vi.03-uva-lawn-plan.jpg; accessed January 27, 2012.

33   "Modern Campus for School at Beirut Is Designed by U.S. Architect," *New York Times*, March 19, 1961; John Fistere to Stone, October 25, 1971, and Thomas C. Schuller to Good Friends of International College, September 28, 1971, Stone Papers, 2nd acc., box 29; Stone, "U.S. is Becoming Nation of Boxes, Billboard, Bar-B-Q's," *Richmond News Leader*, December 31, 1960.

34   Stone to Nelson A. Rockefeller, June 8, 1962, Stone Papers, 1st acc., box 79.

35   Stone, *Recent and Future Architecture*, 9.

36   Stone and Associate Architects, "1974 Comprehensive Site Plan Updating State University of New York at Albany," July 1968, Stone Papers, 2nd acc., box 43; Stone, "Stone on Stone," *University Review* 1 (Fall 1966): 9; Stone, "The Case for Modern Architecture on the Campus," *Technology Review* 62 (May 1960): 28; Stone, "U.S. is Becoming Nation of Boxes."

37   "Nassau Approves Community College Plan," *New York Times*, June 23, 1964; "Mitchel Field Master Plan for Campus," *New York Times*, March 30, 1975; John Cunniff, "Architect Says U.S. May be on Threshold of Great Things in Construction of Buildings," *(Tulare, California) Visalia Times-Delta*, October 6, 1966.

38   "Designs for World's Fair," Letters to The Times, *New York Times*, December 24, 1960; Wallace K. Harrison to Robert Moses, February 25, 1960, and Moses to Charles F. Preusse, August 14, 1959, Robert Moses Papers, box 106, Manuscripts and Archives Division, New York Public Library, New York (hereafter cited as Moses Papers); Ira Henry Freeman, "Moses to Accept Fair Presidency," *New York Times*, April 1, 1960; Remarks of Moses, May 3, 1960 and Harrison to Moses, May 25, 1960, New York World's Fair 1964–1965 Corporation Records, box 119, Manuscripts and Archives Division, New York Public Library (hereafter cited as WF1964).

39   Jacks, "Elegant Bohemian," 309–10.

40   Stone, "American Landscape," July 13 and August 17, 1960; Moses, June 23, 1965, in "Highways +," Stone Papers, 2nd acc., box 72; Emma Gene Hall, "Directions in Modern Architecture: A conversation with Edward D. Stone," *Gentlemen's Quarterly*, April 1959; Moses to Harrison, June 14, 1960, WF1964, box 119; Moses, draft to Henry Luce, November 7, 1961, WF1964, box 69.

41   Moses to Harrison, June 14, 1960; Moses, memorandum to Stuart Constable, August 14, 1959, Moses Papers, box 106.

42   Moses to Harrison, July 21, 1960, to Thomas J. Deegan, June 23, 1960, and memorandum to Constable, July 21, 1960, WF1964, box 119.

43   Walter Teague to Moses, July 14, 1960, WF1964, box 119.

44   James L. Holton, "World's Fair Planning Slammed," Real Estate, *New York World-Telegram and the Sun*, November 2, 1961; "The Structures Behind the Shapes," *Architectural Forum* 120 (January 1964): 69; Moses, memorandum to Constable and draft to Luce, November 8, 1961, WF1964, box 404; Emerson Goble to Moses, February 9, 1966, WF1964, box 68; Mildred F. Schmertz, "Architecture at the New York World's Fair," *Architectural Record* 136 (July 1964): 143–50.

45   Frank Farrell, "1939 Skeleton for 64 Fair?" *New York World-Telegram and the Sun*, August 12, 1960; Meeting of Executive Committee, August 4, 1960, WF1964, box 119; "1939 Plan for 1964 Fair/Design Board Schemes

Rejected," Meetings and Miscellany, *Architectural Record* 129 (January 1961): 23; Edith Evans Asbury, "Designers Quit Fair in a Dispute on Plan," *New York Times*, December 3, 1960; Douglas Haskell, memo to staff, September 8, 1960, Haskell Papers; Moses to Deegan, August 2, 1960, and Gordon Bunshaft to Moses, July 20, 1960, WF1964, box 119; Moses to Eugene S. Taliaferro, August 30, 1962, WF1964, box 131. See also "The arrested development of the New York Fair," editorial, *Architectural Forum* 113 (December 1960): 63; editorial, *Progressive Architecture* 42 (July 1961): 206; Huxtable, "Architecture: Chaos of Good, Bad and Joyful," *New York Times*, April 22, 1964; "Are Most Cities Too Ugly to Save?"

46 Moses to General William Everett Potter, August 22, 1960, WF1964, box 119; Taliaferro to Moses, August 28, 1962, WF1964, box 131; Committee for Christian Scientist Activities World's Fair 1964–65, "New York World's Fair Activities Progress Report #4," March 1964, WF1964, box 338.

47 Sarah Gordon, "Distinctive Church Meets Wrecking Ball," *San Diego Union-Tribune*, June 17, 2006 (http://www.modernsandiego.com; accessed April 19, 2010).

48 "Religious Exhibits at the New York World's Fair," press release, n.d., WF1964, box 338; "Progress Report #4"; "Ed-U-Cards invites you to Take a Sublime Picture Card Tour that you will treasure always," *New York Times*, April 15, 1964.

49 "The Billy Graham Pavilion, April 17, 1963, Groundbreaking at the New York World's Fair 1964–1965," Billy Graham Center Archives, Wheaton Ill.

50 Hank Beukema to William Ottley, December 4, 1964 and New York World's Fair, press release, August 9, 1963, WF1964, box 338; "Billy Graham Pavilion: One of World's Fair's Outstanding Landmarks," press release, n.d.; "The Billy Graham Pavilion," press release, n.d. and "The 101 Steps," *Decision*, April 1964, WF1964, box 338.

51 Peter John, "An Architect's Trend-Setting Home for the Fair," *Look*, February 11, 1964.

52 "The House of Good Taste," *Interiors* 123 (March 1964): 98–99.

53 Sherman R. Emery, "At the Fair," *Interior Design and Decoration* 35 (August 1964): 75. See also George O'Brien, "Model Homes at Fair," *New York Times*, April 23, 1964; "New York World's Fair," *Interior Design and Decoration*: 82–83; "Patrick Lee Lucas, "Sarah Hunter Kelly: Designing the House of Good Taste," *Interiors: Design, Architecture and Culture* 1 (July 2010): 75–89.

54 Paul Goldberger, "Design Notebook," *New York Times*, June 10, 1982; "Three World's Fair Houses!" *Better Homes & Gardens*, September 1964; "Bold New Plan for Best Land Use," *Life*, September 22, 1958.

55 Stone to Robert W. Dowling, April 16, 1959, Stone Papers, 1st acc., box 70; George E. Spargo to Stone, June 23, 1959, and Stone to Moses and to Spargo, July 8, 1959, Stone Papers, 1st acc., box 39; Hilary Ballon and Kenneth T. Jackson, eds., *Robert Moses and the Modern City: The Transformation of New York* (New York: W. W. Norton, 2007): 238–39.

56 "Hudson Celebration: Theatre-in-the-Park," *Playbill*, Summer 1959; Moses to Newbold Morris, July 23, 1959, Moses Papers, box 106; Spargo to Stone, and Stone to Moses and to Spargo.

57 Huntington Hartford to Moses, October 13, 1959, Moses Papers, box 106.

58 Moses, memorandum to Constable, December 9, 1959, Moses Papers, box 106.

59 Moses to Harrison, January 12, 1960, Moses Papers, box 106. See also Moses, memorandum to Constable, January 19, 1960, Moses Papers, box 106; "Design for Park Café Finished: Work Expected to Begin Soon," *New York Times*, February 2, 1961; "Gift to New York: A $500,000 Café in Central Park," *Progressive Architecture*, 41 (May 1960): 78; Stone, *Evolution of an Architect*, 155, 226.

60 Walter Waggoner, "Art-and-Park Man," *New York Times*, August 21, 1960; Moses to Hartford, November 15, 1960, WF1964, box 51; Moses to Hartford, February 6, 1964, WF1964, box 283. For a detailed account about the café see Stern, Mellins, and Fishman, *New York 1960*, 770–72.

61 Stone, "American Landscape," June 9, 1960.

62 "Suburban office buildings," *Architectural Record* 151 (February 1972): 114; "Offices in the Suburbs," *Time*, February 9, 1971.

63 Rachel A. Antman, "The Donald M. Kendall Sculpture Gardens," *New York Times*, September 29, 2006.

64 "Suburban office buildings": 114.

65 Statement about PepsiCo, n.d., and Kendall to Stone, June 15, 1971, Stone Papers, 2nd acc., box 37.

66 Stone, draft for "The Case of the Tailfin Age," July 15, 1959, Stone Papers, 2nd acc., box 90.

67 "The Architecture Box," *Kansas City (Mo.) Star*, February 2, 1964.

68 (http://www.omahapubliclibrary.org/art-collection-gallery/sunburst; accessed July 22, 2010); Nancy N. Schiffer and Val O. Bertoia, *The World of Bertoia* (Atglen, Penn.: Schiffer, 2003): 174.

69 Perpetual Savings and Loan Association fact sheet, Stone Papers, 2nd acc., box 51; Stone, *Evolution of an Architect*, 157.

70 Esther McCoy, "The Screen of Stone," Bookshelf, *Los Angeles Times*, January 13, 1963.

71 Benjamin Forgey, "Miracle on M Street," *Washington Post*, December 12, 1981.

72 Stone, *Recent and Future Architecture*, 54.

73 Forgey, "Miracle on M Street." See also Huxtable, "National Geographic Society Building Sets a Standard for Washington," *New York Times*, December 13, 1963.

74 Stone to J. William Fulbright, April 13, 1959, Stone Papers, 1st acc., box 70.

75 "New Statehouse for North Carolina, *Architectural Forum* 119 (December 1963): 87.

76 See "North Carolina's Sparkling New Statehouse," *Interiors* 123 (October 1963): 131.

77 "The Toughest Woman in Real Estate is Cecilia Benattar," Close-Up, *Life*, October 1, 1965; Anthony Bailey, "When Better Buildings Are Built," *New York Herald Tribune*, April 4, 1965; Huxtable, "New York's Zoning Law is Out of Bounds," Architecture View, *New York Times*, December 14, 1980.

78 Stern, Mellins, and Fishman, *New York 1960*, 50; Dennis Duggan, "The 'Belly' School of Architecture," *New York Herald Tribune*, December 15, 1963; Thomas C. Abbott to Charles E. Kingdom, May 21, 1963, Stone Papers, 2nd acc., box 28.

79 Stone, "The Skyscraper—What Next," n.d., Stone Papers, 1st acc., box 2; Transcript, Merv Griffin Show: WPTX-TV, Stone Papers, 2nd acc., box 72; "Biggest Glass Panels in G.M. Building," *New York Times*, October 6, 1968; "Construction of General Motors Building Involves 280,000 Square Feet of Glass," press release, n.d., Stone Papers, 2nd acc., box 50.

80 McCandlish Phillips, "Bold New Profile Joins City's East Side Skyline," *New York Times*, October 17, 1967.

81 "To Cherish Rather Than To Destroy," Modern Living, *Time*, August 2, 1968.

82 See "General Motors Files Plans to Build on Savoy Site," *New York Times*, January 27, 1965.

83 Huxtable, *Will They Ever Finish Bruckner Boulevard?* (New York: Collier Books, 1970): 92; Stone, "The Case Against the Tailfin Age," *New York Times*, October 18, 1959.

84 Goldberger, *The Skyscraper* (New York: Alfred A. Knopf, 1981), 141.

85 Huxtable, "How to Kill A City," *New York Times*, March 21, 1965.

86 William D. Smith, "G.M. Introduced New Building on 5th Avenue and Its '69 Cars," *New York Times*, September 27, 1968; Armand Luna to Stone, December 10, 1968, Stone Papers, 2nd acc., box 28.

87 Stone, quoted in Goldberger, "Edward Durell Stone Services Will Be Held Tomorrow," *New York Times*, August 8, 1978; Jim Yardley, "Trump Buying the Landmark G.M. Building," *New York Times*, May 31, 1998; Charles V. Bagli, "G.M. Building Sells for $1.4 Billion, A Record," *New York Times*, August 30, 2003; "Macklowes Sell G.M. Building for $2.9 Billion," *New York Times*, May 25, 2008.

88 Tape recording, July 1, 1964, Stone Papers, 2nd acc., box 81; "Edifice Complex," *Time*, November 10, 1967; "Architect Stone a Self-Styled 'Migrant Worker,'" *Los Angeles Times*, July 21, 1968; "Heights and depths of 1970 Chicago buildings," Rob Cuscaden/Architecture, *Chicago Sun-Times*, January 3, 1971.

89 Stone to Benattar, March 26, 1971, Stone Papers, 2nd acc., box 3; "That anti-Chicago obelisk."

90 "Amoco's Carrara Skin To Be Replaced with Granite," Architecture, *AIA Journal* 78 (October 1989): 26; Theodore H. M. Prudon, *Preservation of Modern Architecture* (New York: John Wiley and Sons, 2008), 496–98.

91 Otto Rank, *The Double: A Psychoanalytic Study*, trans. and ed. by Harry Tucker Jr. (Chapel Hill: University of North Carolina, 1971), 78–79; Paul Gapp, draft for *Inland Architect*, n.d., Paul Gapp Collection, Manuscript Collection, Ohio University Libraries, Athens; "That anti-Chicago obelisk"; Far-

rell to Stone, February 7, 1974, Stone Papers, 2nd acc., box 39. See also Gapp, "Ambiguous statement snarls Center debate," Architecture, *Chicago Tribune*, June 30, 1974.

92 Farrell to Stone.

93 "Mogul Modern," Architecture, *Time*, August 12, 1968.

94 Ishrat Hussain Usmani, April 10, 1966, quoted in Sten Nilsson, "Palaces, camps, capitals: The Resident's authority must be seen or felt…," *Lotus International* 34 (1982).

95 "Statement by Architect Edward Durell Stone on his Design of the Pakistan Institute of Nuclear Science and Engineering," June 7, 1961, Stone Papers, 2nd acc., box 36; "Mogul Modern."

96 Kamil Khan Mumtaz, *Modernity and Tradition: Contemporary Architecture in Pakistan* (New York: Oxford University Press, 1999), 118.

97 Akhtar Mahmood to Stone, August 1, 1961, and Stone to Mahmood, August 21, 1961, Stone Papers, 2nd acc., box 82.

98 Mumtaz, *Modernity and Tradition*, 118; Orestes Yakas, *Islamabad: The Birth of a Capital* (New York: Oxford University Press, 2001); Usmani to Stone, July 6, 1965, quoted in Nilsson, "Palaces, camps, capitals."

99 "Agreed minutes of the discussions regarding planning, designing, and supervision of construction…," 1966, Stone Papers, 2nd acc., box 36.

100 William Borders, "A Shiny New Capital Emerging Slowly in Pakistan," *New York Times*, January 31, 1976.

101 "Edward Durell Stone Named Master Architect for Pakistan's New Capitol," news release, 1966, Time Archives; "Agreed minutes of the discussion," March to July 1966, Stone Papers, 2nd acc., box 36.

102 Qutubuddin Aziz, "Pakistan's Islamabad U: Stone designed, Ford funded," *New York Times*, August 5, 1967.

103 M. Khalilur Rahman to Stone, May 11, 1973, Stone Papers, 2nd acc., box 47.

104 "Memorandum of Understanding," September 3, 1967; Edward D. Stone Jr. and Associates, "University of Islamabad, Design Criteria and Planning Assumptions Outline" and "University of Islamabad, Program Analysis," Stone Papers, 2nd acc., box 47.

105 Sydney H. Schanberg, "Pakstani Capital: Madness to Some, It is 'Lovely Garden City' to Others," *New York Times*, April 10, 1970.

106 Mumtaz, *Modernity and Tradition*, 49–50; Goldberger, "Aga Khan Searches for Islamic Architecture's Roots," *New York Times*, October 10, 1979; AKPIA@ MIT (http://web.mit.edu/akpia/www/page002.htm; accessed July 1, 2010).

107 Philip Herrera, "U.S. Architecture: A Progress Report," Structure and Design, *Fortune*, September 1967; Laurie Johnston, "Central Park Mall May Be Refurbished with Performance Pit and New Lights," *New York Times*, October 4, 1972.

108 Malcolm B. Johnson, "Dickinson Effort Could Be Fatal to New Capitol," *Tallahassee Democrat*, September 12, 1971; "Dickinson Delays Bid To Finance Capitol Planning," *Gainesville Sun*, November 11, 1971.

CONCLUSION *pages 146–149*

1 Buckminster Fuller, "Dymaxion Rating," March 22, 1963, Stone Papers, 2nd acc., box 1.

2 Briefly Noted, *The New Yorker*, January 6, 1968.

3 Editor's note, *Saturday Review*, November 7, 1959; *Dictionary of American Biography*, s.v. "Stone, Edward Durell." See also Ada Louise Huxtable, "Some Sour Notes Sound at Kennedy Center," *New York Times*, September 19, 1971.

4 Stone, quoted in *Celebrity Register* (New York: Harper and Row, 1963), s.v. "Stone, Edward Durell."

5 "More than Modern," *Time*, March 31, 1958.

6 Mary McLeod, "Undressing Architecture: Fashion, Gender, and Modernity," in Paulette Singley, ed., *Architecture in Fashion* (New York: Princeton Architectural Press, 1994), 40.

7 Tom Wolfe, *From Bauhaus to Our House* (New York: Farrar, Straus and Giroux, 1981; Picador, 2009), 70–79.

8 Robert Hughes, "White Gods and Cringing Natives: Tom Wolfe's Look at Architecture Gets It Half Right," *Time*, October 19, 1981; Michael Sorkin, "Wolfe at the Door," Books and The Arts, *Nation* 14 (October 1981): 445, 447; David A. Greenspan, "Right Again?" Books, *Progressive Architecture* 62 (December 1981): 106; Bradford Perkins, "Who Should Be Afraid of Tom Wolfe?" *Architectural Record* 170 (February 1982): 86. See also Edwin McDowell, "Publishing: Anatomy of An Author," *New York Times*, November 13, 1981; Tony Schwartz, "Tom Wolfe: The Great Gadfly," Magazine Desk, *New York Times*, December 20, 1981.

9 Wolfe, *From Bauhaus to Our House*, 70, 72.

10 See Thomas Crow, "Modernism and Mass Culture in the Visual Arts," in *Pollock and After: The Critical Debate*, ed. Francis Frascina (New York: Harper and Row, 1985), 239.

11 See Gillo Dorfles, *Kitsch: The World of Bad Taste (*New York: Bell, 1968).

12 Wolfe, "The Building That Isn't There," op-ed, *New York Times*, October 12, 2003, "The Building That Isn't There, Cont'd," op-ed, *New York Times*, October 13, 2003, and "The (Naked) City and the Undead," op-ed, *New York Times*, November 26, 2006.

13 Susan Sontag, "Notes on 'Camp,' " in Sontag, *Against Interpretation and Other Essays* (New York: Farrar, Straus and Giroux, 1966), 285.

BIBLIOGRAPHY

ARCHIVES

Alden B. Dow Archives, Midland, Mich.: Ingersoll Utility Unit Records.

American Academy of Arts and Letters Archives, New York.

American Institute of Architects Archives, Washington, D.C.: National Institute of Arts and Letters Records.

Archives of the City of Brussels, Belgium: Exposition Universelle et Internationale 1958.

Archives of American Art, Smithsonian Institution, Washington, D.C.: Alfred Hamilton Barr Jr. Papers; American Federation of Arts Records; Architectural League of New York Records; Russell Lynes Papers; Winslow Ames Papers.

Avenue of the Americas Association Archives.

Billy Graham Center Archives, Wheaton, Ill.

Buffalo and Erie County Historical Society, Buffalo, N.Y.: A. Conger Goodyear Papers.

Calder Foundation, New York.

California Institute of Technology, Institute Archives, Pasadena, Calif.: University Records.

Claremont University Consortium, Honnold/Mudd Library, Special Collections, Claremont, Calif.: Claremont Colleges Photo Archive.

Columbia University Libraries, New York: Columbia Center for Oral History; Avery Architectural and Fine Arts Library, Drawings and Archives: Douglas Putnam Haskell Papers; Joseph W. Molitor Photograph Collection; Wallace K. Harrison Papers.

Chevron Corporation, San Ramon, Calif.: Collection of Policy, Government, and Public Affairs.

Condé Nast, New York: Library; Archives.

Cooper-Hewitt, National Design Museum, Smithsonian Institution, New York: Donald Deskey Collection.

Corning Archives, Corning, N.Y.

Dwight D. Eisenhower Presidential Library, Abilene, Kans.

Edward Durell Stone and Associates Records, private collection.

Fairleigh Dickinson University Library, Madison, N.J.: New York Cultural Center Collection.

Fine Arts Commission Records, Washington, D.C.

Frank Lloyd Wright Foundation, Taliesin West, Scottsdale, Ariz.

Getty Research Institute, Research Library, J. Paul Getty Trust, Los Angeles: Julius Shulman Photography Archive; Julius S. Held Papers.

GM Media Archive, Sterling Heights, Mich.

Hallmark Cards Archives, Hallmark, Inc., Kansas City, Mo.

Harry Ransom Humanities Research Center, University of Texas at Austin: Alfred A. Knopf Collection; Norman Bel Geddes Theater and Industrial Design Papers.

Harvard University Library, Harvard University Archives, Cambridge, Mass.: University Records.

Huntington Library, San Marino, Calif.: Maynard L. Parker Collection; Ludwig Lauerhass Papers.

Jane C. Loeffler Collection, Washington, D.C.

John F. Kennedy Center for the Performing Arts Archives, Washington, D.C.

John F. Kennedy Presidential Library, Boston, Mass.: John Kenneth Galbraith Personal Papers; Jarold Kieffer Personal Papers.

Landmark West!, New York: Two Columbus Circle Records.

Library of Congress, Washington, D.C., Manuscript Division: Clare Boothe Luce Papers; Francis Edwin Brennan Papers; Henry R. Luce Papers; Prints and Photographs Division: Gottscho-Schleisner, *Look* Magazine, and *New York World-Telegram and the Sun* photograph collections.

Lincoln Center for the Performing Arts Archives, N.Y.

Lionel Freedman Archives, Los Angeles, Calif.

Lyndon B. Johnson Presidential Library, Austin, Tex.

M. E. Grenadier Department of Special Collections and Archives, University at Albany, State University of New York: University Records.

MIT Libraries, Institute Archives and Special Collections, Cambridge, Mass.: Rotch Travelling Scholarship Records; University Records.

Munson-Williams-Proctor Arts Institute Library, Utica, N.Y.

Museum of Modern Art, New York: Architecture and Design Study Center; Library and Archives.

Museum of the City of New York: Wurts Brothers Collection.

National Archives and Records Administration, College Park, Md.: International Conferences, Commissions, and Expositions Records; U.S. Department of State Records.

National Park Service, Washington, D.C.

New-York Historical Society, New York: Mattie E. Hewitt Photograph Collection.

New York Public Library, Astor, Lenox and Tilden Foundations, Manuscripts and Archives Division, New York: Crowell-Collier Collection; New York World's Fair 1964–65 Corporation Records; Robert Moses Papers.

New York Times Photograph Archives, New York.

Noguchi Museum Archives, Long Island City, N.Y.

Ohio University Libraries, Manuscript Collection, Athens: Paul Gapp Collection.

Queens Borough Public Library, Long Island Division, Jamaica, N.Y.: *New York Herald Tribune* Photograph Morgue.

Rockefeller Archive Center, Sleepy Hollow, N.Y.: Abby Aldrich Rockefeller Papers; Nelson A. Rockefeller Papers.

Rockefeller Center Archives, New York.

Shepley Bulfinch Richardson and Abbott Archives, Boston: Henry R. Shepley Papers.

South Caroliniana Library, University of South Carolina, Columbia: University Records.

Smithsonian Institution Archives, Washington, D.C.

Stanford Historical Society, Stanford, Calif.

Stanford University Libraries, Special Collections and University Archives, Stanford, Calif.

Syracuse University Art Galleries, Syracuse, N.Y.: Mary Petty and Alan Dunn Estate.

Time, Inc., Archives, New York.

UAMS Library Historical Research Center, Little Rock, Ark.

U.S. Air Force Academy, Academy Libraries, Special Collections, Colorado Springs, Colo.: Academy Records.

U.S. Department of State, Bureau of Overseas Buildings Operations, Washington, D.C.: Office of Foreign Building Operations Records.

University of Arkansas, Fayetteville, Ark.: University Museum; David W. Mullins Library, Special Collections: Arkansas Collection; Edward Durell Stone Papers; University Archives; William J. Fulbright Papers.

University of California, Berkeley, Environmental Design Archives: Phil Fein Collection.

University of California, Santa Cruz, McHenry Library, Special Collections: Morley Baer Collection.

Vanderbilt University, Special Collections and University Archives, Nashville, Tenn.: University Records.

Virginia Museum of Fine Arts, Richmond: VMFA Photo Archives.

Wadsworth Athenaeum Museum of Art, The Archives, Hartford, Conn.: A[rthur] Everett "Chick" Austin Jr. Papers.

Walt Disney Archives, Burbank, Calif.

Ward M. Canaday Center for Special Collections, University of Toledo, Ohio: Owens-Illinois Records.

Yale University Library, Manuscripts and Archives, New Haven, Conn.: Chester Bowles Papers.

THE TEXT'S EXTENSIVE CITATIONS OF JOURNALS, MAGAZINES, NEWSPAPERS, AND INTERNET SITES ARE DOCUMENTED IN THE NOTES.

BOOKS

Agrest, Diana, Patricia Conway, and Leslie Weisman. *The Sex of Architecture*. New York: Harry N. Abrams, 1996.

Albrecht, Donald, ed. *World War II and the American Dream: How Wartime Building Changed a Nation*. Washington, D.C.: National Building Museum/MIT Press, 1995.

Allwood, John. *The Great Exhibitions*. London: Studio Vista, 1977.

Alofsin, Anthony. *The Struggle for Modernism: Architecture, Landscape Architecture, and City Planning at Harvard*. New York: W. W. Norton, 2002.

Bacon, Mardges, ed. *"Symbolic Essence" and Other Writings on Modern Architecture and American Culture*. New Haven, Conn.: A Buell Center/Columbia Book of Architecture, 2005.

Ballon, Hilary, and Kenneth T. Jackson, eds. *Robert Moses and the Modern City: The Transformation of New York*. New York: W. W. Norton, 2007.

Banham, Reyner. *Guide to Modern Architecture*. Princeton, N.J.: Van Nostrand, 1962.

———. *A Personal View of Modern Architecture*. London: Architecture Press, 1962.

Bayer, Herbert, Ise Bayer, and Walter Gropius, eds. *The Bauhaus: 1919–1928*. New York: Museum of Modern Art, 1938.

Becker, Ralph E. *Miracle on the Potomac: The Kennedy Center from the Beginning*. Silver Spring, Md.: Bartleby Press, 1990.

Bensman, Joseph, and Bernard Rosenberg. *Mass, Class, and Bureaucracy: The Evolution of Contemporary Society*. Englewood Cliffs, N.J.: Prentice-Hall, 1963.

Bishop, Minor L. *Fountains in Contemporary Architecture*. New York: American Federation of Arts, 1965.

Blake, Peter. *No Place Like Utopia: Modern Architecture and the Company We Kept*. New York: Knopf, 1993.

Bonta, Juan Pablo. *American Architects and Texts: A Computer-Aided Analysis of the Literature*. Cambridge, Mass.: MIT Press, 1996.

Boorstin, Daniel J. *The Image, or, What Happened to the American Dream*. Harmondsworth, U.K.: Penguin, 1963.

Boyer, Paul S. *Promises to Keep: The United States since World War II*. 2nd ed. Boston: Houghton Mifflin, 1999.

Broadbent, Geoffrey, Richard Bunt, and Charles Jencks, eds. *Signs, Symbols and Architecture*. New York: John Wiley and Sons, 1980.

Brooks, Michael W. *John Ruskin and Victorian Architecture*. New Brunswick, N.J.: Rutgers University Press, 1987.

Broude, Norma, and Mary D. Garrard, eds. *The Expanding Discourse: Feminism and Art History*. New York: IconEditions, 1992.

———. *Feminism and Art History: Questioning the Litany*. New York: Harper and Row, 1982.

———. *The Power of Feminist Art*. New York: Harry N. Abrams, 1994.

Burchard, John, and Albert Bush-Brown. *The Architecture of America: A Social and Cultural History*. Boston: Little, Brown, 1966.

Călinescu, Matei. *Five Faces of Modernity*. Rev. ed. Durham, N.C.: Duke University Press, 1987.

Cheney, Sheldon, and Martha Candler Cheney. *Art and the Machine: An Account of Industrial Design in 20th-Century America*. New York: Whittlesey House, 1936. Reprint, New York: Acanthus Press, 1992.

Church, Thomas Dolliver. *Gardens Are for People: How to Plan for Outdoor Living*. New York: Reinhold, 1955.

Cogswell, Margaret, ed. *Ideal Theater: Eight Concepts*. New York: American Federation of Arts, 1962.

Coleman, Deborah, Elizabeth Danze, and Carol Henderson, eds. *Architecture and Feminism*. New York: Princeton Architectural Press, 1996.

Coleman, Laurence Vail. *The Museum in America: A Critical Study*. Washington, D.C.: American Association of Museums, 1939.

Colomina, Beatriz. *Privacy and Publicity: Modern Architecture as Mass Media*. Cambridge, Mass.: MIT Press, 2000.

Colquhoun, Alan. *Modern Architecture*. New York: Oxford University Press, 2002.

Conant, Kenneth John. *Carolingian and Romanesque Architecture, 800 to 1200*. Baltimore, Md.: Penguin, 1959.

Cook, John W., and Heinrich Klotz. *Conversations with Architects*. New York: Frederick A. Praeger, 1973.

Cowan, Henry J. *Science and Building: Structural and Environmental Design in the Nineteenth and Twentieth Centuries*. New York: John Wiley and Sons, 1978.

Cullman, Marguerite. *Ninety Dozen Glasses*. New York: W. W. Norton, 1960.

Curtis, William J. R. *Modern Architecture since 1900*. Englewood Cliffs, N.J.: Prentice-Hall, 2000.

Desilets, Deborah. *Morris Lapidus*. New York: Assouline, 2004.

Diamonstein, Barbaralee, ed. *Collaboration: Artists and Architects in Celebration of the Centennial of the Architectural League*. New York: Whitney Library of Design, 1981.

Dorfles, Gillo. *Kitsch: The World of Bad Taste*. New York: Bell, 1968.

Drexler, Arthur, ed. *The Architecture of the École des Beaux-Arts*. New York: Museum of Modern Art, 1977.

———. *Modern Architecture USA*. New York: Museum of Modern Art, 1965.

———. *Transformations in Modern Architecture*. New York: Museum of Modern Art, 1979.

Dumas, Ann. *Matisse, His Art and His Textiles: The Fabric of Dreams*. New York: Royal Academy of Arts, 2004.

Egbert, Donald Drew. *The Beaux-Arts Tradition in French Architecture*. Edited by David Van Zanten. Princeton, N.J.: Princeton University Press, 1980.

Evenson, Norma. *The Indian Metropolis: A View toward the West*. New Haven, Conn.: Yale University Press, 1989.

Ewen, Stuart. *All Consuming Images: The Politics of Style in Contemporary Culture*. New York: Basic Books, 1988.

Ferriss, Hugh. *Power in Buildings: An Artist's View of Contemporary Architecture*. New York: Columbia University Press, 1953.

Findling, John E., and Kimberly D. Pelle, eds. *Historical Dictionary of World's Fairs and Expositions, 1851–1988*. New York: Greenwood Press, 1990.

Fletcher, Sir Banister. *A History of Architecture on the Comparative Method*. 17th ed. revised by R. A. Cordingley. London: Athlone Press, 1961.

Floyd, Margaret Henderson. *Architectural Education and Boston: Centennial Publication of the Boston Architectural Center, 1889–1989*. Boston: Boston Architectural Center, 1989.

Ford, James, and Katherine Morrow Ford. *Classic Modern Homes of the Thirties*. 1940. Reprint of *The Modern House in America*, New York: Dover, 1989.

———. *Design of Modern Interiors*. New York: Architectural Book, 1942.

Ford, Katherine Morrow, and Thomas H. Creighton. *The American House Today*. New York: Reinhold, 1951.

Form Givers at Mid-Century. New York: Time, Inc./American Federation of Arts, 1959.

Forsee, Aylesa. "Edward Durell Stone: Campaigner for Permanence and Beauty." In *Men of Modern Architecture: Giants in Glass, Steel, and Stone*. Philadelphia: McCrae Smith, 1966.

Frampton, Kenneth. *A Critical History of Modern Architecture*. 3rd ed. London: Thames and Hudson, 1992.

———. *Studies in Tectonic Culture: The Poetics of Construction in Nineteenth- and Twentieth-Century Architecture*. Cambridge, Mass.: MIT Press, 2006.

Frampton, Kenneth, and Yukio Futagawa. *Modern Architecture, 1851–1945*. New York: Rizzoli, 1983.

Frank, Dianne Ludman. *Hugh Stubbins and His Associates: The First Fifty Years*. Cambridge, Mass.: Stubbins Associates, 1986.

Frascina, Francis, ed. *Pollock and After: The Critical Debate*. New York: Harper and Row, 1985.

Fraser-Cavassoni, Natasha. *Sam Spiegel: The Biography of a Hollywood Legend*. London: Time Warner, 2004.

Friedman, Alice T. *American Glamour and the Evolution of Modern Architecture*. New Haven, Conn.: Yale University Press, 2010.

Gaddis, John Lewis. *The Cold War: A New History*. New York: Penguin, 2005.

Galbraith, John Kenneth. *Ambassador's Journal: A Personal Account of the Kennedy Years*. Boston: Houghton Mifflin, 1969.

Garrigan, Kristine Ottesen. *Ruskin on Architecture*. Madison: University of Wisconsin Press, 1973.

Gauguin, Paul. *Noa Noa: The Tahitian Journal*. 1926. Reprint, New York: Dover, 1985.

Gebhard, David. *200 Years of American Architectural Drawing*. New York: Whitney Library of Design, 1977.

Germany, Lisa. *Harwell Hamilton Harris*. Austin: University of Texas Press, 1991.

Gibson, Ann Eden. *Abstract Expressionism: Other Politics*. New Haven, Conn.: Yale University Press, 1997.

Gill, Brendan. "Wallace K. Harrison." In *A New York Life of Friends and Others*, 151–58. New York: Poseidon, 1990.

Goldberger, Paul. *The City Observed: New York, A Guide to the Architecture of Manhattan*. New York: Random House, 1979.

———. *The Skyscraper*. New York: Knopf, 1981.

Goldhagen, Sarah Williams, and Réjean Legault. *Anxious Modernisms: Experimentation in Postwar Architectural Culture*. Montreal: Canadian Centre for Architecture, 2000.

Goodyear, A. Conger. *The Museum of Modern Art: The First Ten Years*. New York: n.p., 1943.

Graham, Margaret B. W., and Alec T. Shuldiner. *Corning and the Craft of Innovation*. New York: Oxford University Press, 2001.

Greenberg, Clement. *Art and Culture: Critical Essays*. Boston: Beacon, 1961.

Grossman, Elizabeth Greenwell. *The Civic Architecture of Paul Cret*. New York: Cambridge University Press, 1996.

Gubernick, Lisa Rebecca. *Squandered Fortune: The Life and Times of Huntington Hartford*. New York: G. P. Putnam's Sons, 1991.

Guilbaut, Serge. *How New York Stole the Idea of Modern Art: Abstract Expressionism, Freedom, and the Cold War*. Translated by Arthur Goldhammer. Chicago: University of Chicago Press, 1983.

Gutheim, Frederick Albert, and National Gallery of Art. *One Hundred Years of Architecture in America, 1857–1957: Celebrating the Centennial of the American Institute of Architects*. New York: Reinhold, 1957.

Haddow, Robert H. *Pavilions of Plenty: Exhibiting American Culture Abroad in the 1950s*. Washington, D.C.: Smithsonian Institution, 1997.

Hamlin, Talbot F. *Forms and Functions of Twentieth-Century Architecture*. New York: Columbia University Press, 1952.

Hanks, David A., with Jennifer Toher. *Donald Deskey: Decorative Designs and Interiors*. New York: E. P. Dutton, 1987.

Hartford, Huntington. *Art or Anarchy? How the Extremists and Exploiters Have Reduced the Fine Arts to Chaos and Commercialism*. Garden City, N.Y.: Doubleday, 1964.

———. *Has God Been Insulted Here?* Chicago: Reilly and Lee, 1952.

———. *You Are What You Write*. New York: Macmillan, 1973.

Harwood, John, and Janet Parks. *The Troubled Search: The Work of Max Abramovitz*. New York: Miriam and Ira D. Wallach Art Gallery, Columbia University, 2004.

Hayden, Dolores. *Building Suburbia: Green Fields and Urban Growth, 1820–2000*. New York: Pantheon, 2003.

Hayward, Mary Ellen, and Frank R. Shivers Jr., eds. *The Architecture of Baltimore: An Illustrated History*. Baltimore: Johns Hopkins University Press, 2004.

Heyer, Paul. *Architects on Architecture: New Directions in America*. New York: Walker, 1966.

Hine, Thomas. *Populuxe*. New York: Knopf, 1987.

Hitchcock, Henry-Russell Jr. *Architecture: Nineteenth and Twentieth Centuries*. 3rd ed. Harmondsworth, U.K.: Penguin, 1968.

———. *Modern Architecture: Romanticism and Reintegration*. New York: Payson and Clarke, 1929.

———. "1930 to the Mid-20th Century." Americas: Art since Columbus. In *Encyclopedia of World Art*, 270–78. New York: McGraw-Hill, 1959.

Hitchcock, Henry-Russell Jr., and Arthur Drexler, eds. *Built in USA: Postwar Architecture*. New York: Museum of Modern Art, 1952.

Hitchcock, Henry-Russell Jr., and Philip Johnson. *The International Style*. 1966. Reprinted with foreword by Johnson. New York: W. W. Norton, 1995. First published in 1932 as *International Style Architecture since 1922*.

Horn, Richard. *Fifties Style: Then and Now*. New York: Beech Tree Books, 1985.

Hunter, Sam. "Introduction." In *The Museum of Modern Art: The History and the Collection*, 8–41. New York: Harry N. Abrams/Museum of Modern Art, 1984.

Hunting, Mary Anne. "Edward Durell Stone: Perception and Criticism." PhD diss., Graduate Center, City University of New York, 2007.

Huxtable, Ada Louise. *Four Walking Tours of Modern Architecture in New York City*. New York: Museum of Modern Art/Municipal Art Society, 1964.

———. *Frank Lloyd Wright*. New York: Lipper/Viking, 2004.

———. *Will They Ever Finish Bruckner Boulevard?* New York: Collier, 1970.

Huyssen, Andreas. *After the Great Divide: Modernism, Mass Culture, Postmodernism*. Bloomington: Indiana University Press, 1986.

Jacks, Ernest E. "The Elegant Bohemian: Tales of Architect Edward Durell Stone." Private collection, 2000.

Jackson, Kenneth T. *Crabgrass Frontier: The Suburbanization of the United States*. New York: Oxford University Press, 1985.

Jacobus, John M. *Twentieth-Century Architecture: The Middle Years, 1940–65*. New York: Frederick A. Praeger, 1966.

Jencks, Charles. *Modern Movements in Architecture*. Garden City, N.Y.: Anchor Press, 1973.

Johnson, Philip. *Writings/Philip Johnson*. New York: Oxford University Press, 1979.

Jones, Cranston. *Architecture: Today and Tomorrow*. New York: McGraw-Hill, 1961.

Jones, Gerre L. *How to Market Professional Design Services*. New York: McGraw-Hill, 1973.

Jordy, William H. *American Buildings and Their Architects: The Impact of European Modernism in the Mid-Twentieth Century*. New York: Oxford University Press, 1972.

Judt, Tony. *Reflections on the Forgotten Twentieth Century*. New York: Penguin, 2008.

Katz, Herbert, and Marjorie Katz. *Museums, U.S.A.: A History and Guide*. Garden City, N.Y.: Doubleday, 1965.

Kentgens-Craig, Margret. *The Bauhaus and America: First Contacts, 1919–1936*. Cambridge, Mass.: MIT Press, 1999.

Kieffer, Jarold A. *From National Cultural Center to John F. Kennedy Center for the Performing Arts: At the Front End of the Beginning*. Fairfax, Va.: privately printed, 2004.

Kilham, Walter H. Jr., "Journeys in Two Worlds." Cornwall, Conn.: privately printed, 1992.

Kornwolf, James D., ed. *Modernism in America, 1937–1941: A Catalog and Exhibition of Four Architectural Competitions*. Williamsburg, Va.: Joseph and Margaret Muscarelle Museum of Art, 1985.

Kostof, Spiro. *A History of Architecture: Settings and Rituals*. New York: Oxford University Press, 1985.

Kulka, Tomas. *Kitsch and Art*. University Park: Pennsylvania State University Press, 2002.

Lamonaca, Marianne, and Jonathan Mogul, eds. *Grand Hotels of the Jazz Age: The Architecture of Schultze and Weaver*. Miami Beach: Wolfsonian-Florida International University/Princeton Architectural Press, 2005.

Le Corbusier. *Towards a New Architecture*. 1927. Reprint, New York: Dover, 1986.

Le Corbusier, and Pierre Jeanneret. *Oeuvre complète de 1910–1929*. 4th ed. Erlenbach-Zurich: W. Boesiger and O. Stonorov, 1946.

Leipold, L. Edmond. *Famous American Architects*. Minneapolis: T. S. Denison, 1972.

Levine, Neil. *The Architecture of Frank Lloyd Wright*. Princeton, N.J.: Princeton University Press, 1966.

Loeffler, Jane C. *The Architecture of Diplomacy: Building America's Embassies*. New York: Princeton Architectural Press, 1998.

Lull, James. *Media, Communication, Culture: A Global Approach*. 2nd ed. New York: Columbia University Press, 2000.

Lynes, Russell. *Good Old Modern: An Intimate Portrait of the Museum of Modern Art*. New York: Athenaeum, 1973.

———. *Taste-makers*. New York: Harper and Brothers, 1955.

Macdonald, Dwight. *Against the American Grain*. New York: Random House, 1962.

MacDougall, Elisabeth Blair, ed. *The Architectural Historian in America: A Symposium in Celebration of the Fiftieth Anniversary of the Founding of the Society of Architectural Historians*. Washington, D.C.: National Gallery of Art, 1990.

Marchand, Roland. *Advertising the American Dream: Making Way for Modernity, 1920–1940*. Berkeley: University of California Press, 1985.

Mason, Joseph B., *History of Housing in the U.S., 1930–1980*. Houston, Tex.: Gulf, 1982.

Mattie, Erik. *World's Fairs*. New York: Princeton Architectural Press, 1998.

McAndrew, John., ed. *Guide to Modern Architecture: Northeast States*. New York: Museum of Modern Art, 1940.

Meister, Maureen. *Architecture and the Arts and Crafts Movement in Boston: Harvard's H. Langford Warren*. Hanover, N.H.: University Press of New England, 2003.

Meyer, Karl E. *The Art Museum: Power, Money, Ethics*. New York: William Morrow, 1979.

Mock, Elizabeth, ed. *Built in USA since 1932*. New York: Museum of Modern Art, 1945.

———. *If You Want to Build a House*. New York: Museum of Modern Art, 1946.

Modern by Edward Stone. Fayetteville, Ark.: Fulbright Industries, 1951.

Modleski, Tania, ed. *Studies in Entertainment: Critical Approaches to Mass Culture*. Bloomington: Indiana University Press, 1986.

Mumtaz, Kamil Khan. *Modernity and Tradition: Contemporary Architecture in Pakistan*. New York: Oxford University Press, 1999.

Münz, Ludwig, and Gustav Künstler. *Adolf Loos: Pioneer of Modern Architecture*. Translated by Harold Meek. New York: Frederick A. Praeger, 1966.

Muschamp, Herbert. *File under Architecture*. Cambridge, Mass.: MIT Press, 1974.

Musée du Jeu de Paume. *Trois siècles d'art aux États-Unis*. Paris: Éditions des musées nationaux, 1938.

Museum of Modern Art. *Art in Our Time: An Exhibition to Celebrate the Tenth Anniversary of the Museum of Modern Art and the Opening of Its New Building*. New York: Museum of Modern Art, 1939.

———. *Buildings for Business and Government: Exhibition, February 25–April 28, 1957*. New York: Museum of Modern Art, 1957.

———. *Modern Architecture: International Exhibition, New York, February 10–March 23, 1932*. New York: Museum of Modern Art, 1932.

———. *The Museum of Modern Art: The History and the Collection*. New York: Harry N. Abrams/Museum of Modern Art, 1984.

———. *What Is Modern Architecture?* New York: Museum of Modern Art, 1942.

Nelson, George, and Henry Wright. *Tomorrow's House: How to Plan Your Postwar Home Now*. New York: Simon and Schuster, 1945.

Newhouse, Victoria. *Wallace K. Harrison, Architect*. New York: Rizzoli, 1989.

The 1940 Book of Small Houses by the Editors of Architectural Forum. New York: Simon and Schuster, 1940.

Noffsinger, James Philip. *The Influence of the École des Beaux-Arts on the Architects of the United States*. Washington, D.C.: Catholic University of America Press, 1955.

Noguchi, Isamu. *A Sculptor's World*. New York: Harper and Row, 1968.

Ockman, Joan, comp. *Architecture Culture, 1943–1963: A Documentary Anthology*. New York: Rizzoli, 1993.

Okrent, Daniel. *Great Fortune: The Epic of Rockefeller Center*. New York: Viking, 2003.

Oliver, Richard, ed. *The Making of an Architect, 1881–1981*. New York: Rizzoli, 1981.

Packard, Vance. *The Status Seekers*. Harmondsworth, U.K.: Penguin, 1966.

Perl, Jed. *New Art City: Manhattan at Mid-Century*. New York: Knopf, 2005.

Peter, John. *The Oral History of Modern Architecture: Interviews with the Greatest Architects of the Twentieth Century*. New York: Harry N. Abrams, 1994.

Pohl, Frances K. *Framing America: A Social History of American Art*. New York: Thames and Hudson, 2002.

Prak, Niels L. *Architects: The Noted and the Ignored*. New York: John Wiley and Sons, 1984.

Prudon, Theodore H. M. *Preservation of Modern Architecture*. New York: John Wiley and Sons, 2008.

Rank, Otto. *The Double: A Psychoanalytic Study*. Translated and edited by Harry Tucker Jr. Chapel Hill: University of North Carolina Press, 1971.

Reich, Cary. *The Life of Nelson A. Rockefeller: Worlds to Conquer, 1908–1958*. New York: Doubleday, 1996.

Riley, Terence, and Barry Bergdoll. *Mies in Berlin*. New York: Museum of Modern Art, 2001.

Riley, Terence, Barry Bergdoll, and Peter Reed, eds. *Frank Lloyd Wright: Architect*. New York: Museum of Modern Art, 1994.

Roberts, Mary Fanton. *Inside 100 Homes*. New York: Robert M. McBride, 1936.

Rogers, Elizabeth Barlow. *Landscape Design: A Cultural and Architectural History*. New York: Harry N. Abrams, 2001.

Román, Antonio. *Eero Saarinen: An Architecture of Multiplicity*. New York: Princeton Architectural Press, 2003.

Rosa, Joseph. *Albert Frey, Architect*. New York: Princeton Architectural Press, 1999.

Rosa, Joseph, et al., eds. *Glamour: Fashion, Industrial Design, Architecture*. New Haven, Conn.: Yale University Press/San Francisco: San Francisco Museum of Modern Art, 2004.

Rosenberg, Bernard, and David Manning White, eds. *Mass Culture Revisited*. New York: Van Nostrand Reinhold, 1971.

Rosenberg, Harold. *The Tradition of the New*. New York: Horizon Press, 1959.

Rowe, Colin. "Introduction." In *Five Architects: Eisenman, Graves, Gwathmey, Hejduk, Meier*. New York: Oxford University Press, 1975.

———. *The Mathematics of the Ideal Villa and Other Essays*. Cambridge, Mass.: MIT Press, 1987.

Rubin, William Stanley, ed. *"Primitivism" in 20th Century Art: Affinity of the Tribal and the Modern*. New York: Museum of Modern Art, 1984.

Ruskin, John. *The Stones of Venice*. Rev. ed. by J. G. Links. 1960. Reprint, New York: Da Capo, 1985.

Rydell, Robert W. *World of Fairs: The Century-of-Progress Expositions*. Chicago: University of Chicago Press, 1993.

Rydell, Robert W., and Nancy Gwinn. *Fair Representations: World's Fairs and the Modern World*. Amsterdam: VU University Press, 1994.

Sargeant, John. *Frank Lloyd Wright's Usonian Houses*. New York: Whitney Library of Design, 1984.

Schiffer, Nancy N., and Val O. Bertoia. *The World of Bertoia*. Atglen, Penn.: Schiffer, 2003.

Schulze, Franz. *Philip Johnson: Life and Work*. New York: Knopf, 1994.

Scully, Vincent. *American Architecture and Urbanism*. New York: Frederick A. Praeger, 1969.

Seiberling, Frank. *Looking into Art*. New York: Holt, Rinehart and Winston, 1959.

Shadegg, Stephen. *Clare Boothe Luce: A Biography*. New York: Simon and Schuster, 1970.

Shanken, Andrew M. *194X: Architecture, Planning and Consumer Culture on the American Home Front*. Minneapolis: University of Minnesota Press, 2009.

Simon, Maron J., ed. *Your Solar House*. New York: Simon and Schuster, 1947.

Singley, Paulette, ed. *Architecture: In Fashion*. New York: Princeton Architectural Press, 1994.

Smith, G. E. Kidder, and the Museum of Modern Art. *The Architecture of the United States*. Garden City, N.Y.: Anchor Press, 1981.

Sontag, Susan. *Against Interpretation and Other Essays*. New York: Picador, 1966.

Staniszewski, Mary Anne. *The Power of Display: A History of Exhibition Installations at the Museum of Modern Art*. Cambridge, Mass.: MIT Press, 2001.

Stern, Robert A. M., Gregory Gilmartin, and Thomas Mellins. *New York 1930: Architecture and Urbanism between the Two World Wars*. New York: Rizzoli, 1987.

Stern, Robert A. M., with Raymond W. Gastil. *Modern Classicism*. New York: Rizzoli, 1988.

Stern, Robert A. M., Thomas Mellins, and David Fishman. *New York 1960: Architecture and Urbanism between the Second World War and the Bicentennial*. New York: Monacelli, 1995.

Stone, Edward Durell. "America—The Not So Beautiful." *New York Herald Tribune*, July 12, 1961.

———. "The American Way of Life." *Congressional Record—Appendix* (May 25, 1959): A436.

———. "An Architect's Religion." In *Faith Is a Star*, edited by Roland Gammon, 104–7. New York: E. P. Dutton, 1963.

———. "Architecture…" In "Is This the Year to Build Your House?" *House and Garden*, February 1947.

———. "Architecture: My Way of Life." *Boys' Life*, March 1965.

———. "Break the Rules!" *Los Angeles Times*, May 8, 1960.

———. "Business, Profits and Architecture." *Think*, April 1959.

———. "The Case against the Tailfin Age." *New York Times Magazine*, October 18, 1959.

———. "The Case for Modern Architecture on the Campus." *Technology Review* 62 (May 1960): 27–29, 44.

———. "Edward D. Stone, FAIA/Design: The Keynote Address." *AIA Journal* 32 (August 1959): 25–28.

———. "Era of Apartments: Abandonment of Single Family Homes Advocated for Metropolitan Areas." *Outlook for Men*, January 1961.

———. *The Evolution of an Architect*. New York: Horizon Press, 1962.

———. In "Fairest Cities of Them All." *New York Times*, January 24, 1960.

———. "For a Moratorium on Trivia." *New York Herald Tribune*, August 9, 1961.

———. "Frank Lloyd Wright: A Tribute to a Personal Hero." *Pacific Architect and Builder* 66 (March 1960): 20.

———. "The Future of Modern Architecture and City Planning." *Annual of Architecture, Structure and Town Planning* 2 (1961): A57–61.

———. "Hero, Prophet, Adventurer." *Saturday Review*, November 7, 1959.

———. "House around a Garden." *Suburbia Today*, June 1962.

———. "Introduction." In *Frank Lloyd Wright: Drawings for a Living Architecture*. New York: Horizon Press, 1959.

———. "Introduction." In *The Everyday Pleasure of Sculpture*, by Maria M. Valentine and Louis di Valentine. New York: James H. Heineman, 1966.

———. In "I Predict: Twenty-Five Farseeing People Tell What They Hope, Fear and Imagine for 1987." *Look*, January 16, 1962.

———. "Kitchens: Efficiency Is Not Enough." *Architectural Record* 9 (May 1962): 5–11.

———. "Modern Architecture on the Campus." *Stanford Review* (November 1960): 12–14.

———. "The National Cultural Center." *County Government* (April 1963): 20–21.

———. "Preface." In *It's the Law! Recognizing and Handling the Legal Problems of Private and Public Construction*, by Bernard Tomson and Norman A. Coplan. Great Neck, N.Y.: Channel Press, 1960.

———. "Progress: Spare That Building!" *Harper's Bazaar*, May 1962.

———. "Progress with Beauty." *Arkansas Democrat Magazine*, January 14, 1962.

———. *Recent and Future Architecture*. New York: Horizon Press, 1967.

———. "U.S. Is Becoming Nation of Boxes, Billboards, Bar-B-Q's." *Richmond News Leader*, December 31, 1960.

———. "What Architecture Should Be." *Show*, March 1964.

Stone, Maria Durell. "Friends." In *About Wright: An Album of Recollections by Those Who Knew Frank Lloyd Wright*, edited by Edgar Tafel, 56–62. New York: John Wiley and Sons, 1993.

[Stone], Maria Elena Torch. "Three Architects' View of Japan." *This Is Japan* (1955): 214–17.

Sudjic, Deyan. *The Edifice Complex: How the Rich and Powerful Shape the World*. New York: Penguin, 2005.

Swanberg, W. A. *Luce and His Empire*. New York: Charles Scribner's Sons, 1972.

Sweetman, John. *The Oriental Obsession: Islamic Inspiration in British and American Art and Architecture, 1500–1920*. New York: Cambridge University Press, 1991.

Thompson, Elizabeth Kendall. "Backgrounds and Beginnings." In *Domestic Architecture of the San Francisco Bay Region*. San Francisco: San Francisco Modern Museum of Art, 1949.

Toffler, Alvin. *The Culture Consumers: Art and Affluence in America*. Baltimore, Md.: Penguin, 1965.

Treib, Marc, ed. *An Everyday Modernism: The Houses of William Wurster*. San Francisco: San Francisco Museum of Modern Art, 1995.

———. *Thomas Church, Landscape Architect: Designing a Modern California Landscape*. San Francisco: William Stout, 2003.

Twombly, Robert C. *Frank Lloyd Wright: His Life and His Architecture*. New York: John Wiley and Sons, 1979.

United States Federal Housing Administration. *The FHA Story in Summary, 1934–1959*. Washington, D.C. , 1959.

Varnedoe, Kirk, and Adam Gopnik, eds. *Modern Art and Popular Culture: Readings in High and Low*. New York: Museum of Modern Art, 1990.

Venturi, Robert. *Complexity and Contradiction in Architecture*. 1966. Reprint, New York: Museum of Modern Art, 2002.

Venturi, Robert, Denise Scott Brown, and Steven Izenour. *Learning from Las Vegas: The Forgotten Symbolism of Architectural Form*. 1977. Reprint, Cambridge, Mass.: MIT Press, 2001.

Von Eckardt, Wolf. *Back to the Drawing Board! Planning Livable Cities*. New York: New Republic Books, 1978.

———. "Introduction." In *Mid-Century Architecture in America: Honor Awards of the American Institute of Architects, 1949–1961*. Baltimore, Md.: Johns Hopkins University Press, 1961.

———. *A Place to Live: The Crisis of the Cities*. New York: Dell, 1967.

Watkin, David. *The Rise of Architectural History*. London: Architectural Press, 1980.

Waugh, Edward, and Elizabeth Waugh. *The South Builds: New Architecture in the Old South*. Chapel Hill: University of North Carolina Press, 1960.

Weber, Nicholas Fox. *Patron Saints: Five Rebels Who Opened America to a New Art, 1928–1943*. New York: Knopf, 1992.

Weingarten, David. *Bay Area Style: Houses of the San Francisco Bay Region*. New York: Rizzoli, 2004.

White, Norval. *The Architecture Book*. New York: Knopf, 1976.

White, Norval, and Elliot Willensky. *AIA Guide to New York City*. Rev. ed. New York: Macmillan, 1978.

Williams, John G. *The Curious and the Beautiful: A Memoir History of the Architecture Program at the University of Arkansas*. Fayetteville: University of Arkansas Press, 1984.

Williamson, Roxanne Kuter. *American Architects and the Mechanics of Fame*. Austin: University of Texas Press, 1991.

Wilson, Forrest. *Emerging Form in Architecture: Conversations with Lev Zetlin*. Boston: Cahners, 1975.

Wilson, Kristina. *Livable Modernism: Interior Decorating and Design during the Great Depression*. New Haven, Conn.: Yale University Press, 2004.

Wilson, Richard Guy, Diane H. Pilgrim, and Dickran Dashjian. *The Machine Age in America, 1918–1941*. New York: Harry N. Abrams/Brooklyn Museum, 1986.

Wodehouse, Lawrence. *Ada Louise Huxtable: An Annotated Bibliography*. New York: Garland, 1981.

Wojtowicz, Robert. *Lewis Mumford and American Modernism: European Theories for Architecture and Urban Planning*. New York: Cambridge University Press, 1996.

Wolfe, Tom. *From Bauhaus to Our House*. New York: Farrar, Straus and Giroux, 1981.

———. "The Luther of Columbus." In *The Kandy-Kolored Tangerine-Flake Streamline Baby*, 233–44. New York: Farrar, Straus and Giroux, 1965.

———. *The Painted Word*. New York: Farrar, Straus and Giroux, 1975.

Woodbridge, Sally, ed. *Bay Area Houses*. Salt Lake City: Peregrine Smith, 1988.

Woods, Randall Bennett. *Fulbright: A Biography*. New York: Cambridge University Press, 1995.

Wright, Gwendolyn. *USA: Modern Architectures in History*. London: Reaktion, 2008.

Wright, Olgivanna Lloyd. *The Shining Brow: Frank Lloyd Wright*. New York: Horizon Press, 1960.

Yakas, Orestes. *Islamabad: The Birth of a Capital*. New York: Oxford University Press, 2001.

PHOTO CREDITS

INDEX

Page numbers in *italic* refer to images.
All buildings cited are by Stone unless otherwise indicated.